A *YANKEE* MAGAZINE GUIDEBOOK

FAVORITE DAYTRIPS
·IN NEW ENGLAND·

❖ ❖ ❖

By Michael Schuman

SECOND EDITION

YANKEE BOOKS

a division
of Yankee Publishing Incorporated
Dublin, New Hampshire

Yankee thanks John Robaton and Harris Smith,
and their photojournalism students at Boston University's
School of Public Communication, Department of Journalism,
for the substantial efforts they extended
to provide illustrations for this book.

Yankee Publishing Incorporated, Dublin, New Hampshire 03444

Second Edition
Second Printing, 1984

Copyright 1982, 1984 by Yankee Publishing Incorporated
Printed in the United States of America

Library of Congress Catalog Card Number 83-50697
ISBN 0-89909-024-9

To my parents, who would have been proud.

Contents

Introduction

New England has a special character that words can only attempt to capture. Its personality has to be discovered by travel and experience. This book, therefore, serves as an introduction to the character of New England, offering a volume of ways you can discover what makes New England unique.

Getting to know New England is easy for anyone who lives within or near the borders of the six-state region, because accessibility is easy. New England is smaller than every other section of the United States. From Boston, you can be in any of the other five states within a few hours. Hartford is only a two-hour drive from places as varied as Brattleboro, Vermont, and Newport, Rhode Island. Northern New Englanders can hop on Interstate 91 or 93 to arrive at sights in Massachusetts or Connecticut in the same amount of time. It's almost as if New England were just one big state itself.

We have divided this book into seven chapters, each woven around a specific subject area. Some trips consist of up-to-date looks at old favorites while others detail worthwhile spots still undiscovered by many. There are daytrips that will appeal to just about anyone as well as some for people with very specific interests. But we chose all of them with three prerequisites in mind: 1) high quality; 2) reflection of the nature and complexion of New England; and 3) geographic distribution such that anyone living anywhere in or near New England will find choices within easy reach. Of course, there are many more spots that meet these criteria; as much as we would have liked to include every worthwhile attraction in this six-state region, there's so much that we would have needed a volume the size of an unabridged dictionary to do so. That's the frustration of living in an area that has so much to do in such a small space.

As you read through this book, we hope you'll keep a few things in mind. First, the word "daily" has several definitions, but we are using it to mean "seven days a week." Second, while we have tried to be as complete as possible regarding all vital details, and while all information is correct as we go to press, there's always the possibility that an attraction listed will suddenly alter its days of operation or that a spot currently free will decide to institute an admission fee. If you're driving a long distance and have your heart set on seeing one special place, you may want to call in advance to be certain nothing has changed. Finally, if two of the trips look familiar, there's a good reason. These two, to Historic Deerfield and Shelburne Museum, were written by Sharon Smith and originally ran in *Yankee Magazine's Travel Guide to New England.*

Every single trip here has been taken recently — every attraction visited, every city toured, and every scenic route traveled. It was, needless to say, a thoroughly enjoyable assignment. And whether you're a native who has never taken the time to put aside the weekend lawn mowing in order to see this region, or a newly arrived transplant who always wondered how the reality of New England would match its images, we are certain you'll find these day-trips as pleasurable as we did.

THEY THAT GO
DOWN TO THE SEA
IN SHIPS
▲ ▲ ▲
1623 ⁓ 1923

CHAPTER I

Rich Men, Fishermen, Soldiers & Heroes

T he mention of the word "heritage" in New England instantly musters up thoughts of those who carried muskets or marched with a fife, drum, or "Don't tread on me" flag in the American Revolution. The area's role in the actual war may at times seem a bit glamorized, especially since relatively few battles were actually fought on New England soil. However, the region, and Boston in particular, served as a hotbed of dissent, setting off sparks that started the war. And most current residents, whether their ancestors landed at Plymouth Rock or at Ellis Island, are undeniably proud of New England's role in begetting the American Revolution.

But heritage in New England transcends the image of the ragged minuteman standing up to the redcoated British militia, and is expressed in a wide variety of current New England lifestyles. For over a century, the nation's super wealthy have used New England's shores as their summer playground. While the idle rich are playing in the water, the fishermen of Massachusetts' North Shore are working in it; Gloucester is still, as it has been for generations, the center of the ever-important fishing industry. And ever since 1636, when Harvard was founded as the first university in America, New England's tidy college towns have attracted students from all over the world.

Bits of all this can be experienced in the following five daytrips — proving that New England has led the country not only in colonial history but in much more as well.

One of the most photographed landmarks in New England is Gloucester's famous Man at the Wheel, *symbol of the centuries of fishing heritage in this area.*

When guests visited William and Alma Vanderbilt, this is where they were entertained — the lavishly gilded Ball Room in Newport's Marble House.

The Rich Men

Even if you've been to the grand European palaces like Versailles or Nymphenburg, you won't fail to be astounded by the sumptuous and stately, majestic and magnificent mansions formerly lived in by nineteenth-century American commercial royalty in Newport, Rhode Island. Furnishings from throughout Europe stock the interiors, and the efforts of the best American designers and architects can be inspected at these summer homes. You'll see significantly less in many museums across the country.

When the Vanderbilts and other families came to Newport in the 1890s, the fashionable trend of summering in this coastal town was already well established. The original warm-weather residents were Southern plantation owners who had come some fifty years earlier to this area of moderate summer temperatures and ocean breezes to escape the torrid Southern heat and humidity. By the 1860s, staying at hotels in Newport for the few warm months of the year was an increasingly popular custom; it was becoming harder and harder to find desirable accommodations in what was evolving into an overcrowded resort.

So, employing Yankee ingenuity to its fullest, vacationers took to building their own summer houses in Newport. Owning one's own summer home in this southern New England oceanside town came to be the utmost in prestige and status, and the privately owned homes that began the trend were soon followed by the luxurious mansions you see today.

Perhaps the most splendid of these is **The Breakers,** summer home of Cornelius Vanderbilt II, grandson of the shipping and railroad magnate. The family had lived in a considerably more modest Victorian estate on the same ocean-front location from 1885 until a fire destroyed it in 1892. The current mansion, built in a remarkably short period of two years, was emblematic of its time; America was growing and was bursting with confidence, and its architecture — whether of a city hall, a railroad station, or a millionaire's home — mirrored that feeling with an engrossment in the grand and monumental. Americans in the late-Victorian period felt that this would go on forever.

Ironically, Vanderbilt, who constructed the glorious palace with the millions he inherited from the family fortune, was a dour individual whose lifestyle was more like that of a refined clergyman than of high society and the idle rich. And this man who would never smoke, drink, or utter an obscene word was known as much for his philanthropy as for his abstinence. While he wouldn't take part in rich men's sports like horse racing or yachting (although he is said to have enjoyed a midwinter sleigh ride around Central Park now and then), he did give often and heavily to innumerable charities and was active in his church. The style of The Breakers, therefore, was one hundred eighty degrees opposite from that of the solemn family man who, it was said, smiled about as often as it snows in Hawaii. (It has been hinted that his wife, Alice, helped architect Richard Morris Hunt in the home's planning.)

Cornelius Vanderbilt, in keeping with his quiet manner, also entertained in a modest way. When The Breakers was opened to local society in 1895 (the event also served as the coming-out party for daughter Gertrude), there were few lavish decorations. True, flowers lined the hallways, and imported French fans (for the ladies) and gold and silver scarf pins (for the gentlemen) were the favors. (And they were *all* ladies and gentlemen.) However, that was the limit; The Breakers itself was all that was needed to overwhelm any guest. And of all, the dining room was then and is still generally considered the most spectacular.

Two gargantuan crystal chandeliers and twelve pillars of red alabaster with bronze Corinthian capitals are prized features of this room. Gilded cornices and garlands top the pillars, and looking down upon all the visitors below is the goddess Aurora, greeting the Dawn in a ceiling painting on canvas. The dining-room table, which seated thirty-four, is carved of oak and inlaid with lemonwood, and the dark-red damask used to upholster the furniture and form the drapes gives the room a royal touch.

When you initially look at the grand salon, another of about fifteen rooms on the tour, you won't be as impressed as when you hear that the entire room was designed and constructed in France, dismantled,

The style of The Breakers was 180 degrees opposite from that of the man who, it is said, smiled about as often as it snows in Hawaii.

shipped to the United States in packing crates, and then unpacked and set right up in The Breakers as if it were part of a child's doll house. The firm that put together this room of gray and gold Ionic columns, bas-relief carvings, and velvet draperies sent its employees over with the furnishings to be certain that the mirrors above the fireplace tilted correctly to reflect the painted ceiling and that the grand piano and the chandeliers were not one inch out of place. Whenever the Vanderbilts scheduled an event that would involve dancing or music, this is where it took place.

From numerous points of view at The Breakers, one can see the waters of Rhode Island Sound, which lap at the very coattails of the Vanderbilts' backyard. On your tour, you get your first look at the huge puddle from the Great Hall, reached by climbing the grand staircase, with its wrought-iron-and-bronze railing and red carpet. The east end of the Great Hall is enclosed in glass, offering a magnificent view of the water; the other three walls are of Caen stone imported from France. It is here that you are also shown a huge (eighteen-by-twenty-four-foot) seventeenth-century Flemish tapestry and the gold-leaf acorn decorations on the ceiling. (The acorn is the Vanderbilt family symbol.)

A brother of Cornelius Vanderbilt, William, and his family moved just up the road in August of 1892 into their summer home, **Marble House.** The name couldn't be more fitting; $7 million worth of imported marble was used in the construction of this $11 million structure. Located on Bellevue Avenue, the home is marked by four high Corinthian columns, which make it easily the most notable building on this elegant street.

Unlike his stoic brother, William Kissam Vanderbilt was a lover of the diversions of the wealthy. He spent his money on parties, polo matches, yachting (his prize boat was the *Alva*, named for his wife), and in the entertainment of his fellow members of high society. He also had a carefree attitude toward marriage, and problems between Alva and him were initially suspected after his yacht was destroyed in a collision and he neglected to name his newly constructed replacement the *Alva II.* The marital troubles were indeed real and led to a divorce. Such things just did not happen in late-Victorian society, and Alva was initially snubbed; then, due to her varied activities among the wealthy of the day, she was more or less reaccepted. Incidentally, in the settlement following the March, 1895, divorce, Marble House was awarded to Alva.

You don't enter Marble House through your basic front door; the entrance here is a sixteen-foot-high and twenty-five-foot-wide steel grille with a gun-metal finish and gilt-bronze adornment. The total weight is ten tons, and because of this weight, the central door is

The entire room was designed and constructed in France, dismantled, shipped here, and then set right up in The Breakers as if it were a child's doll house.

Why go to Versailles to see the Grand Trianon when you can see the similar Rosecliff right in Newport?

set on pivots instead of hinges.

The dining room here, like the one in The Breakers, is a classic beauty. Though it is indeed grand, with its sixty-pound solid bronze chairs made in Paris and its portrait of Louis XIV above a marble mantel patterned after one at Versailles, the total effect of the room is more restrained than in William's brother's counterpart. The walls are lined with dark pink marble from North Africa, giving the room a less cheerful appearance, too.

On the other hand, the overwhelmingly extravagant Gold Ballroom is the visual opposite of the dining room. The wall panels are lavishly gilded in carved relief, and the mirrors and chandeliers only add to the bewildering visual effect of all the gilt. The Gothic Room is yet another contrast to the two prior rooms. The pointed arch, notable in the Gothic style, is utilized to the fullest in the highly detailed relief above the mantel and on the ceiling. In addition, the two bronze chandeliers are also of the Gothic style.

Marble here is ubiquitous. From the yellow Siena covering the walls and floors of the entrance and terrace halls to the dining room's African marble to New York State white marble covering the exterior to the marble-based mantels and fireplaces throughout, you'll see the loveliest of this metamorphic rock.

Again in absolute contrast to Cornelius and Alice, Alva was renowned for her expensive celebrating as well as for maintaining a high social standard for herself and her family. The two came together at one of Alva's most luxuriant parties, held for about five hundred guests late in the summer of 1895. Though it was purported to be daughter Consuelo's coming-out party, the twenty-four-year-old Duke of Marlborough was to be in attendance and Alva had plans for both special guests. Just months earlier, Alva had broken up the romance between Consuelo and another young man, with the intent of introducing her to this gem of English royalty. Flowers and exotic plants that could rival the collection at any arboretum were brought in to decorate the interior and lawns of Marble House, and thousands of dollars' worth of handmade pins and fans were given as favors. Imported Chinese-silk lanterns hung throughout the grounds. All that effort

Seven million dollars' worth of imported marble was used in the construction of this 11-million-dollar structure.

proved fruitful; just over three weeks later, the Duke announced his engagement to Consuelo.

Leaving Marble House for your next stop offers one last bit of fun: a drive out by way of the elegant white-brick-lined, balustraded drive that takes you by the entrance before leading you back to Bellevue Avenue.

If you have ever watched the movie *The Great Gatsby* or *The Betsy*, you'll have already seen many of the highlights of **Rosecliff**, also located on Bellevue Avenue; many of the rooms, including the cavernous ballroom, were settings in those two films. (You may have heard that The Breakers served as the "back lot" for *The Great Gatsby*, but only the kitchen in that mansion was used in the film.)

A seven-room ranch house could fit inside the walls of this single room.

Rosecliff was owned and occupied successively by a number of different families, none of them Vanderbilts. It was constructed from 1899 to 1902 for Mr. and Mrs. Hermann Oelrichs to replace an ample frame house, also called Rosecliff, that had been on the same location. Oelrichs, an agent for a German shipping firm, was a pleasant-natured man from New York, while his wife, the former Theresa Fair, was a product of San Francisco society. She was a grand entertainer who, it is said, saw her functions in society as a business. Regardless of her viewpoint, she was considered one of the best hostesses in Newport at the time. Exotic floral decorations and classic artistic performances, whether by dancers imported from the Russian Ballet or tenors from New York's own Metropolitan Opera, were the rule. She opened the house in 1900 (though the construction wasn't yet finished) with a party embellished by Australian tree ferns, palms, and caladiums — and with music by Berger's Gypsy Hungarian Band. The following year, in honor of her ten-year-old son, she had tents and booths placed on the lawn overlooking the ocean for a combination garden party and circus. Mr. Oelrichs died in 1906 but his widow continued to live here until her death, twenty years later. Three other families subsequently owned this forty-room chateau-style home before it was opened to the public in 1971.

If you've ever seen pictures of the Grand Trianon, the small palace built by Louis XIV as a retreat on the grounds of Versailles, you'll certainly be familiar with the basic design of Rosecliff. Minus a few of the wings, courtyards, and architectural details that were less appropriate in twentieth-century Newport than in seventeenth-century France, the main portion of Rosecliff is highly reminiscent of the royal residence.

Famed architect Stanford White was one of Rosecliff's designers, and his touches are evident throughout your tour. What appears to be stone covering the exterior is actually terra cotta, a semifired near-white ceramic clay, which White discovered on a wedding trip through the Near East. The main staircase, also known as the "sweetheart stairway" because of its heart shape, is a favorite of visitors on the Rosecliff tour. Another White design, it has curved marble steps covered by dark red carpeting and complemented by a wrought-iron railing. Despite the romantic outline, many experts doubt this effect was the primary intent of White and his associates when they designed it; more than likely, the form was loosely based on that of a staircase in an eighteenth-century German palace.

Though at eighty by forty feet the Rosecliff ballroom is the largest in this entire grandiose community, it presents something of an optical illusion. Clouds and sky painted on the ceiling, plus windows facing the sprawling outdoors, give this room an effect of being in the open, but it's hard to comprehend its spaciousness until the guide tells you that a seven-room ranch house could fit inside the walls of this single room. It was here that Mrs. Oelrichs gave her famous *bal blanc* party; white wigs and white gowns were worn by all the women guests, decorations included white flowers and an arbor of white Corinthian columns placed on the east terrace, and the menu consisted entirely of white food. This, combined with the backdrop of white drapes and walls, let the men in their required black evening attire stand out dramatically. It's also believed that this was the party for which Mrs. Oelrichs had artificial boats constructed and stationed in the ocean beneath the cliffs in back of the house to simulate an active harbor.

In addition to these three mansions, you'll find many other homes away from home once occupied by Newport high society and now open to the public. Names like Astor and Belmont joined Vanderbilt and Oelrichs at a time when the derogatory chant of "There goes the neighborhood!" took on a different ring.

White wigs and gowns were worn by all women guests, white Corinthian columns were placed on the terrace, and the menu consisted entirely of white food.

ACCESS

TO GET TO THE NEWPORT MANSION AREA. From Interstate 95 exit 3, take Route 138 east to Newport; then take Farewell Street south to Thames Street south. From Thames Street, turn left onto Memorial Boulevard (Route 138A), then right onto Bellevue Avenue.

THE BREAKERS, MARBLE HOUSE, AND ROSE-CLIFF. Directions: Turn left from Bellevue Avenue onto Ruggles Avenue; The Breakers is at the corner of Ruggles Avenue and Ochre Point. Marble House and Rosecliff are located on Bellevue Avenue, south of Ruggles Avenue. **Season:** April through mid-November. **Days:** Daily. **Admission** charged; combination tickets available. **Allow** 45 minutes in The Breakers and Marble House, 30 to 40 minutes in Rosecliff. **Telephones:** For all of these 3, call (401) 847-1000; for other mansions, call Newport County Chamber of Commerce at (401) 847-1600.

The Fishermen

Gloucester is synonymous with fishing, and the legacy is as deep as its harbor.

He's green, bronze, and weathered, grapples with a ship's wheel, and stares perpetually out to sea. The famed statue *Man at the Wheel* is the *Pietà* of Gloucester and is the biggest "must-stop" on a tour of Cape Ann. Indeed, many visitors stop here just to see this symbol of the area and then rush off to the shops and galleries of Rockport.

Yet, though *Man at the Wheel* is a decidedly important attraction, it is only one attraction. Gloucester is synonymous with fishing, and the legacy is as deep as its harbor, with two fine museums offering substantial explanations of the heritage of this city.

This is not to say you should avoid **Man at the Wheel.** That would be like skipping the Eiffel Tower in Paris. Leonard Craske's work of art on Western Avenue overlooks Gloucester harbor as an emblem of all who have made their livings on the wharves, schooners, and dories in this region. The inscription on this monument, "They that go down to the sea in ships," is well known, but did you know it comes from the Bible? The 107th Psalm says:

> They that go down to the sea in ships.
> They that do business in great waters:
> These see the works of the Lord
> and his wonders in the deep.

Like the Tomb of the Unknown Soldier, *Man at the Wheel* is a symbol. Since Gloucester was founded by a fisherman almost three hundred fifty years ago, it's estimated that over ten thousand men have lost their lives while fishing out of the city. Even today, the industry, whether in the form of catching, processing, or cooking, is the moving force in the city. From the Portuguese and Italian fishermen, whose families have been here for generations, to the newly arrived Moonies, who hold an annual tuna tournament, this is a city of and for the fishermen.

Short of hopping on a trawler yourself, the best way to enter the world of these men who survive by the big catch is to enter the **Gloucester Fishermens Museum,** which abides by a hands-on policy to show visitors an authentic view of the salty lives and gritty experiences of the Gloucester fishermen. Children who usually become bored trudging through endless corridors of more formal museums will love this one, where they are not only allowed, but asked, to put their mitts on almost every exhibit in sight.

"Help us shape this mast," beckons a sign placed over a horizontal ship's mast, inviting you and your children to take some century-old shipwright's tools to the timber. Elbow grease is used to the hilt, as ancient planes can only scrape off what seem like worthless minute strips. In the same corner, there's another way you can blister your fingers: you're asked to try (more than likely, unsuccessfully) drilling a hole with a hand drill into a block. Then read that for a one hundred-foot schooner, about eleven thousand such holes were needed and that electric drills were not invented until around 1920. You'll probably be more successful at pumping a large turn-of-the-century foghorn that emits a sound evocative of your pet dog as he catches his tail in your car door.

But what would a fishermen's museum be without exhibits on the catch itself? On the walls, you'll see models and descriptions of native fish that you've no doubt heard about, whether in the local market or in other seaports you've visited. There are the more recognizable sea creatures, like a squid and a flounder, as well as some rather obscure ocean dwellers like the wolf fish and the silver hake. And, in keeping with the theme of this museum, you'll want to take advantage of the "touchable" displays. Ever wonder if a swordfish's bill is really sharp, or if a seal's skin is slippery, or what a whale's teeth feel like? Hold, stroke, and touch for yourself.

You're also afforded the opportunity to learn something about the schooners that once transported the fishermen across the ocean waters as well as about some of the traps and tools used to do the catching. Scale models of schooners, some partially cut away to show the detailed workmanship involved, are displayed, accompanied by instruments that were kept on board.

In a different part of the museum, you get a close-up view of some weathered lobster traps like those that you have seen from a distance before. Here you're shown through an exhibit just how they work. The lobster, attracted by a bait bag, crawls farther into the "kitchen" of the trap and then even farther into the "parlor," which is the thick of the netting; from here, he makes himself at home whether he likes it or not until the fisherman removes him.

And in another section, there's a collection of sailors' knots including the square knot, the sheet bend, the short splice, and the monkey's fist. They're all precisely and accurately tied and waiting for the approval of an expert.

The Haul of Fame is an area set aside for all the flotsam and jetsam dragged out of the brine. A conglomeration of "collectibles" ranging from a horn from an early-twentieth-century schooner to a shoulder girdle from a whale is exhibited. And as area fishermen discover other treasures from under the ocean waters, more oddities are to be displayed here. It's a continual fishermen's scavenger hunt.

Hungry for more fishy displays? Patient human touches have turned haddock bones into fish models and swordfish and sawfish into tools; these are among the many items you can observe while on the guided tour offered at another museum, the **Cape Ann**

ALEXANDRA MEYNS

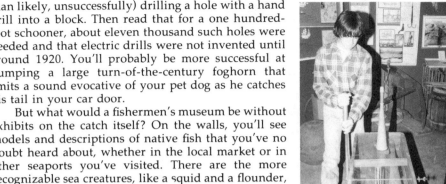

Pull the lever and block your ears. It emits a deafening noise, but the foghorn at the Gloucester Fishermens Museum is a popular hands-on exhibit.

Children are not only allowed, but asked, to put their mitts on almost every exhibit in sight.

Historical Association. Artifacts from the fishing industry are confined to the second floor, while the first floor is stocked with remnants of foreign commerce.

The location of the museum couldn't be more appropriate; it's the 1804 vintage home of a former captain of a merchant ship, Elias Davis, Jr., and the fact that there's a modern wing to the structure isn't the least bit objectionable. The seascapes of Gloucester native Fitz Hugh Lane, decorating numerous walls inside the building, are the pride of the association; this is the largest collection of Lane's paintings under one roof in the world. However, you really don't need to be an art connoisseur to enjoy them; many of the scenes will look familiar to any Gloucester visitor.

Make sure you see the sixteen-by-five-by-two-and-a-half-foot dory in the basement; you'll no doubt be stunned to hear this small boat once sailed across the Atlantic Ocean. Looking at it, it's easy to think you wouldn't trust it in your swimming pool; but, sure enough, this lilliputian vessel sailed from Gloucester to Liverpool, England, on a sixty-six-day voyage a little over a century ago.

Whether admiring the fishing industry's most famous symbol, brushing the skin of a sea creature, or surveying the harbor's turbulent skies on a painted canvas, you will derive a certain insight into the fishing heritage of Gloucester through a visit here. And you will come to understand how the people who see only *Man at the Wheel* and then move on miss so much. In fact, the best advice one can offer is not to *stop* at *Man at the Wheel*. That is simply the best place to start.

ACCESS

MAN AT THE WHEEL. Directions: From the terminus of Route 128 in Gloucester, take a right onto Route 127; follow Route 127 for just over 1 mile to the statue. **Season:** All year. **Days:** Daily. **Admission** free. **Allow** 10 minutes.

GLOUCESTER FISHERMENS MUSEUM. Directions: From the terminus of Route 128 in Gloucester, turn right onto Route 127, then left onto Rogers Street; the museum is at the corner of Rogers and Porter streets. **Season:** All year. **Days:** Daily. **Admission** charged. **Allow** 45 minutes. **Telephone:** (617) 283-1940.

CAPE ANN HISTORICAL ASSOCIATION. Directions: From the terminus of Route 128 in Gloucester, take the first right, onto Washington Street, and go 2 miles; then take a left onto Railroad Avenue, a left onto Prospect Street, and a right onto Pleasant Street. Follow Pleasant Street ½ mile to the museum. **Season:** March through January. **Days:** Tuesday through Saturday. **Admission** charged. **Allow** 45 minutes to 1 hour. **Note:** Metered parking is available across the street from the museum. **Telephone:** (617) 283-0455.

This is the largest collection of Fitz Hugh Lane paintings under one roof in the world.

ALEXANDRA MEYNS

This little boat sailed the Atlantic Ocean. It's on permanent display now at the Cape Ann Historical Association.

The Soldiers

DIANE DE MANGO

Many Massachusetts residents as well as other New Englanders go to Concord and Lexington just twice in their lives: once with their seventh-grade class and once with their relatives from Florida who come to visit and want to see the sights. And even when the out-of-staters come, they may head off to either of the Capes or Plymouth or reborn downtown Boston, totally ignoring Daniel Chester French's famed *Minuteman* statue, the modern visitors' center, the museums, and the authentically reproduced Buckman Tavern with its charming atmosphere. As a result, they miss out on an understanding of the first battle of the Revolutionary War, of the reason Lexington calls itself the "Birthplace of American Liberty," and of the feelings that early battle has stirred in poets and artists ever since. So if your last trip here was years ago with Mrs. Crosby and thirty other thirteen year olds, then you really should take a day to see what Ralph Waldo Emerson called "the rude bridge that arched the flood," and the other associated sights that lie within a few miles of each other.

From the beginning you can throw the old "historical sights never change" theory by the wayside. If you haven't been here since before 1976, you'll be unfamiliar with the **Battle Road Visitor Center** that was constructed for the Bicentennial and is now a permanent fixture. It's located half a mile west of Interstate 95 (there are well-placed signs) and features a film, an audio-visual presentation, and displays of Revolutionary period artifacts and information.

The film, called "To Keep Our Liberty," lasts twenty-two minutes and incorporates some hypothetical reenactments with narration in showcasing the events leading up to April 18, 1775. It's a bit corny at times, with a young colonist telling his side of the story and with scenes of a Tory being attacked and a tax collector being hanged and burned in effigy. But it does afford valuable background material that will help make your visit more than just a look at a collection of historic markers. And some of this information may surprise you.

For one thing, you are told that by the end of the French and Indian War, American colonists were enjoying one of the highest standards of living in the world. And you also hear that the British were not the overbearing oppressors that you might think; on the contrary, their system of government was one of the most liberal in the world's history. So how, you might ask, did trouble start?

The answer is . . . what else? Taxes. The British gained much new territory after the French and Indian War and felt that the colonists should contribute toward the cost of defending it. Basically, the taxes were little more than symbols of Parliament's

The Minuteman *stands sentry to the North Bridge today just as his real-life counterpart did over two hundred years ago.*

DIANE DE MANGO

The "rude bridge" that arches the Concord River where the "embattled farmers stood" is a 1956 re-creation of the original North Bridge.

authority, but they were resented by the colonists as being unconstitutional: Remember "Taxation without Representation"? The Boston Massacre and the Boston Tea Party were manifestations of this sour feeling, and the placement of British soldiers in Boston as a means of keeping order only stirred up the colonists' emotions that much more. The situation between the colonists and Parliament was like that of a pressure cooker about to explode. Fearing revolution, London gave General Thomas Gage, commander-in-chief of Britain's North American armed forces and a strict disciplinarian, orders to confiscate arms and ammunition being stockpiled by the patriots in Concord. So on the night of April 18, 1775, Gage dispatched his soldiers to seize the supplies.

That's where the film ends; to find out what happened next, follow the guide to a small theater, where the five-minute audio-visual display helps you see just where Lexington Green, the North Bridge, and those historic homes in Lexington fit into this whole thing. Paul Revere, whom everyone knows about, and William Dawes and Dr. Samuel Prescott, whom Revolutionary War buffs may be familiar with, all rode to warn of the advance of Gage's forces. Revere, who was a well-regarded Boston silversmith, and Dawes rode out from Boston late at night on the eighteenth, while Prescott, a Concord resident who had been spending the evening with his lady friend in Lexington, joined the duo there.

It was in Lexington that Revere rode up to the Reverend Jonas Clarke's parsonage, where John Hancock and Samuel Adams were staying, and warned the two patriots of the movement of Gage's troops. According to some accounts, militiamen guarding Clarke's house scolded Revere for making too much racket — to which Revere replied by informing them of the reason for the racket. Hancock and Adams, who were already high atop Gage's blacklist as troublesome patriots, scurried off into the woods. It was in the village of Lincoln, not too far from Lexington, that Revere and Dawes were captured; Prescott escaped and went on to bring his message to the militiamen in Concord.

At about two o'clock in the morning of April 19, a large group of colonists under the leadership of Captain John Parker gathered on the Lexington Green to discuss military strategy. When they left, many went to the Buckman Tavern, located just next to the green. About seven o'clock in the morning, however, the drum of sixteen-year-old William Diamond served as a call for the colonists to take their stand on the green once more. British troops, led by Major John Pitcairn, were advancing. Though no order to fire was given by either side, a shot rang out, followed by more shots, and a battle ensued. At the end of this first battle of the Revolutionary War, eight colonists were dead and ten were injured. The British continued their march to Concord.

The battle in Concord took only a few minutes. Lieutenant Colonel Francis Smith, the British commander, led his contingent into the center of Concord, planning to destroy the colonists' military stores; he was successful, setting them on fire and creating billows of smoke. The colonists who had been standing by the Buttrick Farm above the North Bridge saw the smoke and mistakenly thought the entire town was up in flames. Meanwhile, Smith had sent detachments to take control of the North and another bridge, cutting off the entrances into town. Fearing their homes would be burnt to ash if they didn't move, the colonists marched two by two toward the bridge. A few warning shots were fired from British arms into the water; the Americans returned the fire, marching onward; and the British retreated. By noon on the now-illustrious day in American history, April 19, 1775, the British had left Concord. By nighttime, they had followed the Battle Road in reverse all the way back to Boston.

Today's **North Bridge** is a 1956 re-creation based upon engravings of the original done after the battle by a man named Doolittle. It's flanked by two monumental manmade tributes to the event. Daniel Chester French's stately *Minuteman* stands sentry at the west end of the North Bridge; placed here in 1875 as a part of the country's centennial celebration, French's first full-length work bears the opening verse of Ralph Waldo Emerson's world-renowned "Concord Hymn":

> By the rude bridge that arched the flood,
>   Their flag to April's breeze unfurled;
> Here once the embattled farmers stood,
>   And fired the shot heard round the world.

The same hymn was sung on July 4, 1837, at the dedication of another monument by the bridge: the obelisk that marks the spot where the British first fired at the colonists. And a third important marker nearby is the gravestone of two British soldiers who died in the battle. A verse from a poem by James Russell Lowell is inscribed upon it:

> They came three thousand miles and died
> To keep the past upon its throne:
> Unheard beyond the ocean tide,
> Their English mother made her moan.

"Stand your ground. Don't fire unless fired upon. But if they mean to have a war, let it begin here."

If you had lived in Lexington in 1775, you might have spent evenings imbibing flip, just as the Minutemen did in the Buckman Tavern while waiting for the arrival of the British troops.

A ranger, weather permitting, is on duty here to answer questions, offer advice, and distribute the Minuteman National Park pamphlet. There's also a ranger on duty at the visitors' center in the Buttrick House. Built in 1911 by a descendant of Major John Buttrick, the battle hero, this house is about a five-minute walk away. Wonder what you would have looked like if you had lived back then, walking about in a black tricorn hat and a vest, or in a Revolutionary War period bonnet and shawl? These samples of colonial clothing are on display in a room inside the visitors' center, and you are invited to try them on and then examine in a mirror how you'd look as a 1775 Massachusetts minuteman or minuteman's wife. Not as extensive as the Battle Road Visitor Center, this center's other displays are limited to photos of local historic homes, of the North Bridge area itself, and of Daniel Chester French.

Along the path connecting the North Bridge Visitors' Center and the bridge are some markers indicating various points of battle. An offshoot of the path leads to the foundation of the home of David Brown, a farmer and a father of ten, who fought in the battle. A sign indicates where various rooms of the house were.

The battle site that's Concord's inseparable twin in American colonial wartime legend, **Lexington Green,** is attractive and well kept, set apart from any other village green only by a statue of a young, musket-toting minuteman (sculpted by now forgotten artisan Henry H. Kitson), a flagpole with a sign labeling the green the "Birthplace of American Liberty," and a few other monuments and markers; under one monolith lie the remains of those killed in the battle, brought

from another cemetery in 1835. One of the markers, meanwhile, notes the line of the minutemen and is inscribed with Captain Parker's words: "Stand your ground. Don't fire unless fired upon. But if they mean to have a war, let it begin here."

If you mean to park your car, you can do so on the streets bordering the green. It is permitted for two hours, which will give you plenty of time to stroll the green (five minutes or so) and see the two historic houses in the immediate area (Buckman Tavern and the Hancock-Clarke House). The third house, the Munroe Tavern, is on Massachusetts Avenue about a mile east from the green, so you may want to drive to get there.

If you only have time for one house, see the **Buckman Tavern.** Located right across from the green, it's a 1709 gem (with additions over the centuries), and the tours here are wonderful concoctions of wit and fascinating lore combined with history. The first room on the tour is the actual taproom where the minutemen gathered in the wee hours of April 19 waiting for the arrival of the British troops; more than likely, anxious soldiers drank some "flip" that night while warming themselves against the April chill. Flip was a popular drink of the day, comprising two thirds bitter beer, one to two ounces of rum, molasses or sugar to sweeten, and cream or eggs to thicken. The bar itself is not original — it is a reproduction, but believed to be authentic. You're told here that there was no drinking-age limit back then, but if your chin reached the bar, you were considered old enough to drink. No, there wasn't an epidemic of drunken children then; the bar is lower than you might expect simply because the average height for adult men back in the mid 1700s was about five feet six inches.

Behind the taproom is the owner's room, which on one occasion served as a hospital room for two British soldiers wounded in the battle; one died soon after the encounter, and the other rested on the landlord's bed. During that period, a tavern was more or less an inn where travelers stayed overnight; this was primarily a drovers' (or farmers') tavern, a common stopover for those bringing their herds to Boston. Fees of the house were as follows: twelve cents for dinner, ten cents for lodging on a straw mattress, and seven cents if a mattress was shared with another traveler. (Lower your eyebrows; that was a common practice back then!) A quart of flip, by the way, cost three cents.

In the **Hancock-Clarke House,** located 1/3 mile from the Buckman Tavern, you can see Major Pitcairn's pistols, William Diamond's elegantly decorated drum, and the room where Hancock and Adams were sleeping when aroused by Paul Revere. Other battle artifacts, including muskets and personal effects such as a British soldier's pocket watch and a Continental Army surgeon's saddlebag, are displayed in this 1699

Fees of the house were: twelve cents for dinner, ten cents for lodging on a straw mattress, and seven cents if a mattress were shared with another traveler.

ancestral home of John Hancock. Hancock's grandfather, the Reverend John Hancock, built it, but at the time of the battle it was owned by Reverend Jonas Clarke, a strong colonial supporter. You are taken by a guide through the bottom-floor rooms, and are then permitted to walk through the upstairs on your own. There are also colonial household items for your perusal here, including a butter churn, a hand-carved wooden gingerbread press, and some tin and wooden lanterns.

According to some accounts, militiamen guarding Clarke's house scolded Revere for making too much racket!

While the Buckman Tavern was infirmary to just two British soldiers, the **Munroe Tavern** was transformed into a British field hospital during a ninety-minute occupation. Fatigued soldiers were fed and cared for at the tavern, which was owned, ironically, by William Munroe, sergeant of Captain Parker's minuteman company. Brigadier General Earl Percy, in charge of the men at the tavern, later patted himself on the back by writing, "I had the happiness of saving them from inevitable destruction."

George Washington dined here in 1789 while visiting the location of the historic fight; still on view in the house are the table he used and some papers dealing with his visit. The wedding ring, bonnet, and slippers of the owner's wife, the bread trough she used the night before the battle, and taproom artifacts like flip mugs, tables, and chairs can also be examined here.

From the aged artifacts to the actual sites of the musket fire, there's much to see as you take a look at the history behind America's most famous battle. So when your out-of-state cousins arrive, or even before they do, consider a trip to these places right out of the history books. You'll be surprised at how much you don't remember and how much you never saw.

ACCESS

BATTLE ROAD VISITOR CENTER. Directions: From Interstate 95 exit 45W, go west ½ mile. **Season:** April through December. **Admission** free. **Allow** 40 minutes. **Telephone:** (617) 369-6993.

NORTH BRIDGE AND VISITORS' CENTER. Directions: From Interstate 95 exit 45W, go west to Concord Center, then turn right onto Monument Street. **Season:** All year. **Days:** Daily. **Admission** free. **Allow** 45 minutes. **Note:** Free parking is available across the street from the path to the bridge. **Telephone:** (617) 484-6192.

LEXINGTON HOUSES. Directions: From Interstate 95 exit 45E, go east on Route 2A, then left onto Waltham Street. Turn left onto Massachusetts Avenue, and continue to the green. **Season:** Mid-April through October. **Days:** Daily. **Admission** charged; combination tickets available. **Allow** a total of 90 minutes for the 3 tours. **Telephone** for all houses: (617) 861-0928.

It was a moment for the colonists to savor — the Battle of Bennington was over, the colonists had won, and the British prisoners were being counted. This grand painting hangs in the Bennington Museum.

More Soldiers

The two-hundred-year-old flag, frazzled, frayed, and faded, hangs in the Bennington Museum more proudly than any vibrant, newly manufactured Stars and Stripes ever could. And just a musket shot away from the museum, a 306-foot-high obelisk commands the view of the countryside skyline for miles as it marks the site of an old storehouse, once filled with colonial weapons, that was the cause of a major battle in the Revolutionary War.

The Battle of Bennington is marked by these symbols, among others, which a visitor can see today in a trip lasting just a few hours. The museum includes among its varied collections a military-history room that features captured and preserved artifacts from this battle and the Revolutionary War era in general, while the monument offers the visitor an opportunity to take an elevator ride two thirds of the way to the top for an overview of placid southwestern Vermont.

One thing you can't see in Bennington is the location of the battle itself. That, ironically, lies about two air miles away in Walloomsac, New York. (A few historic markers point out the exact spots where altercations occurred, but there is no major attraction there that commemorates the battle.) So while you can't see the historic land in Bennington, you can see the treasured artifacts and symbols; and from the point of view of a visitor who'd like to investigate a little bit of Revolutionary War history and take a look into this smashing colonial victory, the town of Bennington is the place.

The battle, to answer a logical question, is named after Bennington and not Walloomsac because the Vermont town and, most important, the military supplies stored there were the target of British troops coming in from New York State; essentially, these were the reason for the battle taking place. The British, who had won at Fort Ticonderoga a few weeks earlier and then resisted a fiery rear-guard action by the Green Moun-

The Battle of Bennington was a crucial encounter in the chain of events culminating in the British surrender at Saratoga less than two months later.

Dominating the immediate area like a redwood tree in Kansas is the Bennington Battle Monument.

MELINDA MACAULEY

Take the elevator up to the viewing point in the Bennington Battle Monument, and on clear days you'll be able to see into three states.

tain Boys at Hubbardton, were desperately in need of fresh arms and supplies. The storehouse at Bennington seemed conveniently close by.

The colonists, overwhelmed by the seeming ease of the British victories, mustered under the leadership of General John Stark of New Hampshire in anticipation of a British attack led by General John Burgoyne. Stark learned of the British advance on August 13, 1777, and it was on August 16, "precisely at three o'clock in the afternoon," according to General Stark, that the fighting began. By five o'clock the British and their German mercenaries appeared to have been defeated; but a second enemy unit appeared, taking the tired and hungry colonists by surprise. However, as the Americans were giving ground and appeared to be losing, a band of the famed Green Mountain Boys, led by Colonel Seth Warner, came overland from Manchester. Though this was more of a morale booster than a manpower supplement, it was enough of an uplift to help the colonists halt the advance and force the British to flee to the west as darkness fell.

The Battle of Bennington is regarded by many historians as the most crucial encounter in a chain of events that culminated in the British surrender at Saratoga less than two months later. It was at Walloomsac that the British momentum was stopped, and it was at Saratoga that General Burgoyne surrendered his total command of some eight thousand troops, including British, Hessians, and Brunswick Grenadiers.

Four British cannons were captured during the battle, and General Stark, the only American present who was knowledgeable in the skill of loading and firing, personally took over the act of firing one such weapon. One of the captured cannons is now housed at the **Bennington Museum,** as are a few crumbling, baseball-sized cannonballs that were found at the battle site and could actually have been fired from the cannon on display.

There are other weapons on exhibit here, including the sword used by Colonel Baume (who led one unit of the British troops), and a Spanish-made sword used by the colonists. But by far the pride of the museum, if not of the entire town, is the five-and-a-half-by-ten-foot Bennington '76 flag, protected by glass and hanging grandly on the wall so that even one not entering the military-exhibit room can see it while just passing by. Considered to be the oldest Stars and Stripes in existence, this was the one that was flying over the supply storehouse that was the target of the British. Years of wear and exposure have caused the colors to completely vanish, but you can still discern the oversized "76," the thirteen stars, and the twelve wide but now colorless stripes (one is completely torn off the two-century-old flag).

It will become obvious to you why the British were called "redcoats" when you take a look at a small boy's jacket here. To give you an idea of what the colonists were wearing in the days of the Revolution, you can eyeball the buckskin trousers commonly worn by frontiersmen of that day as a kind of colonial blue jeans.

The drum may be the instrument most associated with the colonial period, and at the museum there's one that was captured from the British and is in remarkably good shape. Though the drum is a little worn, you can easily see the redcoat on the black horse as well as the "1757" painted on the side. The date refers to the year it was made, and while the drum was twenty years old at the time of the battle, it is thought of as being rather typical of the day. Some canteens, a powder horn, and captured instruments for drawing and map making are also exhibited.

Other artifacts relating to the Battle of Bennington? You'll find a small statuette of General John Stark, although this time raising his arms in victory at the Battle of Bunker Hill, and a six-by-twelve-foot painting depicting British prisoners being gathered and counted at the Bennington Meeting House following the battle. A key, across the narrow hall, identifies the major personalities in this 1938 Leroy Williams work of art.

Before heading to the monument, you might want to explore the other rooms inside the museum. In addition to the military gallery, there are excellent collections of Grandma Moses paintings, early-American glass, and Bennington pottery.

Not far from the museum is the **Bennington Battle Monument.** Dominating the immediate surroundings like a redwood tree in Kansas, the monument sits neatly in a circle of grass surrounded by a roadway. The blue dolomite structure was constructed in 1891 at a cost of one hundred twelve thousand dollars, and you may be interested to know that its weight is estimated at about three hundred thousand tons.

An elevator takes you up about two hundred feet, and from this viewpoint you can peruse a 360-degree panorama of the southern Green Mountain countryside. The southern exposure offers a bird's-eye view down Monument Avenue, the stately street you just drove along to get here. When skies are clear, you can see portions of the Bennington battlefield in New York State. Looking east you'll see a less congested part of Bennington, with Woodford Mountain in the distance. Facing north, you'll see various scenic peaks of the Green Mountains, including 3,816-foot-high Mount Equinox, forming a backdrop for Bennington College and other town structures. And to the west are country roads winding into pastoral scenes of the farms and white frame houses of New York State. (Binoculars are helpful if you're searching for specific landmarks.)

On a clear day, you'll also be able to distinguish Mount Anthony, highest peak in the immediate Ben-

Considered to be the oldest Stars and Stripes in existence, this was the one flying over the supply storehouse that was the British target.

COURTESY
BENNINGTON MUSEUM/MARTIN LEIFER

Protected by glass, this original 1776 American flag is the pride of the Bennington Museum.

nington area. In wind or rain, however, you could be in for a disappointment. In any kind of winds, glass doors at the top remain closed; and though you'll see for miles straight ahead, you'll find yourself peeking through corners for a glimpse of the scenery that's off to the sides.

The most popular time for visitors? It's estimated that the fall-foliage season wins with flying colors. But if you're looking for distance, we recommend a visit in April, between the showers and before the foliage has had a chance to grow and thicken. Another reason for coming to Bennington in April is that, since you'll be avoiding the height of the tourist season, the elevator operator may well have time to point out several notable sights when you arrive at the lookout point. Otherwise, with no diagrams or displays pointing out significant landmarks, you're on your own; you may enjoy the view, but whether you know just what you're looking at will depend on your own familiarity with local geography.

We recommend a visit in April, between the showers and before the foliage has had a chance to grow and thicken.

While you're waiting for the elevator, take a look at the authentically re-created diorama downstairs. You'll see models of Colonel Seth Warner's Green Mountain Boys facing off against troops of mercenary soldiers from Brunswick, Germany, in the second engagement of the battle. Hanging above the diorama is a massive iron kettle that was used for cooking by General Burgoyne's troops. The kettle was left on the ground for many years simply because of its great weight, but after it was finally removed, it was used for a long while by area farmers during hog-killing time.

The kettle, though an impressive antique, is also a representation. And that sums up the attractions of Bennington. From the 1776 flag to the battle monument itself, this is a town of representations. And that, in the end, may be much more important than the actual battleground.

ACCESS

BENNINGTON MUSEUM. Directions: From the junction of routes 9 and 7, go west 1 mile on Route 9 (West Main Street) to the museum. **Season:** March through November. **Days:** Daily. **Admission** charged. **Allow** 1 hour to 90 minutes to see the entire museum; allow 30 minutes to see the military exhibits only. **Telephone:** (802) 447-1571.

BENNINGTON BATTLE MONUMENT. Directions: From the junction of routes 9 and 7, go west on Route 9, past the Bennington Museum, to Monument Drive. Turn onto Monument Drive; the monument is straight ahead. **Season:** April through October. **Days:** Daily. **Admission** charged. **Allow** 20 to 30 minutes. **Notes:** Free parking is available north and northeast of the monument. Tickets should be purchased in the gift shop, the little white house next to the northeast parking area. **Telephone:** (802) 447-0550.

The Heroes

"Did you know that the Civil War began and ended in Brunswick, Maine?" asks our guide at the Pejepscot Historical Museum. Eyebrows are raised and
shoulders shrugged as we think back on Bull Run and
Appomattox, neither of which seems to have anything
whatsoever to do with this college town hundreds of
miles to the north. "Well," she states after hearing no
answers, "Harriet Beecher Stowe wrote *Uncle Tom's
Cabin* here, and later on, when President Lincoln met
Stowe, he said, 'So you're the little lady that started
this big war.' And it was at Appomattox that a Brunswick man and Bowdoin College professor, Joshua
Lawrence Chamberlain, accepted General Lee's surrender sword." That's just the beginning. As we tour
this museum that seems virtually to be Brunswick's
attic, we hear stories abut the military memorabilia,
the kitchen, the trades room, and more.

We learn, for instance, that it was two Bowdoin
alumni who were the first to reach the North Pole and
are today honored in Bowdoin's Peary-MacMillan
Arctic Museum. And that when a work from little-
known artist Winslow Homer became a part of Bowdoin's collection in 1894, it was viewed as a novel piece
of modern art; today, a substantial collection of his art
forms an exhibit in the Bowdoin College Museum of
Art. These three museums constitute a daytrip that
permits you to see three different aspects of this college
town, evidence that in Brunswick there are very
definitely both a college and a town.

If you start in the morning, you'll commence in
one of the college museums since the Pejepscot
Historical Museum doesn't open its doors until the
afternoon. The Peary-MacMillan Arctic Museum and
the Museum of Art directly face the college's main
quadrangle. While strolling to your destinations, direct
your eyes to some of the nineteenth-century architecture around you; though Bowdoin officially opened in
1802 (with eight students), the majority of buildings
found along the east end of the quad were constructed
between 1808 and 1855, while most of those lining the
quad's west side were built between 1861 and 1894.
Hubbard Hall, which flanks the south end and is the
home of the Arctic Museum, is a 1902-1903 creation;
the Walker Art Building, where you'll find the collection of oils, etchings, and sculpture, was erected from
1892 to 1894.

Neither museum offers guides — you walk about
at your own pace and can read the well-labeled displays for information. So when you see Admiral
Robert Peary's (class of 1877) shabby-looking two-
foot-wide and more than twelve-foot-long sledge in
the Arctic Museum, you'll read that the wood sides are
lashed together by sealskin thongs — but that this
rickety sledge could support from one thousand to

*Portraits of local heroes, like
James Bowdoin II, as well as
those of national heroes decorate
the walls in the Bowdoin College
Museum of Art.*

*"So," President Lincoln
said when he met
Harriet Beecher Stowe,
"you're the little lady
that started this big
war."*

Mother and Child, *pastel on buff paper by Mary Cassatt, one of many intriguing works displayed in the Bowdoin College Museum of Art.*

twelve hundred pounds on level surfaces. Other implements you can see that Peary and his chief assistant, Admiral Donald B. MacMillan (class of 1898), used in their 1909 expedition? There's an ice lance that could be a lethal weapon even today, an arctic T-shirt looking comfortably warm, and combination wood and rawhide snowshoes.

The camera was just coming into its own at the time of the expedition, and there are some "vacation" photos here far different from your neighbors' color slides of Mexico. A Kodak Model 3A Autographic was used to take a picture of the explorers' supply ship *Erik*, and another of some friends named Eningwah, Ootah, Segloo, and Ooqueah, four Eskimos who reached the Pole with Peary and another assistant. You won't find any Hawaiian-shirted tourists with Instamatics in these photos.

The rear section of the museum is devoted to arctic exploration following Peary's expedition and continuing through the first half of this century. Eskimo sculptures and carvings, used for both religious and practical purposes, make up a formidable portion of the exhibits here. Tupilak carvings from East Greenland depicting part-human and part-animal beings were thought to cause harm to one's enemies; it was believed they were brought to life by singing magic songs. Just the thought of a human body with a shark's head could be enough to frighten anyone's enemy!

The clothing on display ranges from the quite practical to the overpowering — and that means all the way from a child's sealskin parka and boots to a woman's multicolored outfit from Greenland and children's netted collars incorporating blue, white, red, and green beads. And while you probably wouldn't want to chance walking down the streets of your neighborhood wearing the wooden snow goggles with two small slits, you can't argue with the functional design; these were worn in the spring, when the light reflecting from snowy fields could cause a naked eye to go snow blind.

Art aficionados surely will enjoy spending time in the **Bowdoin College Museum of Art.** But even if you're the type who could take an afternoon nap on a tour of the Louvre, you may be interested in the Gilbert Stuart portraits hanging here. The most recognizable subject is Thomas Jefferson, painted by Stuart between 1805 and 1807; this oil on canvas measures about forty-eight by thirty-nine feet, and was given to the school by benefactor James Bowdoin III. There's also a Stuart portrait of Bowdoin, and one of President James Madison, as well as numerous others lining the walls of the gallery. Glass cases here harbor Paul Revere II silver and American pewter objects in the forms of porringers, syrup jugs, basins, and a fireman's speaking trumpet, looking like a miniature horn.

The Winslow Homer exhibits are downstairs.

Homer, a Boston native who worked for many years out of Prouts Neck, Maine, began his professional career by working for a Boston lithographer in 1854 and 1855. After illustrating and painting Civil War subjects from 1863 through 1865, he went on to work in France, the Adirondacks, and Gloucester. He settled in Prouts Neck in 1883 and lived there until his death in 1910. In addition to his etchings, water colors, and some illustrations, you can also inspect his personal possessions such as a canvas knapsack, a casting net, and a canteen. To let you see what he looked like, there's a portrait of the dark-haired and bushy-mustached Homer on the wall.

Other modes and styles to be seen here? There are Italian temperas on panels from the fifteenth and six-teenth centuries, a German woodcarving from around 1600, examples of French Limoges from the sixteenth century, and a 1603 Spanish oil on panel of King David — just the highlights of the European paintings, sculptures, and furniture in the Boyd Gallery. The Hal-ford Gallery, downstairs, is filled with ceramics from the Far East and art objects from ancient Greece and Rome.

To learn a little something about the town where the prestigious college is located, and to get a few good laughs as you study some of the relics of Brunswick's past, plan some time at the **Pejepscot Historical Museum.** You'll probably want to take your car from campus (if you walk, expect a thirty-minute stroll) to get to the museum, where you can learn about Brunswick's connection to the Civil War, see how a cracker stamp was used in early American kitchens, or crank a siren that was once a part of an early fire engine. And chances are good that if you visit this brick building with green shutters at 11 Lincoln Street more than once, you'll get to see something different each time; there are so many items here relating to an earlier time in Brunswick that exhibits are constantly rotated. (One thing that never changes is the name; Pejepscot was the Indian name for the lands where present-day Brunswick and the adjoining towns of Harpswell and Topsham sit. It translates to mean "crooked like a diving snake," probably a reference to the winding lower Androscoggin River that today forms the border between Brunswick and Topsham.)

Chances are great that the exhibits in the adjacent garage won't change either; here is the fire tug *Niagara #3*, which the guide will tell you can hold one hundred men. (We couldn't believe it either.) The siren that you can crank (more than likely, your kids will get a bigger charge out of it than you will), was once lent to Arthur Fiedler when he was a guest conductor of the Portland Symphony; the bell that kids can ring on the fire engine boasts no such claim to immortality but makes a lot of noise and does add charm to this vehicle.

The museum staff is also pleased with the displays

"Come on in if you want to see a bunch of naked ladies," our guide said.

At Brunswick's Pejepscot Historical Museum you can learn about everything from the practical applications of a cracker stamp to the history behind a Revolutionary War era drum.

"Not all Brunswick doctors were successful," the guide stated as she showed us the coffin plates.

There are wax dolls, bisque dolls, papier-mâché dolls, doll costumes, doll accessories, and so many other dolls and associated artifacts, that only a limited portion can be displayed at a time.

of dolls (which include wax, bisque, and papier mâché faces) and of clothes and costumes here. The numbers of collections are so great, however, that only a limited portion can be displayed at one time. In fact, when we toured the museum, we caught the staff smack in the middle of an exhibit change; "Come on in if you want to see a bunch of naked ladies," our guide said, directing us to some denuded mannequins waiting for new outfits to show off.

That irreverent sense of humor was evident in most of the tour that we were given. "Not all Brunswick doctors were successful," the guide stated while showing us the coffin plates in the trades room. And of course, there's that information most of us never knew about the Civil War starting and ending in Brunswick. Along the same line, you're given a chance to brush up on your own knowledge of trivia. After showing us a war club and some hair necklaces that Brunswick sailors brought back from the Sandwich Islands during the last century, our guide asked us where the Sandwich Islands were. The answer, we were embarrassed to learn, is the South Pacific — these islands now are known collectively as Hawaii.

There are a total of eight rooms here and each is stocked with memorabilia when you arrive (if you don't happen upon a transition period as we did when we met up with nude mannequins). All tours are guided, and if you're lucky enough to get director Bette Copeland to give your tour, you are in for a treat. She's got a wonderful personality and a marvelous sense of humor, and offers a most upbeat way to end the third leg of your look inside Brunswick's time capsule.

ACCESS

PEARY-MACMILLAN ARCTIC MUSEUM AND BOWDOIN COLLEGE MUSEUM OF ART. Directions: From Interstate 95, take the Brunswick-Bath exit onto Route 1 (Pleasant Street); head east on Pleasant Street, then take a right onto Maine Street. Follow Maine Street .3 mile to the college campus. **Season:** All year. **Days:** Summer, Tuesday through Saturday days and evenings, plus Sunday afternoon; rest of the year, shorter hours. **Admission** free. **Allow** 30 to 45 minutes in the Arctic Museum and 45 minutes to an hour in the Museum of Art. **Telephone** for both: (207) 725-8731.

PEJEPSCOT HISTORICAL MUSEUM. Directions: From Interstate 95, take the Brunswick-Bath exit onto Route 1 (Pleasant Street); head east on Pleasant Street, then take a right onto Maine Street, followed by a left just before the railroad tracks; turn left onto Park Row, where the museum is at the intersection with Green Street. **Season:** All year. **Days:** Monday through Friday afternoons. **Donation** requested. **Allow** 30 to 45 minutes. **Telephone:** (207) 729-6606.

CHAPTER II

Of Pen & Palette

Perhaps it's because New England was one of the first regions settled in the country. Perhaps it's because the beauty of each changing season served as irresistible inspiration. Or perhaps the tradition of thinkers and creators calling New England home was, once begun, self-perpetuating. Whichever, there is no question that a disproportionate number of artists have written and painted while living here.

Some, like John Greenleaf Whittier and Ralph Waldo Emerson, were natives while others, such as Mark Twain and Herman Melville, were immigrants from other parts of the United States. And then there were the summer residents like Daniel Chester French and Augustus Saint-Gaudens, lured from New York City to New England's verdant hills (Saint-Gaudens thought enough of the area to eventually make it his year-round residence).

The homes, studios, and birthplaces of many of these geniuses are still around and are open to the public. In some, you'll get to see everything from original manuscripts to the coats the artists wore when they stepped outside in the cold northern air. Others hold few or no original furnishings and serve mainly as galleries or visual tributes to past eras. But all offer an insight into what inspired and propelled the famous artists who lived here.

French, Melville, & Wharton

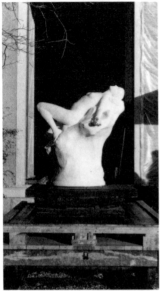

French's tribute to the modern woman, Andromeda, *was his last major work before his death; it's on view today at his Stockbridge home.*

Though down-to-earth in character, French had a somewhat stuffy veneer, always working in his studio attired in a tie and jacket.

The Great Emancipator, the great whale, and a great tragedy were creations of the hands and minds of three of Massachusetts' greatest residents. Daniel Chester French, who kept a summer home and studio in Stockbridge, Massachusetts, sculpted works including the *Seated Lincoln* housed in Washington, D.C.'s, Lincoln Memorial. Herman Melville, some twenty-five years earlier, penned *Moby Dick* in a home in Pittsfield. And Edith Wharton, the author of *Ethan Frome*, lived in a Mediterranean-style mansion in Lenox for a decade before settling permanently in Europe. The Berkshire homes of all three are open to the public.

The tour at **Chesterwood,** French's warm-weather abode tucked into the hills above Stockbridge, combines a layman's explanation of the art of sculpturing with a look at the house of this proper gentleman. The studio, subject of one of three guided-tour segments at Chesterwood and perhaps the most popular, affords the visitor an inspiring look at some of French's works and miniature working models. You can examine a plaster cast of the notable *Seated Lincoln* and a model of the *Minuteman*, which French was commissioned to create in 1873 at the wizened old age of twenty-three and which today sits at the North Bridge in Concord, Massachusetts. These are both working miniatures that look as if they've been through the spin cycle a few times, but the curvaceous *Andromeda*, on the other hand, reclines luxuriously in full glory. The nude female figure was French's tribute to the modern woman; created from 1929 to 1931, it was French's last major work before he died at age eighty.

Today, *Andromeda* sits atop a railroad car and once in a great while still makes a short journey on the studio's railroad tracks, passing through the colossal double doors and out into direct sunlight. The use of the tracks is indicative of the utmost diligence and fetish for detail that French was noted for; as part of his sculpturing process, the artist would place a near-finished work on the car and wheel it outside. Whether it looked its best in sunlight or in shadows — conditions it would be subjected to while sitting in a park or other public site — would be decided at that point.

Small sculptures, busts, working models, and even antique beer and cereal containers are inside the barn gallery, usually the subject of the first portion of the tour. A brief explanation of the items displayed is sprinkled with trivia regarding the art itself. You are then permitted to wander about at your leisure. The bust of Ralph Waldo Emerson is always on view, but exhibit information, such as the fact that models in French's day were paid seventy-five cents per hour (actually forty-five minutes with a fifteen-minute

"I spend six months of the year up here. That is Heaven. New York is — well, New York," French once said. This home, Chesterwood, was his Heaven.*

break), also makes tour-goers stop and think.

You learn, too, about the man himself. He was down-to-earth, yet carried what some may interpret as a stuffy veneer, always working in his studio while attired in a tie and jacket. French was a member of the New England and New York upper crust (born in Exeter, New Hampshire, and living in Concord, Massachusetts, before his move to work in New York), and his subjects reflected his upbringing; he often chose to sculpt notable Americans like Lincoln, John Harvard, General James Oglethorpe, and Thomas Gallaudet as well as mythical and allegorical figures. His style is perhaps summed up best by his *Minuteman.* In a literal sense, it commemorates one of the most illustrious moments in America's history; in a more abstract interpretation, its likeness has been used on many an occasion to replace Uncle Sam or the bald eagle as a representation of the country. During World War II, for example, it decorated defense bonds, stamps, and posters. In the year it was dedicated, 1875, a reporter described *Minuteman* as "a thorough Yankee." Not much different from its creator.

In 1875, a reporter described Minuteman *as "a thorough Yankee." Not much different from its creator.*

Which is why when you tour the 1900-1901 Colonial Revival residence, the other main portion of your visit to Chesterwood, you'll see columns in the first-floor hallway topped not with capitals of an Ionic or Doric mode, but with something purely American: carved ears of corn. And in addition to hearing about the rest of the furnishings, you also will be told about the single preserved rose on display; according to the guide, this was the flower that was placed on the body of Abraham Lincoln at his funeral. It was ultimately removed and given to the French family.

While discussing his summer home, French once said to a reporter, "I spend six months of the year up here. That is Heaven. New York is — well, New York." Herman Melville, a native New Yorker, may not have specifically tagged this region of western Massachusetts "Heaven," but he thought enough of the Berkshires to move to his home at **Arrowhead** at age thirty-one with the full intention of putting down roots. Apparently very much a young man in search of his niche in society, Melville, during just a decade and a half prior to his move to the Berkshires, had been employed as a bank clerk, a factory worker, a schoolteacher, a sailor, and a writer; he had also worked on a whaling ship, and had studied engineering and surveying in the vain hope of landing a job on the building of the Erie Canal.

It was the publication in 1846 of *Typee*, a novel of the South Seas based upon Melville's eighteen months spent there after deserting the New Bedford whaling ship *Acushnet*, that made him think seriously about making writing his career. Melville married in 1847, wrote a second South Seas romance called *Omoo* that same year, and then went off to England and continental Europe for a short visit a few years later, returning to the United States with his eye on settling down in western Massachusetts.

The house he bought, located in Pittsfield just over the Lenox town line, is a former inn, constructed in 1780. When Melville purchased it from a local doctor in 1850 (the building ceased being an inn in 1845), he had no idea that he would be selling it just thirteen years later due to lack of both recognition and commercial success as a writer.

The study in Arrowhead, where Melville did most of his writing during those thirteen years, features a captivating view of Mount Greylock poking above the open countryside, and is perhaps the most popular room on the tour. Though the author's original desk is long gone, a duplicate sits where his did, by a window with an eastern exposure; he would awaken early, the guide explains, to tend his farm animals and then retire to the desk to write from eight o'clock to two o'clock. Melville, who had an eye problem, could only write by natural light; once the early afternoon sun had passed overhead, he could no longer see well enough to do any work. Tiny eyeglasses and a scrimshaw letter opener (which is rather appropriate considering the subjects of much of his writing), both of which it's believed belonged to Melville, are displayed here.

The chimney room downstairs offers a two-faceted representation of Arrowhead's history. The furnishings, including a curved-back settle perpendicular to a brick-lined fireplace, plus a grandfather clock tucked into a corner, fit the mood of an eighteenth-century inn. However, you're told to look above the fireplace along the mantel where Melville's brother, Allan, inscribed quotations from one of the writer's short stories, called "I and My Chimney." The story was basically a quarrel between the narrator, who wanted to keep an old chimney, and his wife, who wanted it destroyed. (They kept the chimney.) By the fireplace is Arrowhead's only piece of Melville's original furniture, a toy chest containing toy flatware he gave to his young daughter, Frances.

Though there is no other furniture here that was owned by Melville, the Berkshire Historical Society has attained a fairly good idea of the house's mid-nineteenth-century appearance from the author's own written recollections, and has filled most rooms in

The story was a quarrel between the narrator, who wanted to keep an old chimney, and his wife, who wanted it destroyed. (They kept the chimney.)

Arrowhead with period pieces to re-create its appearance during Melville's time. (The chimney room is an exception.) Society members have even gone as far as to rebuild, on the home's south side, a piazza that had been removed by later owners. For inspiration, Melville often paced repeatedly on the piazza while gazing dreamily at Mount Greylock. All this time searching for brainstorms paid off; it's estimated that about one third of his literary output was churned out at this house, including a collection of creativity called, appropriately, *The Piazza Tales*.

You hear during your tour that *Moby Dick*, which Melville scripted in the upstairs study, didn't make one cent until a Melville revival in the 1920s, some thirty years after his death. The same held true for his equally famous novel *Billy Budd*, which no one knew even existed until an historian went through some of the novelist's papers in 1924 and discovered this unpublished manuscript. In fact, of Melville's many books, the only two that made any money during his lifetime were *Typee* and *Omoo*, now long forgotten by most except some Melville scholars. When the former mariner moved into the wilderness of the northern Berkshires, he explained that the view of the mountains and the quiet pastoral lifestyle were the ultimate sources of inspiration. His work showed the effects of this atmosphere, you realize, but it took the mass public some seventy years to notice.

After leaving Arrowhead, Melville worked for a couple of decades as a deputy customs inspector for the port of New York until retirement in the mid 1880s, continuing to write poetry on the side. After he retired, he composed *Billy Budd* over a period of three years, beginning in 1888 and finishing it about six months before his death, which went largely unnoticed by the general public. He never did live in the Berkshires again and died believing himself to be a total failure. He is buried in New York City.

Unlike the preserved Chesterwood or the two-hundred-year-old, heritage-filled Arrowhead, **The Mount,** located in neighboring Lenox, is only now undergoing substantial restoration. In fact, it would not be entirely appropriate to call this summer home of Edith Wharton a bona fide tourist attraction. There is, as at other famous home museums, an organized monolog filled with information on the house and its noted resident, but thanks to years of neglect, you won't see any great number of rare, well-preserved treasures or rooms that look like Wharton just left them and went outside for a walk. You will see, however, where she lived, worked, and entertained, and you'll gain understanding of her thinking.

There's another difference between the Mount and other such attractions: this estate serves a dual purpose. It is the home of a burgeoning professional Shakespearean company as well as a monument to

Moby Dick *didn't make a cent until a Melville revival in the 1920s, some thirty years after the author's death.*

Edith Wharton, with the backyard and the house's terrace serving as the stage for various productions. And it is the staff of Shakespeare & Company that gives the tours at The Mount. (Though Shakespeare is their primary forte, they are thoroughly familiar with Wharton and often present a play dedicated to her.)

Don't be disheartened if you couldn't place Wharton's name. She's one of those authors who is often remembered more for her works than by her own name, so it's likely that you'll recall discussions of *Ethan Frome* that you had as a high-school sophomore rather than the woman who conceived it. However, this novelette about infatuation and frustration in a stark New England village was rather untypical of most of Wharton's works. More often, she used her writing as a vehicle to expose what she considered the hypocrisy of Manhattan society, in which she was born and raised. In *The House of Mirth*, her first widely acclaimed novel, written in 1905, she tells the story of socialite Lily Bart, whose poor judgments regarding her romances and diversions like gambling drop her a few rungs down the social and financial ladder; unaccustomed to working for a living, she can't maintain the lifestyle of her youth. Wharton's 1920 Pulitzer Prize winning novel, *The Age of Innocence*, focused on two unfulfilled lovers in the "innocent" world of New York high society. Many of her other short stories and novels also take place in this setting of her growing and learning years.

Wharton was a close friend of writer and critic Henry James, and many students of literature consider the writing styles of the two very similar. James spent two summers visiting Wharton and her husband, Teddy, at The Mount although the torrid summer temperatures, which could strike even this part of the Berkshires now and then, would take their toll on James; the two authors would often go for drives together through the area as a means of relieving James from the heat. It was on one of these drives that Wharton stumbled upon the village of Plainfield, which she used as the setting for *Ethan Frome*.

No unrestrained extrovert, though, Wharton craved privacy when not dutifully involved in enter-

"Privacy," Wharton once said, "should be one of the requisites of a civilized life."

This twenty-nine-room mansion was the home of Edith Wharton. If you visit, you can get a close-at-hand look at the painstaking work of restoring a lovely old building.

taining. This is demonstrated when you're led from one private room to another directly or by way of the terrace, deliberately avoiding a public hallway (although there are doors to the hallways as well). "After all, privacy should be one of the requisites of a civilized life," she once said.

Another such requisite of Wharton's was the constant use of symmetry, which she referred to as "sanity of decoration." This is pointed out dramatically in the library and the writing room. In the library, for instance, a liquor cabinet is explicitly designed to match a door just for the purpose of balance. The same applies to the writing room, where the entrances are perfectly harmonious. Incidentally, the writing room was that in name only; although she wrote personal letters there, all her professional work was created as she lay propped up in bed.

Throughout the tour, you're made aware that restoration is an ongoing thing. You're shown where tapestry panels and gilt mirrors used to be and you're invited to look at photos lining hallway walls and depicting The Mount's interior when Wharton lived here from 1902 to 1911. Not that all adornments are gone; there are original oil paintings along staircases and naked cherubs above doorways.

The fact that the house is currently undergoing a long restoration does not have to be taken as a negative, especially if you've ever wondered about the extensive work involved in restoring other famous homes. Here, you get to see and hear firsthand about the extensive labor required. And no matter what the stage of the restoration process when you visit, you will assuredly be given a good look into the personality of a colorful and admired American author.

She wrote personal letters in the writing room, but all her professional work was created as she lay propped up in bed.

ACCESS

CHESTERWOOD. Directions: From Interstate 90 exit 2, go west on Route 102 for 2 miles beyond the center of Stockbridge; then take a left onto Route 183 and follow the signs. **Season:** May through October. **Days:** Daily. **Admission** charged. **Allow** 90 minutes. **Telephone:** (413) 298-3579.

ARROWHEAD. Directions: From Interstate 90 exit 2, go north on Route 20 (which also becomes Route 7) to Holmes Road. Turn right onto Holmes Road; Arrowhead is ahead on the left. **Season:** June through October. **Days:** Daily. **Admission** charged. **Allow** 30 minutes. **Telephone:** (413) 442-1793.

THE MOUNT. Directions: From the southern junction of routes 7 and 7A, head east on Plunkett Road for ½ mile; The Mount driveway is on the right. **Season:** Mid-June through August. **Days:** Wednesday through Sunday. **Admission** charged. **Allow** 20 to 30 minutes. **Telephone:** (413) 637-3353. Restoration update: (413) 637-1899.

Emerson & Friends

Emerson and Hawthorne lived here, and Emerson's grandfather watched from his window as the British and the colonists battled at the North Bridge. Today, The Old Manse is open for touring.

Ripley wrote his sermons while standing, resigning himself to the fact that when his feet were tiring, the sermons were long enough.

There are states in the union that would give up their state flowers for a chance to boast some of the literary giants who have called Concord, Massachusetts, their home. Louisa May Alcott, Nathaniel Hawthorne, Ralph Waldo Emerson, Margaret Sidney, and Henry David Thoreau are some of the well-known writers who resided in this historic community during the nineteenth century. With the exception of Thoreau's, you can still see the actual homes in which these individuals lived.

Which is not to say you won't need a scorecard to keep track of who lived where. They were a highly mobile group who seemed to make a habit of playing musical homes. Pencils up! The Alcotts, Hawthorne, and Sidney, at various points, all lived in The Wayside; the Alcotts also lived in Orchard House, next door. Emerson's ancestors originally made The Old Manse their home, although Hawthorne also rested his quill pen there for a few years. Emerson, though born in Boston, lived in The Old Manse twice before moving into his almost brand-new home, now called simply The Emerson House, in 1835. Among Emerson's frequent visitors was Thoreau. Pencils down!

With so many authors and so many homes, you may view coming here as you would cleaning a child's room; it's hard to tell where to start. The organized way to tour these famous homes, we feel, is in chronological order; therefore, the commencing point would be **The Old Manse,** located on Monument Street right next to the North Bridge.

"Between two tall gateposts of roughhewn stone (the gate itself having fallen from its hinges at some unknown epoch) we beheld the gray front of the old parsonage, terminating the vista of an avenue of black ash trees," is the way Nathaniel Hawthorne described The Old Manse when he moved in during the year 1842. The "gray front" is now brown, although the "two tall gateposts" still stand as sentinels to this august abode of ministers and authors. It was built in 1769 and 1770 by Reverend William Emerson, grandfather of the poet, who on April 19, 1775, stood guard between his home and the North Bridge while his family watched the battle from the upstairs windows.

The reverend died after contracting "camp fever" while serving as chaplain for some Concord militiamen at Fort Ticonderoga, New York, and his widow later married Reverend Ezra Ripley. You can still see Ripley's writing desk in an upstairs bedroom; he wrote his sermons while standing, resigning himself to the fact that when his feet were tiring, it meant the sermons were long enough.

Mrs. Ripley's grandson, Ralph Waldo Emerson, was close to his grandmother, and lived here as a child in 1813. He moved in again in 1834 and stayed a year, long enough to compose his first book of essays, called *Nature*. However, it was Nathaniel Hawthorne, who rented The Old Manse from Ezra Ripley's son Samuel from 1842 to 1845, who left his mark — literally — on the house. On a window pane in the dining room downstairs and on another in the upstairs study, Hawthorne and his wife, Sophia, inscribed some passing thoughts with her diamond ring. Downstairs, Sophia wrote of their baby daughter Una's first look at winter, "Una Hawthorne stood on this window sill January 22, 1845, while the trees were all glass chandeliers, a goodly show which she liked much, tho' only ten months old." In the study, Sophia wrote, among other notions, "man's accidents are God's purposes," while husband Nathaniel simply identified the room as his study.

It was Nathaniel Hawthorne who left his mark — literally — on the house.

Hawthorne's most famous work produced during these early years was a collection of short stories titled *Mosses from an Old Manse;* though it was a moderate success, it did not give him any great monetary rewards. Hawthorne left here when one of the Ripley family returned in 1845.

Most of the furnishings you'll see on your seven-room tour of The Old Manse were used by Hawthorne and Emerson but were Ripley property. The four-poster bed, the 1864 vintage Steinway grand piano, and the blue-and-white Canton china all belonged to members of the Ripley family during the 170 years The Old Manse was in their hands. The stately grandfather clock in the dining room, however, was bought along with a long dark coat by William Emerson for the grand sum of twenty dollars; he wrote in his diary that he thought he got a "good bargain."

Keeping things in the family, **The Emerson House,** that white frame structure that sits at the hectic intersection of the Cambridge Turnpike and Route 2A, is a logical second stop. This is where the famed writer and his second wife resided from 1835 until their respective deaths in 1882 and 1892. It is also where most of his works were written.

Except for the furniture in the study, which is the first room you see on the tour here, everything in the house is authentically Emerson's. In a downstairs hallway, you can hear about the three small chairs, the middle one of which has a little drawer under the seat; this was hand wrought by Thoreau for his friend Emerson as a place to store his Sunday gloves before he went to church (although he wasn't a regular churchgoer by any means).

Rare green Mintonware china (it's usually blue) from England in addition to a cannonball bed where all four of Emerson's sons were born highlight one of the upstairs bedrooms, while the double table is the biggest conversation piece in the dining room. Both Emerson's bride, Lydian (originally Lydia, but altered by Emerson to prevent the inevitable Bostonian mis-

Henry David Thoreau was one of the most frequent visitors at Ralph Waldo Emerson's house in Concord.

Take a look at the mirror underneath the "petticoat table," which would indicate to Lydian whether hers showed or not.

treatment, which would sound something like "Lydieremerson"), and he had dining-room tables prior to their marriage. A possible disagreement as to whose table to use was avoided when both fit perfectly together to form one big table that would seat eighteen. They didn't have sixteen children, but they did entertain many of the local intellectual community and the seats were often filled.

The parlor was the other main gathering place for visitors to the Emersons' house, and discussions here were often devoted to review of the thoughts and ideas of other prominent writers and philosophers of the day. In this room, you'll be told about Lydian's love for mirrors, many of which are to be seen throughout the house; take a look here at the mirror underneath the "petticoat table," which would indicate to Lydian whether hers showed or not.

Thoreau was probably the most frequent guest at the house. On two different occasions, he lived there for a number of months while his host was out of town. After a while, the Emerson children started to look upon Thoreau, who was fourteen years younger than their father, as an older brother.

Before the children were old enough to understand the thoughts of Thoreau and their father, they would have spent more time in the nursery than with the family's guests. In this upstairs room, you can today see a number of artifacts that belonged to members of the family. A rocking horse dating from 1750 is one of the more ancient items here, while the standard-sized badminton birdies in the toy-filled chest dominate the unbelievably tiny racquets. Emerson's candle holders and some tickets to one of his 1861 lectures are also worthy of your notice. The bathroom on this floor was once used as Thoreau's guest room before it was set up in its current form; the conversion of this room to a bathroom was considered something of a luxury at the time and was a sure sign of success.

The tours here are given whenever a group shows up; there is no waiting, since if you come when a tour is in progress, you join it immediately and then later on see the rooms you missed.

Again, if you're interested in some kind of chronological order, head next to **The Wayside,** the Alcotts' first Concord home, and save Orchard House until you learn a little about the family here.

The Alcotts only resided here for three years, and it is the influence of the home's later literary occupants, Hawthorne and Sidney, that is in evidence as you take the guided tour here. However, you're also reminded that this house stood for about 130 years before the Alcotts wrote their first words. It was initially sold around 1717 (the exact date it was built is forever lost in oblivion) as a four-room saltbox home, and occupants before the Alcotts included Concord minuteman Samuel Whitney, Harvard scientist John Winthrop, and a number of artisans. The house is a tribute to man's ability to adapt his surroundings to his individual needs, and the metamorphosis of this house is evident as you go through each section.

For instance, when Bronson Alcott, his wife, and his four daughters, Anna, Louisa May, Elizabeth, and Abba May (immortalized as Meg, Jo, Beth, and Amy in Louisa May's Little Women), moved here, the house was not nearly large enough to comfortably accommodate them. Hence, two downstairs and two upstairs bedrooms were added onto the west end of the house for the girls; also part of that addition was a study for Bronson Alcott. At the east end of the house, a wing provided the Alcotts with both a bathroom (a rarity in those days) and a woodshed.

The Alcotts did not come here as a wealthy family, however. Bronson, a philosopher and teacher as well as a leader of the transcendentalist movement, arrived following a disastrous attempt at communal living at Fruitlands in nearby Harvard, Massachusetts. Thrilled to be in Concord with his friends Thoreau and Emerson, Alcott settled in as a farmer, working eight acres of land loaned by Emerson. He called this home Hillside, and when you look out the back window, you'll be able to tell why. But Boston contained more opportunities for this revolutionary educator and in 1848, the family relocated to the city.

DIANE DE MANGO

The parlor inside The Wayside, home of the Alcotts, Hawthorne, and Sidney. The gables above the windows are Hawthorne's addition; he had been impressed by some he had seen in Italy.

One of the first marks to be made on the house by the next tenant, Nathaniel Hawthorne, was a change in name. Hawthorne called it The Wayside, which, he wrote in a letter to a friend, "seems . . . to possess a moral as well as a descriptive propriety." But that was hardly Hawthorne's only alteration of the house. The gabled effect of arches over the windows inside was a Hawthorne addition. So were the maid's quarters constructed over the kitchen and a bedroom for his daughter built over the Alcotts' west wing. But the major Hawthorne variation was a three-story addition at the house's back end with the bottom floor a parlor, the second a guest room, and the third Hawthorne's study tower.

The family had rented a cottage in 1850 and 1851 in Lenox, Massachusetts (a replica of the little red structure is used today as a practice room for Tanglewood musicians), but did not care for its cramped conditions. So from the financial success of Hawthorne's two classics, *The Scarlet Letter* and *The House of the Seven Gables*, the family, who had never before owned a home, was able to purchase this property from the Alcotts. And they were able to afford the many additions as well.

But it is interesting to hear that after spending the time and money to build the study tower, Hawthorne rarely wrote there. Instead, he preferred the open outdoors of the hillside in back, and the stand-up desk that you see in the tower was hardly used. It may seem unfortunate that Hawthorne didn't take advantage of the scene of the forest, mountains, and sky that's painted on the ceiling, although you can take his place when you view it on your tour. A word to those with weak legs: the stairway to the tower is steep and narrow, reminiscent of an Amsterdam canal house. So be prepared.

Hawthorne lived in Europe from 1853 to 1860, but then returned to The Wayside and lived here until his death at age sixty in 1864. Mrs. Hawthorne remained here four years afterward.

Though the house went through a few changes in ownership and even served as Mary Pratt's School for Young Ladies from 1873 to 1879, it was once more to be the home of a literary family. In 1883, Boston publisher Daniel Lothrop purchased it; it stayed in the Lothrop family until 1965, when the National Park Service acquired it.

Margaret Lothrop is hardly a household name, but those of you who remember the children's book series *The Five Little Peppers* will note that the author was Margaret Sidney. Sidney was the pen name of Margaret Lothrop, and you can see a collection of the series on the shelves of Mrs. Hawthorne's drawing room (later a memorial room to Margaret's husband, Daniel Lothrop). The Lothrops were deeply concerned with history, and this being one reason for their

The "mood pillow" reflected Mrs. Alcott's disposition: up meant she was cheerful, while down meant "keep your distance."

purchase of this legendary house made few changes regarding the structural condition of it. They did repaint the dining room and the sitting room and they added central heating and electricity, but felt a need to preserve Hawthorne's influence.

Next door to The Wayside is **Orchard House,** home exclusively of the Alcotts. After you pay your admission here, you're invited to take a look at the barn-like School of Philosophy, teaching place of Bronson Alcott, located up a small hill from the residence itself. All the furniture, mainly five rows of chairs and benches and a small podium, is original, with the exception of a pipe organ in a corner. A display on the wall describes the tenets of transcendentalism. This school is today regarded as the first school for adult education in the history of the country.

The Alcotts had lived in twenty-three houses in twenty-one years prior to their residence in Orchard House, but they stayed here for twenty years. They bought this house in 1857 — the house itself dates from the 1600s — and because of its neglected condition, worked on it for a year before living here.

Orchard House is on a par with Utopia for an Alcott admirer. Throughout the tour, you see the personal items used by the father, the mother, and the daughters. There's the small bust of Socrates that Bronson carried in his pocket wherever he went to speak, the cylindrical "mood pillow" Mrs. Alcott used to reflect her disposition — up meant she was cheerful,

Mrs. Alcott's mood pillow. You knew she was happy it if was positioned like this.

It's Utopia for an Alcott admirer. Orchard House was the family's home for twenty years.

while down meant "keep your distance" — the half-moon desk tucked in a corner where Louisa May wrote *Little Women*, and many of Abba May's paintings (she was the artistic one).

Louisa May wrote *Little Women* in response to a publisher's request that she write a girls' book since there were few about at the time; the only girls she knew were her sisters. Downstairs in the kitchen, you can see the soapstone sink the family bought after the first money came in following *Little Women's* success. And the book was, you inevitably hear, an instant triumph.

The Alcotts, Sidney, Emerson, Hawthorne, Thoreau. Names synonymous with American literary greatness. And visits to the homes in which these authors once lived will afford you a greater understanding of their works, their lives, and their thoughts.

ACCESS

THE OLD MANSE. Directions: From Interstate 95 exit 45W, go west on Route 2A, bear right toward Concord Center, then turn right onto Monument Street. The Old Manse is on Monument Street, right next to the path to the North Bridge. **Season:** April through October. **Days:** June through October, Thursday through Monday; April and May, weekends. **Admission** charged. **Allow** 30 minutes. **Note:** Parking is available in a lot across the street. **Telephone:** (617) 369-3909.

THE EMERSON HOUSE. Directions: From Interstate 95 exit 45W, go west on Route 2A to the junction with the Cambridge Turnpike; the house is just past the corner on the Cambridge Turnpike. **Season:** Mid-April through late October. **Days:** Thursday through Sunday and holidays. **Admission** charged. **Allow** 30 minutes. **Note:** Parking is available on the street in front of the house. **Telephone:** (617) 369-2236.

TO GET TO THE WAYSIDE, AND TO ORCHARD HOUSE AND THE SCHOOL OF PHILOSOPHY. From Interstate 95 exit 45W, go west on Route 2A about 3½ miles. Free parking is available in a lot on Hawthorne Street, across from The Wayside.

THE WAYSIDE. Season: April through October. **Days:** Thursday through Monday. **Admission** charged. **Allow** 45 minutes. **Telephone:** (617) 369-6975.

ORCHARD HOUSE AND THE SCHOOL OF PHILOSOPHY. Season: Mid-April through early November; winter by appointment. **Days:** Daily. **Admission** charged. **Allow** 35 minutes. **Telephone:** (617) 369-4118.

Whittier & Whistler

He saved money from a job as a shoemaker to go to school, subjected himself to mobs while he spoke against slavery in the decades prior to the Civil War, and was a firebrand whose vigorous abolitionist essays enraged masses. Yet today, John Greenleaf Whittier is known by most as the kindly looking old man who wrote such nostalgic odes to rural New England as "Snowbound" and "Barefoot Boy." Both his birthplace and his home, in Haverhill and Amesbury, Massachusetts, are still around today and can be visited by Whittier admirers as well as by those to whom Whittier's name is blurred with other poets and authors studied in a survey course of American literature.

About the time Whittier was starting to sound off against slave owners, one of America's most gifted artists was born just a couple dozen miles down the road, in Lowell. James Abbott McNeill Whistler's brush with history occurred when he captured the likeness of his maternal parent on canvas; since then, *Whistler's Mother* has been as famous to Americans as the *Statue of Liberty*. His birthplace, located smack in the heart of downtown Lowell, is open to the public primarily as an art gallery but also as a tribute to Whistler and his family. You can see this house, as well as both Whittier buildings, on a daytrip to northeastern Massachusetts.

Although it seems like maneuvering in reverse, you may get a little more out of this trip by stepping into the **Whittier Home** before looking at his birthplace. The Quaker poet wrote what's regarded as his best work, "Snowbound," as sort of a memorial poem from his home in Amesbury; he was then a fifty-eight-year-old man remembering the warm hearth he'd sat by with his beloved family, many of whom had died in recent years. The birthplace is therefore more meaningful as seen through the eyes of an adult looking back.

By the time Whittier had moved to 86 Friend Street in Amesbury, at age twenty-nine, he was already known as a fervent abolitionist. A farm worker and cobbler as a youngster, he took some of his money from his latter job and entered Haverhill Academy, where he took a liking to the poetry of Robert Burns. But it was his strong Quaker background as well as the influence of abolitionist editor William Lloyd Garrison, who had published his first poem, that led him to introduce the northern cause into his writings. (Whittier moved to Amesbury because of the Quaker Meeting House that was located nearby.) His staunch antislavery pamphlet, "Justice and Expediency," was published in 1833 and was probably the most significant work of his early years, kicking off over three decades of abolitionist writings. Yet, though he so firmly supported abolition, he was a pacifist and

Home of John Greenleaf Whittier for fifty-six years, this house saw his transition from fiery young abolitionist to nostalgic old man.

This is how Whittier's home looked when he wrote "Snowbound," and this is how it looks today. Which is probably the way he would have liked it.

opposed the civil war that seemed to be the inevitable consequence of any attempt to end slavery; at one point he wrote he would rather see the South secede than risk war. Inflaming abolitionists with his harsh antiwar stance, Whittier made enemies on both sides.

It's ironic that Whittier is best known today for his nonoffensive looks back at pastoral New England, while it was his rabble-rousing that propelled him into the national spotlight. One explanation is the lack of interest shown in writing advocating a cause once that cause has long ceased to be an issue. Another focuses on the fact that "Snowbound" was Whittier's first poem to make substantial money. Regardless, it was the publication of "Snowbound," in 1866, that made the name John Greenleaf Whittier illustrious.

The house in Amesbury where Whittier lived for fifty-six years is, for the most part, nothing to look at from the outside. It has had more face-lifts than a society matron, and because of that, even the curator couldn't categorize it as being one particular style. A "four-room cottage" when Whittier moved here in 1836 (it was probably built around 1820), the house is now a green-shuttered, rambling white structure that is camouflaged well by the other old homes on this downtown street. In fact, it's easy to miss unless you keep an eye out for the house number or small sign above the doorway labeling it the "Whittier Home."

Thanks to the Whittier Home Association, which purchased the residence in 1918 from family heirs, most of Whittier's furnishings are still here to be viewed. In the Manuscript Room, you can see the secretary desk upon which he wrote "Snowbound"; the desk is so narrow that it looks barely big enough to support pencil and pen. You are then told that as a man of, at best, modest income for most of his life until his success with that memorable poem, he never had the money to spend on frills; after earning ten thousand dollars in commissions from the sale of "Snowbound" (he made ten cents on each one-dollar copy), he could afford an extravagance now and then. As evidence of that, you are shown the newer, more modern desk that he purchased.

The poet's green-velvet-covered lounge chair, sort of a predecessor to today's recliner, sits in the guest room, and if wear is any sign of utilization, it must have been employed to the fullest. His mother's spinning wheel, the family's fainting couch (which women wearing the day's stylish tight corsets would "faint" onto), his sister's homespun candlewick bedspread, and Whittier's own colorful dressing gown can, with other family furnishings, be seen. The dressing gown is a fascinating piece; although it might indicate that Whittier was a man who enjoyed the garish, you are told that, on the contrary, he was colorblind.

Are you the type that can't write a letter to Mom without making so many lines and X's that your paper looks like a school crosswalk? If so, you'll want to take a look in the Manuscript Room, at drafts of some of Whittier's poems in his original handwriting and with so many marks and scribbles that they can't help inspiring anyone who has ever had trouble putting thoughts into words. But there's more than writing on the walls; family pictures decorate the parlor, and a chromo-lithograph of the Haverhill birthplace will give you a preview of what to expect on your next stop.

However, the most popular feature in the **Whittier birthplace** is the fireplace, which has to rank as one of the most renowned in American literary history. It's the first thing you'll see on a tour of the nearly three-hundred-year-old structure in Haverhill — a building that, perhaps as fate's ultimate honor to the poet, has escaped the onslaught of progress and is still relatively isolated.

> Shut in from all the world without,
> We sat the clean-winged hearth about,
> Content to let the north-wind roar
> In baffled rage at pane and door,
> While the red logs before us beat
> The frost-line back with tropic heat;

"While the red logs before us beat / The frost-line back with tropic heat," wrote Whittier, referring in "Snowbound" to the hearth in his birthplace.

So said Whittier in "Snowbound," and the fireplace where he and his family huddled, oblivious to the frantic north wind, still looks like it could warm a family on a frigid December night. As we view the bellows and kettles and flax-spinning wheel to the side, the guide tells us that although the house was built in 1688, the fireplace wasn't added until some time in the 1700s and this main room was later expanded into the main kitchen. Fervent Quakers, the Whittiers often held Quaker meetings while sitting by the sparkling fire. And if you have read "Snowbound" and remember Whittier fondly recalling when "The mug of cider simmered slow," take a close look: the glazed-pottery cider mug still sits on a shelf to the upper left of the fireplace.

But don't feel that you have to have done a dissertation on Whittier to enjoy the birthplace. The curator says that a substantial number of visitors are not familiar with the poet, but are simply fascinated by old homes and learn more about Whittier upon taking the tour. Indeed, "Snowbound" and Whittier lore aside, one of the prime points of fascination in this farmstead is the mother's bedroom, located next to the kitchen and raised a few steps from the rest of the main floor. The reason, you find out, is that the room was built over a boulder that was too big to move.

Although John Greenleaf Whittier left the ancestral home when he was twenty-nine, there are a number of his original possessions here. You can see baby clothes that belonged to him and others of his family as well as, in the mother's bedroom, the black wool suits that he wore as an adult. An original family

Whistler is regarded mostly as a flamboyant ladies' man whose talent for putting visions on canvas was outshone only by his sharp tongue.

The birthplace of artist James Whistler, possibly the only place in the world where you can see not only a painting of Whistler's mother, but one of Whistler's father as well.

Bible sits upon a small Hepplewhite table in the borning room; it is opened to the twenty-fifth Psalm, his mother's favorite. And there is, hanging in the same room, the only portrait of the Quaker poet painted from life. It shows a young, clean-shaven Whittier, and while that's not the way most followers would remember him, it's likely the way he'd want to be remembered — as a young rabble-rouser rather than a sentimental old man.

James McNeill Whistler, on the other hand, is recalled as neither. He's regarded mostly as a flamboyant ladies' man whose talent for putting visions on canvas was outshone only by his sharp tongue.

Unlike Whittier, who spent many years in his homes, Whistler only lived at the **Whistler House** and what is now the Parker Gallery until age three, and there is no original Whistler furniture here. However, this may be the only place in the world where you can see a painting not only of Whistler's mother but also of Whistler's father. And some other very fine works of art as well, by both Whistler and others.

Located on a side street in downtown Lowell, the blue frame house looks as lost as a bed of roses on an airport runway. It was built in 1823, but the Whistlers didn't reside in it until 1833; James was born on July 10, 1834. His father, an engineer, had been brought to Lowell to help design engines for some of the early railroads; in 1837, the family moved to Springfield, Massachusetts (the home there has long been destroyed); and when James was nine years old, the family moved to Saint Petersburg, Russia, where Whistler's father helped design some of the first Russian railroads. Mr. Whistler died while in Russia and young James came back to the United States when he was fifteen.

Much of the color that James Whistler was known for during his lifetime was emitted not only from his paintbrush but also through his own personality. He lived in London during most of his years, taking up a Bohemian lifestyle and living with an Irish mistress during the heat of the stuffy Victorian era. He made as much news with his biting wit and passionate hatred for critics as he did with his art. When failing to be re-elected president of the Royal Society of British Artists, he shrugged, "It is all very simple. The RSBA has disintegrated. The 'artists' have come out, the 'British' remain."

In fact, Whistler's disdain of critics briefly took art out of the studio and into the courtroom. A critic, John Ruskin, described one of Whistler's paintings showing in an 1877 exhibition thusly: "I have seen, and heard, much of Cockney impudence before now; but never expected to hear a coxcomb ask two hundred guineas for flinging a pot of paint in the public's face." Whistler took Ruskin to court, claiming slander. For his trouble, he was awarded damages of one farthing, roughly equivalent to a quarter of a penny. Whistler took to wearing the farthing on his watch chain following the conclusion of the trial, then published a book entitled *The Art of Making Enemies.*

For a number of years, Whistler was the only American painter who had a work in the Louvre in Paris. Although that distinction no longer holds true, *Whistler's Mother* (which, incidentally, was originally called *An Arrangement in Grey and Black* and later changed by Whistler to *Portrait of My Mother)* is still an object of captivation and curiosity. The full-sized replica (which is larger than you might think) on display here was painted by Whistler's mother's great-grandniece, Edith Fairfax Davenport. The painting is surrounded by a Whistler frame, just like the original.

Original Whistler etchings also decorate the walls. Some are of members of his family while others are of scenes in Chelsea, England, another of the many places he called home. The guide will also point out the clever way Whistler signed his paintings with his initials in the shape of a butterfly. In the main lobby, you'll see the painting of the black-frocked, strong-nosed man who was Whistler's father. (It was another painter, W.S. Elwell, who immortalized the elder Whistler in about 1842.) And there are many other paintings in the house at 243 Worthen Street not by the building's eponym. Some are scenes of Lowell, while others are by artists who lived in the area. The second floor, also seen on a tour, consists of local historical and cultural exhibits.

Whistler took to wearing the farthing on his watch chain following the conclusion of the trial, then published a book entitled The Art of Making Enemies.

ACCESS

WHITTIER HOME. Directions: From Interstate 495 exit 54, go north on Route 150 to Main Street; take a left onto Main Street, then another left onto Friend Street. The home is at 86 Friend Street. **Season:** May through October. **Days:** Tuesday through Saturday. **Admission** charged. **Allow** 30 minutes. **Telephone:** (617) 388-1337.

WHITTIER BIRTHPLACE. Directions: From Interstate 495 exit 52, go north 1 mile on Route 110. **Season:** All year. **Days:** Tuesday through Saturday, plus Sunday afternoon. **Admission** charged. **Allow** 30 minutes. **Note:** Free parking is available on the side of the road and across the street, by the barn. **Telephone:** (617) 373-3979.

WHISTLER HOUSE. Directions: From Route 3, take the Lowell Connector to Gorham Street and then take a left; at the junction with Merrimack Street, take another left, then take a third left onto Worthen Street. **Season:** All year. **Days:** Tuesday through Friday afternoons, plus Saturdays in July and August. **Admission** charged. **Allow** 30 minutes. **Telephone:** (617) 452-7641.

Mark Twain's mid-Victorian home has been visited by literature lovers from Hartford to Haifa and from Bridgeport to Berlin.

Twain, Stowe, & Webster

Back when Hartford's total population was about double the seating capacity of today's Civic Center arena, Mark Twain and Harriet Beecher Stowe were moving into their newly constructed homes in the almost rural western part of the city. Over a century earlier, American lexicographer Noah Webster had been born in a four-room farmhouse in the wilds of what is now West Hartford. Today the homes of all three are preserved as testaments to the skills and life-styles of Hartford's most renowned literary minds.

"Everywhere the eye turns it is blessed with a vision of refreshing green. You do not know what beauty is if you have not been here."

Twain, when he initially visited Hartford in 1868, wrote the following of the city: "Everywhere the eye turns it is blessed with a vision of refreshing green. You do not know what beauty is if you have not been here." Indeed, the neighborhood where he resided, **Nook Farm,** was one of the most desirable in the community, and a number of stalwarts of mid-nineteenth-century American culture became the best of friends and neighbors here. Stowe and Twain (pen name for Samuel Clemens) were doubtless the most famous. Today, his 1874 home (he originally moved to Hartford in 1871 but lived in a leased home until his was built) is a mid-Victorian oasis in a desert of storefronts and brick apartments; it can be assumed that if Twain could see what has happened here, he would have some disparaging remark regarding progress.

The home of perhaps America's most famous

writer, Twain's house has been toured by visitors who have come so far that Hartford, to them, may seem almost next door to Hannibal. Names from Australia, Israel, West Germany, and Great Britain can be found on the pages of the guest register, in addition to entries from every one of the fifty states. They have come not only to examine the furnishings of a wealthy man's Victorian home but also to gain an insight into Twain's character.

His cynicism is discovered in one of the first highlights of the tour you can take here. An antique butter-stamp phone in the drawing room acts as a prop for the guide's comment about Twain's disturbance over interruptions due to the newfangled invention. You then listen through the phone to a tape of Hal Holbrook's Mark Twain impersonation, wishing a merry Christmas and good will to all with the possible exception of the inventor of the telephone.

But you also see a warm side of Twain as a devoted family man and a gracious host. The library, which was actually a sort of family room, was often the center of family and social activities. Twain's nephew, Jervis Langdon, wrote, "One of the pleasantest neighborhood customs that grew up in the Hartford home was the gathering, of an evening, around the library fire while Mr. Clemens read aloud. He liked stirring poetry, which he read admirably, sometimes rousing his little audience to excitement and cheers."

Many of the rave reviews came from his favorite audience, his three young daughters. He often told them bedtime stories by the fireplace here, basing them on the pictures and figurines that still surround the mantel. In return, his daughters would perform plays in this room now and then for their parents.

The girls' nursery, in addition to their schoolroom, is a specimen of pure Victoriana. The dolls, rocking chairs, and English-printed wallpaper, which is based on the poem "Ye Frog He Would A-Wooing Go," highlight the nursery, while the study-turned-schoolroom features an 1880 Fischer upright piano,

You listen through the phone to "Mark Twain" wishing a very merry Christmas and good will to all with the possible exception of the inventor of the telephone.

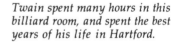

Twain spent many hours in this billiard room, and spent the best years of his life in Hartford.

Neatness is the rule in the Stowe House kitchen. Shelves are deliberately narrow, so that no article is allowed to hide behind any other.

This was Harriet Beecher Stowe's retirement cottage, where she lived her last twenty-three years. Most of us could easily handle a "cottage" such as this.

vintage textbooks, a window seat based on one that existed in a Middle Eastern monastery, and a fireplace where the girls actually did roast chestnuts on an open fire on those cozy winter nights.

The billiard room on the third floor could perhaps make Minnesota Fats drool; it was a room that Twain used to its fullest for both business and pleasure. Though he often wore out his guests with innumerable games of billiards (after which he would continue knocking billiard balls into pockets on his own), Twain also found this third-floor room most conducive to working. Twain's original billiard table, as well as decorations of cues, pipes, and cigars that line the ceiling, and translucent marble panels in the south wall, illustrate Twain's use of this room as an adult play area. The antiquated typewriter is emblematic of his more serious moments in this room. You learn on this tour that he was one of the first writers to type his manuscripts, but that he did most of his serious writing at his wife's family's farm in Elmira, New York.

Twain's years in Hartford were the best of his life. He was already acclaimed throughout the world when he bought the house, and his best known works — among them *The Adventures of Tom Sawyer, The Adventures of Huckleberry Finn, The Prince and the Pauper,* and *A Connecticut Yankee in King Arthur's Court* — were written during his stay in Hartford. It was after the death of his twenty-four-year-old daughter, Suzy, in 1896, that he left Hartford, and from that time on he was never to enjoy the same happiness again.

The case with Harriet Beecher Stowe is quite different. Although she was a Connecticut native, she spent the most productive years of her life, from ages twenty-one to fifty-five, elsewhere; her work that changed America's thinking, *Uncle Tom's Cabin,* was written in Brunswick, Maine. By the time Stowe moved back to Hartford in 1864, her best known deeds had been completed. The home on Nook Farm, in which she lived from 1873 until her death in 1896, was basically her retirement "cottage."

A "cottage" that most of us could handle as a permanent residence, this fourteen-room, slightly Gothic structure features many Stowe-family heirlooms and is furnished as it was when Harriet Beecher Stowe lived here. Sunlight literally brightened her day, and she let as much into her house as she could; translucent curtains, and sometimes plants instead of *any* curtains, graced her windows to achieve this. In the upstairs study, you can see the desk she used for writing and a small bureau that she once painted. Atop the bureau is a small box of medicines that she probably would have taken in her declining years; the wallpaper in this room features flowers and ferns, emphasizing her love for nature and gardening.

No permanent record was kept of the kitchen downstairs, so it has been redecorated in the style mentioned in the book she and her sister, Catharine, wrote in 1869: *The American Woman's Home,* a compilation of homemaking hints. "If parents wish their daughters to grow up with good domestic habits, they should have a neat and cheerful kitchen," the book said. In this room, neatness is the rule; shelves are narrow so no package or utensil is allowed to hide behind another, while early kitchen instruments like an eggbeater, a pie holder, and a soap cage rest upon the table in their proper places.

But don't let Stowe's domesticity fool you. "She was a dynamo, though a quiet woman," our guide told us, "a powerful person in her own being." Her husband, Calvin, a highly regarded scholar himself, originally suggested that Harriet write about slavery since he thought her style was more readable than his pedantic wordings. However, it was more than her style that made *Uncle Tom's Cabin* a household name and something that was to be translated into forty-two languages. Her feelings were more visceral, we are told. She had been the target of discrimination — denied, because of her sex, her desire to become a minister like some of her family's male members. And, having experienced incisive sorrow and pain after losing children, she could relate to similar feelings experienced by slaves.

Stowe's talents for expressing her feelings stretched beyond the creative use of pen and paper. She belonged to the school of thought that says writers should not be artists and vice versa. She maligned her own attempts at painting. However, many others thought her ability was much more than satisfactory in capturing sights and moods on canvas. You can judge for yourself, as many of the walls here support her attempts at art. The gouache of Casco Bay, painted in Brunswick, is one of her more memorable efforts.

For a look at another side of Hartford's literary heritage, head a few miles west off Interstate 84 in West Hartford to the saltbox **Noah Webster House,** where the dictionary writer was born in 1758. The house itself is somewhat older; it is believed to date from somewhere between 1710 and 1740, but there is

"If parents wish their daughters to grow up with good domestic habits," the sisters wrote, "they should have a neat and cheerful kitchen."

Plants served as substitutes for curtains in Stowe's bedroom. It was her way of letting as much sunlight as possible into her house.

no documentation of the exact year.

Since Webster lived at this house at 227 South Main Street only until he left for Yale at age sixteen, and since most of his professional years were spent in New Haven, this building isn't packed with Webster memorabilia. In fact, the only article in the house that actually belonged to Webster is a desk he used in his later years while residing in New Haven. However, considering that this was the man whose name has become synonymous with the American dictionary (How many times have you simply said, "Let's look it up in *Webster's*?") and who helped Americanize the formality of the mother country's English (thanks to Webster, "honour" has become "honor" and "musick" is now "music" in America, for example), his desk is the most appropriate of his possessions that could be displayed.

Although you can view a fifteen-minute audio-visual presentation on Webster's life and accomplishments, the proposed purpose of the displays in this house is to give the visitor a glimpse of both the accouterments and the techniques of farm life two centuries ago. The accouterments include authentic eighteenth-century articles like a gate-leg table, Windsor and fiddleback chairs, kitchen woodware, baby and doll cradles, and pewter and porcelain. The techniques are demonstrated during the house's regular hours, making use of some of the old-fashioned implements there. A loom like the one the Websters owned, a spinning wheel commonly used in the era, and the beehive oven next to the cavernous kitchen fireplace are utilized today in the same manner they were when Noah was learning to say his very first words. Today's youngsters can also get a feel of the way life was in Noah's early years since they are permitted to try a hand at the spinning wheel now and then.

COURTESY
NOAH WEBSTER FOUNDATION

The man whose name is synonymous with the dictionary was born in this saltbox house in West Hartford in 1758.

ACCESS

NOOK FARM. Directions: From Interstate 84 exit 46, head north onto Sisson Avenue, then take a right onto Farmington Avenue; the homes are on your right. **Season:** All year. **Days:** June through August, daily; rest of the year, Tuesday through Saturday, plus Sunday afternoon. **Admission** charged; combination ticket available. **Allow** 50 minutes for Twain house tour and 40 minutes for Stowe house tour. **Telephone:** (203) 525-9317.

NOAH WEBSTER HOUSE. Directions: From Interstate 84 exit 41, take a right onto South Main Street; the house is on the left. **Season:** All year. **Days:** All day Monday through Thursday, plus Sunday afternoons. **Admission** charged. **Allow** 1 hour for tour. **Telephone:** (203) 521-5362.

Saint-Gaudens & Parrish

In the days when American citizens jumped at the possibility of having sculptures displayed on their own town greens, the name Augustus Saint-Gaudens was synonymous with excellence in the respected art. Not long after Saint-Gaudens began garnering world fame, Maxfield Parrish was becoming one of the most favored painters on the planet; in 1936, for instance, when Parrish was well into his career as an established artist, *Time* magazine reported that van Gogh, Cézanne, and Parrish were the three most popular artists in the world in terms of sales of expensive reproductions. The homes and studios of both artists are located minutes from each other in west-central New Hampshire, in the towns of Cornish and Plainfield respectively.

If you've ever walked by *The Shaw Memorial* on the Boston Common, you've already made yourself familiar with the work of Augustus Saint-Gaudens. The bronze monument, showing Colonel Robert Gould Shaw on horseback leading his black Civil War regiment, took the sculptor fourteen years to create. (Shaw was killed while commanding this group of Massachusetts volunteers at Fort Wagner in Charleston Harbor.) On the grounds of the **Saint-Gaudens National Historic Site** in the New Hampshire hills is a plaster cast of the memorial. In addition, you can see Saint-Gaudens' house, two sculpture studios, and much more.

"No one ever succeeded in art unless born with an uncontrollable instinct toward it," Saint-Gaudens has been credited with saying. His own efforts were propelled by a constant desire to reach perfection; Saint-Gaudens put in enough hours that today he would have been called a workaholic. (Even in his early years, though he disliked his school work greatly, he was always anxious to be dabbling in art.) In whatever spare time he had, he nurtured a wonderful camaraderie with actors, architects, and other artists. The Cornish Colony, a group of fellow artists who lived in this area, began with Saint-Gaudens' initial summer stays from 1885 to 1897; others then followed in his northerly footsteps. By the time the artist moved here permanently in 1900 (following a three-year residence in Paris), dozens of artists and writers were calling this village by the Connecticut River "home". Saint-Gaudens and they had a fine relationship as a community of artists.

The home here was called Aspet, named after the village in France where Saint-Gaudens' father was born. (The sculptor himself was born in 1848 in Ireland during the heart of the potato famine, and came to New York with his family as an infant.) A widely discussed story has it that New Yorker Saint-Gaudens' initial reaction to the thought of buying his eventual

"No one ever succeeded in art unless born with an uncontrollable instinct toward it."

Saint-Gaudens' statue, Diana, *is in the Philadelphia Museum of Art. However, you can see a copy in the Little Gallery at the sculptor's home.*

> "Saint-Gaudens held up the mirror and no more; he meant to ask a question, not to give an answer."

It was originally known as "Huggins' Folly," a seldom-used turn-of-the-century inn. Saint-Gaudens bought it, renamed it Aspet, and lived and worked here for many years.

home here was disgust. Aspet was then regarded as "Huggins' Folly," an inn that two Huggins brothers had built and that had fallen into neglect when the main coach road was built elsewhere. The story goes on to say that Saint-Gaudens was planning a statue of Abraham Lincoln, and a lawyer who owned property in Cornish tempted the artist. He claimed that there were many "Lincoln-shaped" men to be found among the thin, hard-working Yankee population who could potentially be used as models. That, combined with the thought of spending another unpleasant summer in New York, helped make up Saint-Gaudens' mind that a move would be worth it.

Your tour of Aspet itself is the only guided part of your visit. A ranger takes you through the white-brick structure, pointing out certain pieces of furniture or wall hangings; the house has been left essentially as it was when Saint-Gaudens lived here. The Flemish tapestries, the Japanese grass mattings, and the Victorian sofa were all his. Instead of belaboring details of every item in the house, the guide encourages you to ask questions regarding any specifics that pique your interest, then lets you explore the rest of the grounds on your own.

There are dozens of sculptures inside the Little Studio, and it's here that you'll see one of Saint-Gaudens' most notable departures from the style of other nineteenth-century sculptors: he abandoned classical dress, opting instead for contemporary clothing that was typical of the day. It was common for him to place his sculpted figures in military dress, for instance, and the heroes he depicted therefore looked truly American. Additionally, while other established sculptors leaned toward creating forms of allegorical figures, Saint-Gaudens' best efforts went into memorials and portraits. The model of the *Standing Lincoln* that you see in the Little Studio is typical. Also representative of the artist's style are the bronze bas-relief of Robert Louis Stevenson (modeled after five sittings with the author in 1887), the eight-foot-high plaster statue of former Princeton University President James McCosh (examine the detail in his hand as it reaches out), and a bust of Admiral David Farragut (reduced in size from that of the monument), which are found in another gallery, the New Gallery.

Ironically, two of Saint-Gaudens' better known works were not based on real heroes. One, *Diana*, a copy of which is exhibited in the Little Gallery, depicts the nude goddess; it once stood atop the Madison Square Garden Tower and is now in the Philadelphia Museum of Art. Another, the Adams memorial, presents a shrouded sitting figure. (The original of this can be seen in the Rock Creek Church Cemetery in Washington, D.C., while a copy can be viewed here on the grounds.) It was commissioned by historian Henry Adams for his wife's grave. No title was ever given to the meditative figure; Adams said, "Saint-Gaudens held up the mirror and no more; he meant to ask a question, not to give an answer."

This historic site serves as a tribute to the art itself as well as to the artist, and to help visitors gain an appreciation of sculpturing, a sculptor in residence ·is on duty in yet another studio. Garbed in smock, old shirt, and jeans, she was putting the finishing touches on a plaster mermaid when we visited. Don't be scared to interrupt the artist with any questions you have; that's what she's there for. Ever wonder just how a bronze work of art is formed? You've got your own personal expert to explain.

Many visitors finish off a day here by taking a look inside the stable filled with sleighs and carriages of Saint-Gaudens' day, then pausing for a moment at the pillared marble monument called *The Temple* — which marks the family's grave site — or strolling along the two nature trails on the property. Of course, you can wrap up your stay just by taking a deep breath and viewing the green hills that envelop the peak of Mount Ascutney in the distance or admiring the flowers that bloom by your feet. Mixed gracefully with the sculptures that decorate the grounds, nature here is also at its showiest — and you can't find better combinations of manmade and natural beauty.

The **Maxfield Parrish Museum,** just a few miles away, is also located in a spot of natural splendor. Parrish was a painter, not a sculptor, so his works are all inside behind protective doors. And from inside the house there are wonderful views of the verdant hills beyond — the view that inspired the artist in the later years of his career.

Most who come here, though, are interested in seeing the paintings first, then the scenery. Even if you don't recognize Parrish's name, you will probably recall his style. Think back to the whimsical covers you saw long ago on covers of magazines like *Life, Collier's,* and *Scribner's,* most of which featured fairy-tale-like figures against a background with some hint of blue. No doubt you'll be remembering Parrish in his prime.

At the museum, you'll not only see the original oils for those magazine covers but also other fantastical Parrish gems that served to advertise everything from electric power to chocolate miniatures, and still others that became illustrations for books over a half century ago. Many of his early paintings had a distinctive subject: one or two young maidens, sparsely dressed and sitting on a rock or by a tree, with mountains or water in the background. *Air Castles,* which you can see hanging in the museum, is a typical Parrish fantasy. A young girl, lounging by water's edge, dreamily looks up at the sky, which is filled with bubbles, clouds, and a Cinderella-like castle. *The Garden of Allah* is one of Parrish's most famous works, originally painted to decorate a box of Crane's Chocolates; here, three

Garbed in smock, old shirt, and jeans, she was putting the finishing touches on a plaster mermaid when we visited.

young women repose on a wall in a garden embellished with radiant sunshine. The women are framed by two urns, a common Parrish touch, and one woman looks into water at the bottom of the painting to see the reflection of herself and her companions.

About the time that Parrish was reaching his sixtieth birthday, he decided to change his style radically. It was in 1930 that Parrish is claimed to have told a reporter that he wanted to concentrate on landscapes. Said the artist: "I'm done with girls on rocks. I've painted them for thirteen years and I could paint them and sell them for thirteen more. That's the peril of the commercial art game. It tempts a man to repeat himself. It's an awful thing to get to be a rubber stamp. I'm quitting my rut now while I'm still able.

"There are always pretty girls on every city street, but a man can't step out of the subway and watch the clouds playing with the top of Mount Ascutney. It's the unattainable that appeals. Next best thing to seeing the ocean or the hills or the woods is enjoying a painting of them."

The metamorphosis is captured perfectly in his painting *Dreaming*, initially called *October* and for a long time recognized by most people by that name. Very characteristic of early Parrish, it portrayed a naked young girl sitting on a rock by a tree in a setting replete with forest and water. After tiring of that style, the artist painted out the girl with the intent of transforming it into a landscape. He never got around to completing it, so you see an unfinished painting.

But you do more than look at paintings here; you tour Parrish's studio and learn a little about the man's lifestyle and character. He was a tinkerer who always liked to dabble with gadgets and inventions. Elaborate locks on doors, a conveyor belt that brought firewood from the basement to the living room, and a hidden narrow stairway leading to an overlook of his studio were some of the additions he made here. (Parrish lived in this studio in his later years; his earlier home, named The Oaks for those plentiful trees on his property, was destroyed by fire in 1979.)

Parrish, although born to a wealthy family in Philadelphia, was drawn to the wilds of Cornish by the intellectual and artistic community there; his father, Stephen Parrish, also an artist, was already one of the residents. Even before his 1898 move, the younger Parrish was a successful painter and illustrator, having to his credit a *Harper's Weekly* cover and illustrations for the children's book *Mother Goose in Prose*, by L. Frank Baum (who would later author *The Wizard of Oz*). A copy of the Mother Goose book can be viewed at the museum.

During his years as an established painter, Parrish became widely known not only for his subject matter of girls on rocks but also as a commercial artist. From 1917 to 1934, he did calendars (many of which are on

"I'm done with girls on rocks. I've painted them for thirteen years and I could paint them and sell them for thirteen more."

display) for General Electric's Edison Mazda Lamp Division and for many years, illustrated children's and adults' books such as nursery rhymes and Edith Wharton's *Italian Villas*. These commissions, in addition to his magazine covers and product advertisements, led to negative criticism of Parrish by purists who dubbed him a commercial artist. Still, he was regarded as a talent, and his use of Parrish blue (created by grinding lapis lazuli) in his distinctive skies and waters made his works well recognized. Though his popularity faded in the forties and fifties, it revived a few decades ago; Parrish lived long enough to see that revival, painting through 1962 and living in Plainfield until his death at age ninety-five in 1966.

The Maxfield Parrish Museum contains a gallery where paintings from widely known artists, including Parrish, are sold.

One word of caution: the museum is fairly new, having opened only in 1978. Tours are casual and vary in length and detail, depending on your particular guide. If the guide doesn't discuss a specific painting, an illustration, or a piece of furniture that interests you, be sure to ask about it.

Though west-central New Hampshire is not a nationally known bastion of art today, tours of these artists' homes can show you remnants of the time when it was. Although Saint-Gaudens and Parrish are both gone, their art lives on. And so do the views that inspired them.

ACCESS

TO GET TO THE MUSEUM AREA. Northbound: From Interstate 91 exit 8, take Route 5 north, then turn right onto Bridge Street in the town of Windsor. Southbound: From Interstate 91 exit 9, take Route 5 south, then turn left onto Bridge Street in the town of Windsor.

SAINT-GAUDENS NATIONAL HISTORIC SITE. Directions: From Bridge Street, cross the covered bridge, then follow the signs to the historic site. **Season:** Late May through mid-October. **Days:** Daily. **Admission** charged. **Allow** 1 to 2 hours. **Telephone:** (603) 675-2175.

MAXFIELD PARRISH MUSEUM. Directions: From Bridge Street, cross the covered bridge, then turn onto Route 12A north and continue for about 4 miles; turn left at the sign for The Oaks. **Season:** May through October. **Days:** Tuesday through Sunday. **Admission** charged. **Allow** 1 hour to 90 minutes. **Telephone:** (603) 675-5647.

Among his additions here: a hidden narrow stairway and a conveyor belt that brought firewood from the basement to the living room.

ROSS CONNELLY

By the time Maxfield Parrish had made this studio his permanent home, he was well into his second career, as a painter of landscapes.

CHAPTER III

The Way It Used To Be

What is it about days long past that sparks the curiosity of late-twentieth-century Americans? Is it the "good old days" syndrome that makes us yearn for a time when life was simpler and slower moving? Or is it a craving to see the opposite — a period when medical care, plumbing, and transportation were still in the dark ages — so we can appreciate modernity even more?

Whatever the reason, thousands flock every spring, summer, fall, and in some cases, winter to inspect in New England's re-created villages the ways in which persons lived and worked during years gone by. They go to see the village blacksmith forging horseshoes with authentic tools, the apothecary shop brimming with pillboxes and early surgical instruments, and the white-steepled village meeting house filled with seat-torturing hard wooden benches. And more and more and more.

The specifics that you see depend on the time depicted — ranging from the eighteenth to the mid nineteenth century, with a wide variety of contemporary developments and inventions — and the locale — types of trades and overall lifestyles were vastly different along the Connecticut shoreline and in the woods of Maine. In other words, expect to see something distinctive at each.

An advisory is in order for those who have limited time: if you can't stay at a re-created village for at least three hours (the smaller Willowbrook in Maine is an exception), it would be best to postpone your visit. The early New England that's simulated in these villages is of a slower pace than today's world; these are places not to be sampled but to be savored.

There was a time not too long ago when chopping wood for fuel was a matter of staying alive, not just heating cheaply. At a place like Old Sturbridge Village, you can take a step back into that era.

Dressed in contemporary 1830s fashion, two Old Sturbridge Village "residents" huddle against the winter chill while strolling through the heart of the town.

Old Sturbridge Village

It may be the extensive and realistic setting; after visiting the homes and stores of the center village, you walk through the tree-lined woods to the countryside with its farmstead, mills, and craftsmen. On the other hand, it may be the authentically costumed guides, or the fact that you can see brooms and barrels and bread made just as they were a century and a half ago. Or it just may be the fact that **Old Sturbridge Village** in Sturbridge, Massachusetts, has been around for over thirty years and has been growing continuously; or that all the buildings you see are authentic, having been moved here from other locations throughout New England. Whatever the reason, Sturbridge today is the re-created historic village to which all others in New England, and some outside as well, are compared.

What you visit here is a rural inland New England village of around 1830. (In the past, personnel set the date portrayed as between 1790 and 1840, but now they're targeting the setting more specifically as the decade of the 1830s.) The Industrial Revolution was just beginning to affect New Englanders' everyday lives, as evidenced by the whirring machinery in the carding mill here; yet, the agricultural lifestyle was slow to die, as you can tell when you see two farm hands chasing a pig around a barnyard, attempting to force it into a pen. It was a time of transition in New

England, exemplified, however subtly, by the activities, dress, conversation, and furnishings you see and hear while at the village.

The **Thompson Bank,** in the center village, is a prime example. The banker behind the counter in this pillared brown building tells you about the day's business; borrowers were all commercial enterprises, looking for financial backing for new inventions that would help make life a little easier. Consumers interested in saving opted for the mattress as opposed to the village bank.

Some of the farmers' money at that time went for support of the state church, housed locally in what was called the **village meeting house.** The guide inside this archetypal white-steepled Congregational Church mentions that all state citizens, whether parishioners or not, paid taxes for its support — at least until 1832, when Massachusetts became the last New England state to abolish the state church. And everyone who *was* a Congregationalist bought a pew as he would any other property and therefore paid taxes on the pew as well. It was common for the owners to decorate the pews with their own seat-soothing cushions (red and green were the most popular cushion colors) and in some cases, wallpaper. On cold days, a churchgoer would place on the floor by his pew a coal-heated foot warmer or a less sophisticated warmed soapstone; examples are on view here today.

Not to imply that all religious villagers were Congregationalists. At the **Quaker meeting house** almost next door, elders — though not ordained ministers — sat on benches in front, and everyone in the congregation was permitted to speak; women were especially encouraged. The Quakers, you hear, rejected the conventional Roman names for days and months, which they considered to be of pagan origin. Instead, they simply used "First Day," "Second Day," "First Month," and so on.

The village parson lived, naturally, in the **parsonage,** located between the law office and, ironically, the tavern. Wallpaper was becoming common by the 1830s, and its use here, along with the canopied beds, makes for an attractive atmosphere. You go through the attic — where herbs hang drying and a spinning wheel sits idly, thanks to the advent of textile looms in surrounding communities — before heading downstairs to a back bedroom that would probably have been rented by a ministry student.

There were, of course, other village residents besides the parson. The housekeeper in the nearby **Fitch Home** had just finished making a tomato pie when we arrived. The concoction, displayed on the kitchen table before us, was made from tomatoes, eggs, nutmeg, sugar, and cream, with a rich pastry crust. A nineteenth-century recipe book stated that this was an "excellent and much approved pie." No book said any-

All food prepared at Sturbridge is baked using early nineteenth-century recipes and methods. This turkey was cooked in a tin reflector oven on an open hearth.

White-shirted farm hands with suspendered pants maneuver a full hay wagon pulled into the barn by yoked oxen.

And then there are those "exhibits" that happen to pass by as you're walking down one of the country lanes, across the covered bridge, or by the village common.

Old-time skills are kept alive at Sturbridge. Here a shoemaker employs nineteenth-century techniques in crafting shoes by hand.

thing about the flies, however, which were attracted by the sweet fragrance and entered uninvited through the open windows. The little pests made us stop and consider that the invention of window screens was some time in the future.

A detail like the lack of window screens signifies the fact that authenticity is the rule at Sturbridge. You can also see that in one of the other center-village homes. The **Fenno House,** which with a 1704 construction date is the oldest building in the collection, has been set up as the home of a couple whose children have all grown and left. The house has been through plenty of generations, and the furniture is not of the latest styles. In the upstairs bedroom, for example, are some backless step-down Windsor chairs, made around 1820 in some nearby chair factories that ran on waterpower.

You see other instances of the same quest for historical realism throughout the village. In addition to the brass candlesticks, curry powder, bellows, and Staffordshire china sold at the Knight Store are fustic, madder, and Irish moss. Fustic and madder are plants whose roots were scraped, boiled, and then used as dyes, while Irish moss is a seaweed that was commonly used in everything from soups to jellies to medicine. Another example of authenticity? Take a glance at the informal dresses worn by the women in the center village and in the countryside; the fancier, puffed-out leg-of-mutton sleeves that you saw in town are not worn by most of the women in the country.

The best look at country-style Sturbridge is at the **Pliny Freeman Farmstead.** Farm animals are bred as they were in the last century, and you can see the results: tiny chicks following every footstep of a mother hen while a baby calf pokes its head out from behind a barn. White-shirted farm hands with suspendered pants maneuver a full hay wagon pulled into the barn by yoked oxen; then, with hayforks, they pitch the harvest of fodder into the loft. The womenfolk at the farmstead, meanwhile, are inside the house yarn-stitching a woolen hearth rug. The rug, they explain, was used as an early means of fire prevention; it would catch a wild spark and then smolder, emitting an odor that would warn the residents. As they work on the rug, bread is baking in the beehive oven while herbs like sage, parsley, and thyme dry above the fireplace.

As would have been the case on an average day back in 1830, someone is always working on farm property. We saw some hearty young men scything in the fields. You may observe helpers tending the peas, corn, or other crops on the farm. For other looks at the ongoing activities in the countryside, you'll want to head to the **mills and shops** that are located on the outskirts of town. The village shoemaker uses a wooden shoe form to shape the footwear he's making. The broom maker weaves his house-cleaning instruments from broom corn, actually a sorghum plant that was at one time grown in New England; the plant was cultivated for the express purpose of making brooms. The cooper, while explaining barrel staves, explains that the name of his profession comes from a Latin term meaning "maker of containers."

And then there are those "exhibits" that happen to pass by as you're walking down one of the country lanes, across the covered bridge, or by the village common. Don't be surprised if the oncoming clip-clop of horses alerts you to step aside and let the two-seat buggy pass. Or if the sonance of fifes and drums starts getting closer and closer, the result of a band of "early-American" musicians. Or if a team of musketeers assaults your eardrums with other kinds of attention-grabbing sounds. Something is always going on here, whether you're entering an established old building or merely strolling down a dirt road.

Special events almost make a mockery of the word "special" since they occur so often.

There is so much more to Old Sturbridge Village. In addition to the active exhibits, there are some intriguing museum-like buildings devoted to clocks, glass (in all forms, from paperweights to an early-American optical kit), military artifacts (cannonballs, drums, and tricorn hats), and lighting (from whale-oil lamps to candle making). And special events almost make a mockery of the word "special" since they occur so often. Typical distinctive events that have taken place in the past include: the Ladies Benevolent Society Picnic, a representative nineteenth-century social event; Fall Militia Training Day, in which an 1830s militia unit trains; days where old-time crafts like theorem painting, sheepshearing, blacksmithing, and fireplace cooking are explained and demonstrated; and Thanksgiving, when you can enjoy the same dishes that a New England family would have eaten a century and a half ago. Some of the foods baked in Sturbridge's brick ovens, as well as many of the crafts and other hand-wrought items made on the premises, are for sale in the village's gift and food shops every open day. You won't find bargains, but you will see top quality.

Perhaps so many people compare other re-created villages to Old Sturbridge Village because so many have been there time and time again. And that's the key. It's a place where something is always happening, and you can find it just as fascinating visiting the second, third, and fourth times as you did the first.

ACCESS

OLD STURBRIDGE VILLAGE. Directions: Follow signs from Interstate 86 exit 3. **Season:** All year. **Days:** April through late October, daily; rest of the year, Tuesday through Sunday. **Admission** charged. **Allow** 4 to 8 hours. **Notes:** Wear comfortable shoes. Picnic tables are set up in a pine-shaded area. Food is available for purchase. **Telephone:** (617) 347-3362.

RUSS KENDALL

Just as George Sheldon ordered. Visitors still peer through the hole in the "Old Indian House Door" to see Sheldon's portrait in Memorial Hall.

Historic Deerfield

Deerfield. A mixture of private schools and public homes, dedicated to the education of the young and the preservation of the old (houses, that is). Visitors to northwestern Massachusetts often take a quiet detour from Interstate 91 to tour the twelve houses of **Historic Deerfield,** weathered structures, primarily from the eighteenth century, that line Deerfield's mile-long main street (called simply "The Street"). What they discover is that Historic Deerfield never can be totally separated from the town of Deerfield itself.

The houses of the restoration have not, for the most part, been moved here from other locations, and so most of them stand where they were first built — interspersed with other, often equally historic buildings that are still private residences. In addition, some space within each of the twelve structures that are Historic Deerfield is almost always reserved for a twentieth-century tenant — often a faculty member from Deerfield Academy. In Deerfield, people don't just preserve history and study it; they live with it — and it fits as comfortably as the proverbial old shoe.

The Deerfield tradition of living with and preserving local history is vividly reflected in the restored homes of Historic Deerfield, and it's a tradition that stems in large part from the characters of those homes. Not character, though they have plenty of that, too, but characters.

George Sheldon was a character. One of the first forces in the move for preservation at Deerfield, Sheldon used to talk town residents into loaning their historic treasures to the collection now housed in **Memorial Hall** and owned by the Pocumtuck Valley Memorial Association — and, worse than the notorious neighbor who borrows garden tools, he never returned a thing. It's said that when a Deerfield resident died, Sheldon arrived as soon as the undertaker, and while the deceased went on to the graveyard, his effects often went to George's museum.

But the most prized piece in the entire museum is an old door with a hole in it: the well-known "Old Indian House Door." Back in 1704 this door sturdily guarded the home of Ensign John Sheldon (an ancestor of George) during an Indian massacre, until attackers finally chopped a hole in it with their tomahawks and

It's said that when a Deerfield resident died, George Sheldon arrived as soon as the undertaker, and while the deceased went on to the graveyard, his effects often went to George's museum.

fired at random through the opening, killing Ensign Sheldon's wife. The house was torn down in the mid-nineteenth century, but the door was preserved — and when it ended up in Memorial Hall, George Sheldon positioned it so that visitors peering through the hole in the door would find their gaze focused on a portrait of him. (George Sheldon's home, the **Sheldon-Hawkes House,** is part of Historic Deerfield and is open to the public today.)

Miss C. Alice Baker was a cousin of George Sheldon's, and she was a character, too. She bought the fading **Frary House** in 1890, announcing she planned to live in it, to make a home for her mother in it, and to dance in it. Some of the townsfolk thought she might as well dance in the looney bin — even in Deerfield, restoration wasn't a popular cause at the time (witness the fate of the Old Indian House), and for a *woman* to have such ideas . . . !

But restore the place she did. She made a home here for herself, two friends, and her mother, and when the restoration of the ballroom and fiddlers' gallery was complete she hired a dancing master from Boston, rented eighteenth-century costumes, and gave a ball that set Deerfield on its heels. Today the Frary House is one of the best in Historic Deerfield for children; not only can they climb up into the fiddlers' gallery and peer down on the grand ballroom, but they can also explore the "touch-it room," handling wooden plates, lifting heavy iron pots, and trying their hands at carding wool.

At the far end of town from the Frary House, you can visit **Ashley House** and learn the story of a Deerfield character from another period: Reverend Jonathan Ashley. Ashley lived in Deerfield from 1732 until his death in 1780, and his story, complete with myths and legends, sums up much of the fierce antagonism between Deerfield Whigs and Tories. The song that accompanies the Historic Deerfield slide-show orientation program tells the story best:

Reverend Jonathan Ashley had his salary and even his firewood supply cut off when he continued his unwavering support for England even after the beginning of the Revolution. This is where he lived.

> Parson Ashley, Parson Ashley
> Mixed Britannia with his theology.
> You can only get to heaven if you
> stand behind the King.

Shortly after the Boston Tea Party, Ashley held a tea party of his own to demonstrate his allegiance to Britain. Even after the Revolution began, his sympathies continued to be so ill concealed that his parishioners eventually cut off both his salary and his supply of firewood, and on one occasion even barred him from entering his own church. Today you can see in his house the sermons that inspired such wrath: pages of tiny script, sitting on a writing desk directly in front of a pair of spectacles. "One hopes," our guide commented, "that he memorized his sermons."

Most of the homes of Historic Deerfield date from

the eighteenth century, but the town's history goes back well beyond that. Deerfield was settled in 1669, subjected to brutal Indian massacres in 1675 and 1704, and resettled each time. It saw heavy disputes between Whigs and Tories during the Revolution, later settling down and trading swords for plowshares and pupils. (The town is now home to three private schools.) The preservation of the area's history, begun by George Sheldon, was continued more formally when Henry N. and Helen Geier Flynt established the Heritage Foundation (since renamed Historic Deerfield) in 1952 and began the restorations you can see today.

There are many more characters who preserved the town and/or whose memories are preserved in Historic Deerfield. You'll find evidence of their stories in the Asa Stebbins House, the first brick residence in Deerfield; the Wright House, built by Asa Stebbins as a wedding gift for his son Asa, Jr.; the Wells-Thorn House, where a fortified 1717 section contrasts dramatically with an addition from a later, less dangerous period; the Dwight-Barnard House, with relatively bright paint that really *is* authentic; the Allen House, where the Flynts lived for many years; and a number of other small collections.

Modern visitors to these ghosts of the past come here to inspect the impressive collections of scallop-topped tables and Hadley chests, to pace off rooms and measure floorboards in anticipation of restoring their own homes, to attend forums (past forum subjects have included Windsor chairs and early New England cookery). Experts come to study outstanding architecture, antique furniture, lighting fixtures, embroidery, ceramics, and silver.

No matter what your interest, we join the staff of Historic Deerfield in recommending that you not try to take in too much in one visit, and thus avoid the plague one visitor labeled "visual indigestion": the psychological equivalent of eating a pizza with anchovies followed by a butterscotch sundae followed by sweet and sour chicken. Take time to see the slide-show orientation and plan to visit just a sampling of the houses in a single daytrip. Or stop at neighboring Memorial Hall and see the Old Indian House Door. Don't hesitate to space your visits out. There are a lot of characters here, and it takes time to get acquainted.

Miss C. Alice Baker announced that she planned to live in the fading Frary House, to make a home for her mother in it, and to dance in it. Townsfolk thought she might as well dance in the looney bin.

ACCESS

HISTORIC DEERFIELD. Directions: From Interstate 91 north exit 24 or south exit 25, take routes 5 and 10 north about 6 miles, and follow the signs to Historic Deerfield. **Season:** All year. **Days:** Daily. **Admission** charged; combination tickets for several houses available. **Allow** approximately ½ hour per house. **Note:** Parking is available along The Street. **Telephone:** (413) 774-5581.

Mystic Seaport

A taste of nineteenth-century New England life with a seaside flavor is an appropriate way to describe Mystic Seaport, located in the southeastern corner of Connecticut in the town of Mystic. Watching the sail-setting demonstrations, scrutinizing the scrimshaw in the Stillman Building's extensive collection, listening to the village shipsmith explain how iron was forged into ships' tools, and bending down to observe the storage areas in the low-ceilinged blubber room of the only surviving wooden whaling ship made in this country are simply a few of the activities that will occupy your time here.

With an old village street, a few museums filled with maritime exhibits, and some classic boats that were used by ancient mariners, this re-created seaport town encompasses a great deal in its presentation of an era gone by.

Some of the buildings here have guides who explain how certain items were sold or how procedures were carried out 150 years ago; others are unstaffed, but keep informative labels on or descriptions of the antiquated articles inside. The **shipsmith**, who probably would have been known as a blacksmith in an inland town, for instance, will tell you about the harpoons or ship's fittings he's creating. If you come in late and miss his demonstration, be sure to ask about those huge bellows hanging from the ceiling; they were operated by pulling on a connecting handle, so it's easy to see what kept the shipsmith's other arm in shape while he was diligently banging on the sizzling hot metal.

In **Schaefer's Spouter Tavern,** a typical waterfront tavern or boarding house straight out of the 1850s, there is no guide. You read here that life was tough for the transient sailor, and that the inexperienced were particularly vulnerable to all sorts of skullduggery that parted them from their money. Upon entering this former New Hampshire tavern, which was moved to this location in the 1950s, you can smell the musty aroma so typical of a dockside bar.

And then there's the antithesis to the lifestyle where rowdiness was rampant and vice was the rule. "Honest labor could bring a person closer to God than any other worldly action, except, of course, prayer," explains the posted description of the **Fishtown Chapel.** The hard benches inside the chapel epitomize the stern tenets of the parishioners, as does the interior of the **Boardman School,** right next door. Eight harsh gray desks huddled around a wood stove are topped with small slates or books such as *McGuffey's Reader.*

Back then, when a woman wasn't at home cooking, she'd likely be shopping at the general store; at Mystic Seaport's **G.H. Stone General Store,** the "clerk" tells all about the odd-looking kitchen equipment, the

Square-rigged masts form the foreground for early New England buildings at Mystic Seaport, where life in a nineteenth-century oceanside village is portrayed.

Life was tough for the transient sailor, and the inexperienced were particularly vulnerable to all sorts of skullduggery that parted them from their money.

Have you ever seen scrimshaw on desk-clock stands, rolling pins, and corset holders?

If you have ever wondered how those thirty-foot-long whaling boats carried men with all that gear, you'll find the answers when demonstrations such as this one are given.

old-time tin containers, and maybe even that ice skate with the paper-thin blade on which even Eric Heiden would feel gimpy kneed.

The brightly painted hand-carved figures of subjects like a beautiful young woman, an admiral, a mythical goddess-like creature, an old sea hag, and a sea captain that you see inside the **Wendell Building** were not for sale anywhere. These stunning wooden likenesses are figureheads, which were placed on the bows of ships and at one point thought to bring good luck. They're typical of the contents of this museum, one of a few at the seaport that contain superb memorabilia of Mystic's heyday as a shipbuilding center and of nautical nineteenth-century New England.

Reproductions of 1840s advertisements recruiting sailors and a series of stained-glass windows depicting historically famous vessels can be seen while touring the three floors of exhibits in the **Stillman Building,** which holds one of the most impressive collections. Allow a good half hour to absorb all that this carpeted, modern, and very well-organized museum has to offer. The bottom floor creates a time-tunnel effect, sectioning off displays into the periods to which they pertain: "The First Settlement," "Colonial Trades and Industry," "The War of 1812," and so on. The first-rate scrimshaw exhibit on the second floor shows you the most astonishing feats of scrimshawing. We've all seen pendants, necklaces, and earrings made from etching and carving whales' teeth and walruses' tusks. But have you ever seen desk-clock stands, rolling pins, corset holders, and pie-cutting jagging wheels made in this fashion? And designs here include likenesses of President George Washington and General William Tecumseh Sherman as well as a view of Connecticut's Wesleyan University. While up here, be sure to take time to examine the healthy number of ship models, and then concentrate on their details to appreciate the patience involved in creating one of those authentic reproductions.

And after you've beheld the miniatures, how about taking a look at, or better yet, hopping on board, the real thing? You won't be able to walk around the grounds here for ten minutes without hearing about the **Charles W. Morgan,** the only surviving American wooden whaling ship. The most famous of the half dozen or so classic vessels on display here, this National Historic Landmark was built in New Bedford, Massachusetts, in 1841 and served as a whaling boat until 1921. The blubber pots on the deck emblematize the purpose of this majestic, fully rigged ship; below deck, you can inspect the blubber room, literally a low-overhead operation with a five-foot three-inch high ceiling. You'll gasp in disbelief with the rest of the visitors when you see the tightly packed double bunks that sailors slept on during their voyages.

Though the *Morgan* is the most popular of the boardable boats, it's not the only one docked here. The **Joseph Conrad,** a training ship built in 1882 for the Danish merchant service, and the **L.A. Dunton,** a classic Gloucester fishing schooner first launched in 1921, are also here for you to climb on and look at from a seafarer's point of view. In addition, the **Sabino,** built as a passenger ferry in East Boothbay, Maine, in 1908, is still used as an excursion boat. Trips lasting a half hour are offered to Seaport visitors for an additional charge during prime season, and at night, anybody can enjoy a ninety-minute cruise that features entertainment. At some point over the next few years, several of the boats here will have some repair work performed upon them, so they may not be in their regular berths. While this may be a bit disappointing to those who won't see a particular ship sitting on the waves in its full glory, it will afford an opportunity to see a rarity: the actual reconstruction of a classic boat in progress.

There are also constantly scheduled opportunities to see how those nineteenth-century mariners set or furled the sails on their ships. And if you've ever wondered how those thirty-foot-long whale boats carried all those men and all that gear, you'll be able to see for yourself when you visit Mystic on any summer day or during a weekend in the fall or spring, when these maritime skills are demonstrated periodically. Other ongoing activities you can check out include: lobster-pot making; salting, splitting, and drying codfish; and the playing of instruments, like the button organ, the concertina, and the banjo, that were usually on board the glorious old vessels.

Celebrating a part of history as Mystic does, it makes sense that Memorial Day and Independence Day are observed here in a grand manner. Try to be here on either holiday; you'll be able to take part in a Mystic experience not regularly offered. Programs featuring the singing of sea chanteys or other music of the era are often slated. You may also see re-creations of battle encampments or drills of the nineteenth century, and children might be invited to take part in hundred-year-old children's games like hoop rolling and stilt walking on the village green. Schedules are slightly different on each holiday each year, but the price never varies from the daily admission fee.

Boats are for boarding at Mystic Seaport. The L. A. Dunton is a classic Gloucester fishing schooner that was first launched in 1921.

ACCESS

MYSTIC SEAPORT. Directions: From Interstate 95 exit 90, head south on Route 27 for 1 mile. **Season:** All year. **Days:** Daily. **Admission** charged. **Allow** 4 to 7 hours. **Note:** There are 2 entrances (north and south of the museum); parking is available at both. **Telephone:** (203) 572-0711.

Horsepower was a literal thing in mid-Victorian era Maine, and the scenes from the harness shop, blacksmith shop, and carriage barn at Willowbrook at Newfield attest to that.

Willowbrook at Newfield

The small, boxy-looking wood-frame post office is a throwback to an earlier time, when the friendly bespectacled neighborhood postmaster sorted your mail in a modest structure just down the road a bit. The narrow country thoroughfare that runs by the building looks perfectly suited for a horse-drawn vehicle to roll by. And the surrounding New England countryside smacks of a past day in a still-undeveloped New England.

But wait! This is the actual village of Newfield, Maine, the location of the re-created village of Willowbrook at Newfield. Willowbrook itself lies next door to and across the street from the post office, straddling both sides of the sharply curving street. This is one of two features that set Willowbrook at Newfield apart from other re-created villages; you already feel a part of the era Willowbrook represents before you even set foot in any of the buildings. Willowbrook is one re-created village that does not sit a half mile off a busy interstate highway. It's located a good fifty miles inland from the busy southwestern Maine coast, and you have to drive along a maze of back roads through country towns and peaceful farmland to get here. There are no fast-food restaurants or chain hotels just up the street, just as there were none for Maine villagers in the nineteenth century.

And this leads to Willowbrook's second major difference from other such establishments. The period portrayed here is years later; it's the heart of the mechanical revolution in America and there are a couple dozen buildings filled with antiques ranging from washing machines to snowshoes to a potato-seed cutter. Willowbrook is, as the printed combination guide and map calls it, "country Victorian." Emphasis on the word "country." During this period in history, new and better equipment was being churned out to make life easier for the farmer. The advances to be brought on by the introduction of the horseless carriage, however, were still a few decades away, so sleighs and carriages (horse drawn, that is), were the modes of transportation. While there are no active demonstrations of any Willowbrook equipment, the substantial collections here are a testament to the lifestyle of workers in the mid nineteenth century.

Greatest in number are buildings sporting examples of antiquated agricultural equipment in a variety of shapes and sizes. Housed here are: a big red-and-yellow corn-harvesting contraption, three Maine potato-digging plows, a cornstalk chopper for cattle feed, a clover seeder that once planted a twelve-foot swath, one of Maine's first horse-drawn manure spreaders, and more and more and more. The **Durgin Barns,** the first buildings you examine, hold an ample collection of antique farm equipment, and inside you can peek at the last item made in the old mill that was located in Newfield — would you believe a *round* chicken crate?

Inside the **Carriage House** is a nostalgia addict's heaven — Currier and Ives in three dimensions. (In fact, posted alongside the many scrubbed and polished sleighs and carriages are Currier and Ives prints showing similar vehicles in action.) There's the brown-and-white Eben Davis tinker's sleigh, which once belonged to a peddler who sold his goods around southeastern New Hampshire and southwestern Maine; piled on top today are kitchen and other household implements. There's a doctor's black sleigh with an overhanging roof to protect precious medical equipment from precipitation. And there's the D.A. Moore milk wagon, realistically stocked with old milk bottles and complementing a bigger red, green, and yellow milk wagon near the rear of the barn.

The most novel among the collection are the red-seated white wedding sleigh — note the bells — and the squatty foul-weather sleigh. The latter, local legend has it, was made for a minister by the town fathers, who wanted him to be able to arrive at church on inclement Sunday mornings without getting his sermon all wet. The fact that it's low to the ground, added to the heavy overhang, made it difficult for the horse to pull; while it is said that the minister would arrive with sermon intact, he usually was late.

Though the sleigh and carriage collection is doubtless the most complete on Willowbrook's grounds, it's hardly the only extensive collection. Nineteenth-century women's gowns, musical instruments, shoes, and household items like vacuum cleaners and typewriters make up one additional iota of the potpourri of articles on display in the Durgin Barns. But there were producers as well as consumers in Maine a hundred-odd years ago; to see the types of things that were manufactured in this region, grab a look at the goods in the **Roscoe Whitman Machine Shop,** the **Silas P. Hardy Bicycle Shop,** and the **Carpenter Shop.** In another unit, labeled "The Trades of Yesteryear," there's the village barbershop, the photographer, the toy shop, the bank, and the fuel-implement shop (the burning of kerosene was the most modern advancement at the time, and everyone knew that the supply would be plentiful forevermore).

A costly fire that burned out much of Newfield in 1947 spared the **William Durgin Homestead,** built in 1813 and now decorated wholly in pure Victoriana. The homestead was converted in 1832 to an inn and the bedrooms upstairs let by weary transients. (Take a quick study of the antique sewing machines in one of the upstairs rooms; they look almost like shrunken versions of today's seamstresses' helpers.) Downstairs, the elegant room with the grand piano and sofa was once the inn's pub.

Inside you can peek at the last item made in Newfield's old mill — would you believe a round *chicken crate?*

You can be a guest in Dr. Isaac Trafton's house while visiting Willowbrook. He was a Newfield country doctor and his kitchen reflects that of a family of modest means in the mid 1800s.

Near the end of your visit to Willowbrook at Newfield, you'll be able to tour a different former private home. **Dr. Isaac Trafton,** who practiced in the village for a number of years, constructed this house in three stages, beginning in 1856. Again, this is a tribute to "country Victoriana"; it includes the doctor's office (complete with a case full of medicine jars and a desk supporting an open ledger), the kitchen, the parlor, and the marine room (filled with nautical artifacts in a display that's interesting though a little out of place) downstairs. Upstairs you'll find two bedrooms and a nursery, the latter containing toys like a rocking horse, building blocks, and a tea set. Don't walk by the hall wall without noticing the framed set of greeting cards called "The Greatest Moments in a Girl's Life." The list includes: "the proposal," "the trousseau," "the wedding," "the honeymoon," "the first evening in their new home," and finally, with the third member of the family, "their new love."

For those girls who never got to enjoy all those greatest moments, there's the unmarried maiden's room. Her room was small, with its own private entrance to give her all the time she'd need to herself, a small wash basin, a placard that says "God Bless Our Home," a black gown and hat, and a lone bed.

As with many other New England attractions, any visit during the school year could put you on a collision course with groups of schoolchildren. Although at other places you'd avoid those masses of ten year olds as you would blackflies, it may not be a bad idea to tag along here; the school groups are the only recipients of guides' monologs, so they get to hear some delightful background information. (By the way, you may notice that some of Willowbrook's prized possessions appear to postdate the declared Victorian period. While this does seem to preclude total authenticity, the artifacts are noteworthy and will bring back memories to many.)

Willowbrook's a lovely place for a picnic lunch, and there's a screened-in area for your picnicking pleasure. If you would rather leave the cooking to others, you can make use of the snack bar and ice-cream parlor on the premises. Willowbrook's gift shop, Christmas Etcetera, is located across the street next to the post office; it's a good place to walk off calories — and it's also a gentle transition back to the world of the twentieth century.

ACCESS

WILLOWBROOK AT NEWFIELD. Directions: From Interstate 95 exit 2, go north about 20 miles on Route 109, then north about 13 miles on Route 11. **Season:** Mid-May through September. **Days:** Daily. **Admission** charged. **Allow** 2 to 3 hours. **Telephone:** (207) 793-2784.

Shelburne Museum

A national historic landmark, the Ticonderoga *is the last side-wheeler existing in America. Its permanent home is the Shelburne Museum.*

Why is it that children and their grandparents always seem to have such one-way conversations? Grandma gets to hear all about the latest report card, the new tree house, and the scraped knee, but just let her *try* to get a word in edgewise about herself. One hint that the conversation is about to turn to the "good old days" and the kids start fidgeting in their seats and whispering that it's time to go home.

Maybe it's time to turn the tables and to let the kids learn something about Grandma's life for a change. Did we hear snoring? Wake up; we're going to Shelburne.

Shelburne Museum is forty-five acres and three centuries of fascinating Americana tucked away in a corner of northern Vermont. What child wouldn't love to put Mom in the stocks and Dad in the pillory in front of the old jail? If they let you out, you can show *them* the dunce cap and stools in the schoolhouse or let them play the toy shop's 1890 music box. The whole family can explore the old railroad train, search for the queen in the live bee exhibit, or inspect the delightful range of carousel figures and old posters in the Circus Parade Building. And just wait till you get to the general store; after Grandma finishes explaining to the kids how those string holders work, there won't be any generation gap left.

Explore the old railroad train, search for the queen in the live bee exhibit, or inspect the delightful range of carousel figures and old posters in the Circus Parade Building.

Although Shelburne is officially a museum, you'll find no stuffed buffalo or stuffy documents here. What you *will* find is a look at the way generations of earlier Americans lived. And since those "earlier Americans" included the kids' own grandparents, you may well find that Grandpa recollects perfectly those dental pliers that make the kids cringe.

Where to start? One of the first things you'll see after entering the grounds is the ship **Ticonderoga,** recently restored. Before you have a chance to consider

Shelburne's Stagecoach Inn is the home of an eclectic collection of cigar-store and carousel figures, weathervanes, and tavern and trade signs.

There's a direct correlation here between the age of any visitor and the number of items he can identify.

anything else, you'll have to go on board to catch up with the kids.

And you'll be glad you did. The *Ti*, as she's affectionately known at the museum, is a side-wheeler, the last of its type in America, and a national historic landmark. The *Ti* steamed across the waters of Lake Champlain for almost the entire first half of this century. After it was removed from service in the fifties, the 220-foot ship was actually transported two miles overland from the lake to its present site in Shelburne; the story of its last voyage is told dramatically in a film shown aboard the *Ti*. (Check at the museum entrance for show times.)

But you're really here to explore the ship itself. You'll find lots of gleaming metal; frosted glass windows; the ship's wheel from the battleship *Vermont;* and old clippings from, among others, *Life, National Geographic,* and the *Illustrated London News.* The pumps and gauges in the fo'c's'le date from 1906, and children can be absolutely entranced by the coal bunkers, boiler room, and steam-driven dynamo.

On the same deck you'll find the now-closed Temperance Cafe, where only soft drinks were served, and a barber shop with a collection of shaving mugs and a sign: "Teeth Extracted without Pain by O.B. Comfort, Dentist." Elsewhere the ticket office is full of memorabilia, and a dinner table is set for ten.

But there's much to see on land, too, and the next stop is the **Electra Havermeyer Webb Memorial Building.** Mrs. Webb and her husband J. Watson Webb were inveterate collectors of art and Americana, and they founded Shelburne Museum in 1947. In 1960, after their deaths, six rooms of their seventeen-room Park Avenue apartment were re-created in the museum's Webb Memorial Building.

Here you'll find Greek figurines from 350 B.C., ribbonback Chippendale chairs, and Georgian paneled rooms. There are four Monets in one room and a pair of Manets in the next — and Rembrandt, Degas, and

Whistler are represented in other parts of the house. In the library you'll find walls of English cowhide leather, but you'll also find a very personal atmosphere, evoked largely by the numerous displays of family photographs. In many ways, the Webb Memorial Building is a personalized microcosm of what the museum is all about — a collection of art and Americana that lets the visitor see, and sometimes feel, how our predecessors lived.

More eclectic examples of earlier lifestyles can be found in the **general store,** not far away from the *Ticonderoga.* The collections here cross quite a time span, but they all bring oohs and ahs from those who discover the high button shoes, coffee grinder and roaster, top hats, cracker barrel, butter churn, and even an old-fashioned device for making a rag mop. There's a direct correlation here between the age of any visitor and the number of items he can identify — but youthful visitors, or those with poor memories, will find their curiosity satisfied by a helpful staff member.

Be sure, too, to visit the **apothecary** next door. This isn't a huge shop, but three of its walls are packed with medicines and potions from earlier times. After you've picked out "Saturday night ambition pills" and "pink pills for pale people," ask the guide here to explain how the glass cups in the display case were once used for bloodletting.

Prefer the finer things in life? In the far corner of the museum grounds you'll find the **Hat and Fragrance Unit,** with its varied display of gowns from the late nineteenth and early twentieth centuries. Here, too, are samplers, laces, huge hair combs, an old-fashioned birdcage, and a number of old doll houses. We counted seventy-five quilts in just *one* of the rooms, and the guides are prepared to answer your questions about all of them.

And that's just the beginning. There's a weaving display, an old meeting house, the Beach Hunting Lodge, a sawmill — the list seems to go on forever. Get there when the museum opens at nine o'clock in the morning and take a minute to study the map you're given before you start out; with thirty-five buildings and a ship to see, you need to be pretty selective in the morning or you'll end up jogging through "just one more" display at five minutes of five. Come on a sunny day, and wear your walking shoes. Bring the kids — and don't forget Grandma.

SEAN KARDON

How would you like to put your children in the stocks? Or your parents? You'll get the chance at Shelburne.

After you've picked out "Saturday night ambition pills" and "pink pills for pale people," ask the guide to explain how the glass cups in the display case were once used for bloodletting.

ACCESS

SHELBURNE MUSEUM. Directions: From Interstate 89 exit 13, take Route 189 west to Route 7, then follow Route 7 south through the town of Shelburne. **Season:** Mid-May through mid-October. **Days:** Daily. **Admission** charged. **Allow** 5 to 8 hours. Telephone: (802) 985-3344.

COLIN LEE

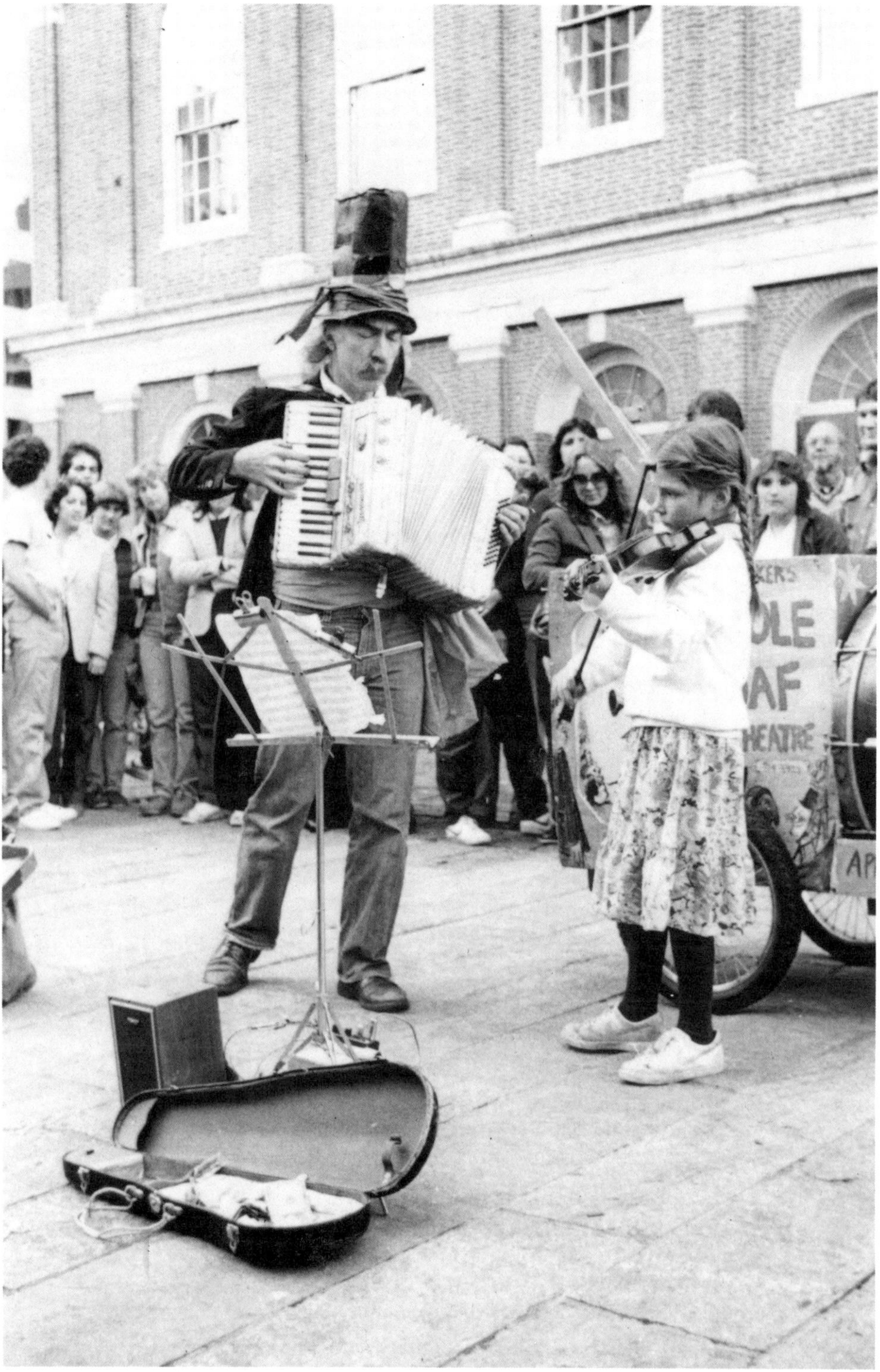

CHAPTER IV

Downtown!

A funny thing happened on the way to the suburbs. Fuel, construction, and transportation costs hit all time highs in the 1970s, blocking the well-traveled path. All over America, and, specifically, right here in New England, leaving long-neglected downtowns for greener suburbia reached a limit in appeal. The situation was no different whether you were a downtown dweller, shopper, diner, or worker. It became obvious that the "raze and raise" theory of knocking down the old and creating the new wasn't always worth it.

The answer sat right under the noses of urban developers in the form of solid gold disguised as tin. New England downtowns harbored buildings that were decaying and ignored. Yet many were beautiful works of architecture and just needed some sprucing up, both inside and out, to look their best. After thorough cleansing, they were filled with businesses, families, restaurants, stores, and museums; this adaptive re-use proved that these buildings could be as useful and esthetically appealing as they were originally — and *that*, in most cases, was over a century ago.

The restaurants, stores, and museums are what interest visitors most; reborn downtowns have proved to be wonderful places to shop, dine, sightsee, and simply walk around. While some renovations — like Faneuil Hall Marketplace in Boston, The Richardson in Hartford, and The Arcade in Providence — have been confined to individual complexes and buildings, others are devoted to entire downtown areas in small cities, like Portland and Brattleboro. And then there are those downtowns that are, in effect, museums themselves; in Lowell and New Bedford, you can explore and learn about the days when these cities were centers of nationwide industry.

If you're planning a day of shopping, remember that old blue laws are in effect in most New England downtowns. Unless otherwise noted, downtown stores here are closed on Sundays like Arizona ghost towns. But on the remaining six days, take your best pair of walking shoes, a healthy wallet, and your trusty camera — and head downtown.

Keeping in tune with the times, cities all over New England are refurbishing their historic downtown areas, just as Boston has in its historical Faneuil Hall Marketplace.

Faneuil Hall Marketplace

The building's the same; only the carriages have been changed. And Faneuil Hall Marketplace still bustles just as it did one hundred years ago.

You'll find scrimshanders, weavers, potters, Portuguese foods, street theater, and musical performances.

Pizza, yogurt, cookies, hot dogs, quiches, bagels, and egg rolls practically yelled out, "Eat me!" as we paraded by the palate-tempting food stalls in the hundred-and-fifty-year-old Quincy Market; we offended vendors of none of the above when we finally settled on falafels. After sufficiently filling ourselves, we browsed through the specialty shops in the North and South Market buildings that sandwich Quincy Market, a couple of the closest things this earth has to shoppers' heaven. In between the eating and the shopping, we caught the antics of some street acrobats on one of the cobblestoned pedestrian malls between the buildings. It was, basically, a pretty typical day at Faneuil Hall Marketplace.

While not the first urban redevelopment of this type, the complex by the Boston waterfront is often used today as the yardstick by which others of this type are measured. It is one of the most visible redeveloped centers and one of the most famous.

The date was August 26, 1826, when some nine dozen food merchants opened stalls to sell a variety of meats and fish in a spanking new market building by Boston's waterfront. Special ceremonies and formal pronouncements heightened the public's excitement regarding this opening, which would relieve the overcrowded conditions of the old market that was huddled around Faneuil Hall. The mayor of Boston, Josiah Quincy, dedicated the new complex.

A total of 150 years later to the day, **Quincy Market** was rededicated and reopened, with Mayor Kevin White and other principals in the redevelopment process on hand at the ribbon-cutting ceremony. And Bostonians, as well as others interested in downtown preservation, relished the thought of the electric atmosphere around the marketplace, which would draw both locals and visitors who otherwise would never have headed into this part of downtown. In the subsequent two years, the South Market building and the North Market building both opened, completing the complex today known as Faneuil Hall Marketplace.

What had happened to Quincy Market over the years between these two occasions is not too different from what had occurred across the country; architecturally attractive buildings that had once served useful purposes had fallen into disrepair for one reason or another. Quincy Market had become an overcrowded, often neglected wholesale-food building, and North and South Markets had regressed into little more than warehouses. It was in the early 1960s that renewal plans were first considered, and after years of comprehensive study it was decided that these buildings should be saved and restructured to fulfill their original purposes.

The outsides of the buildings are very much as

they were a century and a half ago. All three were designed in the Greek Revival style by architect Alexander Parris, a disciple of Charles Bulfinch (who designed Faneuil Hall as well as the Old State House in Hartford) and all three granite structures are listed in the National Register of Historic Places. Incidentally, this is their second time around not only as commercial centers but also as examples of urban renewal; when they were first designed and built, it was on land once used as a town dock that they were placed. Since the opening of the complex was kicked off by a city government that utilized reclaimed land, the 1826 Quincy Market project is regarded by many as the original example of urban renewal in the United States.

Its successor is also one of the most popular, and a morning, afternoon, or entire day can help you attest to that. It's estimated that, on the average, about a million people pass through Faneuil Hall Marketplace each month — which may have been what prompted the *Boston Globe* to call it "Boston's Forum Romani." Basically, it's just one fun place to be. Cruising up and down the aromatic aisles inside Quincy Market and trying to decide on the day's repast will tease you into forgetting any notion of dieting; unless you possess the strongest will power, you'll find you have to try a little of this and a little of that, and a little of this for dessert.

Where to devour the feast you've assembled? You'll see picnic tables set up in the rotunda under the landmark copper dome. Finding a seat there at a peak hour, however, can be on a par with locating a vacant parking space outside Fenway Park at game time. If it's a nice day, you can sit outside on the benches amid the trees on North and South Market streets, both now pedestrian malls, and watch the rest of the world go by as you munch away. For those who prefer not to run and eat, there are sit-down restaurants in some parts of Quincy Market. Outdoors, under weatherproof glass canopies, there are more of the same as well as specialty shops and booths for browsing and buying.

You'll find more places to have a meal, and significantly more items to decorate your coffee table or kitchen wall, in the **North and South Market** buildings. Altogether there are about seventy-five establishments, and you could spend hours browsing in them. While clothing shops — with merchandise ranging from designer fashions to sportswear to hard-to-obtain imported items — make up the largest category of types of stores, the one-of-a-kind specialty shops vie for the most attention. Looking for a ready-to-put-together kite kit, a Vermont-made quilt, a marionette just waiting for you to pull its strings, a real old-time music box, or an imported African carpet? These items, and others you've probably never dreamed of looking for, are representative of some of the more special stores here.

Be forewarned. Observing food vendors at the marketplace can be hazardous to one's diet.

Looking for a Vermont-made quilt, a marionette just waiting for you to pull its strings, or an imported African carpet? You'll find it here.

"Your company will fire you," the waitress snapped, "if you keep eating at cheap places like this."

COLIN LEE

Those who plan on dining at Durgin-Park in the North Market building had best be prepared for some good food and for waitresses who could pass as stand-ins for Don Rickles.

In the North Market building is a Boston tradition called **Durgin-Park,** a restaurant that has been around since the last nail was hammered into the market building's original frame. The saltiest thing in the place may be the attitude of the waitresses who, for all practical purposes, could pass as stand-ins for Don Rickles. When a young woman sitting near us asked for a receipt for business purposes, we overheard the waitress snap, "Your company will fire you if you keep eating at cheap places like this." Later on, a man ordered one of the meat dishes without realizing it is always cooked to order and then asked what the delay was. His waitress replied, "Haven't you ever ordered this before? If you want it raw, we'll give it to you raw." She then walked away without allowing the man time to even think of a response. It's all part of the show here, but be forewarned. As it's been said, "If you can't take the heat, get out of the kitchen."

There's a considerably more gentle atmosphere surrounding the rest of the marketplace, and that especially holds true for North and South Market streets, where the benches are as welcome to exhausted patrons as a swimming pool on a muggy August day. If you still feel somewhat energetic, you can look at or buy some of the flowers, food, or crafts for sale on the movable carts that dot the grounds. But if your eyes say go while your body says no, relax and enjoy some of the daily **street entertainment** that abounds in the spring, summer, and early fall. This is where, in addition to mimes, stand-up comedians, and jugglers, there are usually a capella singing groups, one-act comedy players, or acrobats performing quite often.

The glass canopies at Quincy Market close up to shut out the cold air during the winter months, but that's about all that closes up. An urban pumpkin patch is one way to describe the outside areas just before Halloween, and the Merry Merry Marketplace takes over during the Christmas season. During tinsel time, all the trees on North and South Market Streets are decorated with one hundred thousand white lights, the pushcarts are used to display sellable items that range from holiday apple pies to candy canes to Christmas stockings, and the sounds of caroling can provide a feeling of cheer even among the surliest of waitresses over at Durgin-Park.

ACCESS

FANEUIL HALL MARKETPLACE. Directions: From the Southeast Expressway (Interstate 93) southbound, take the Callahan Tunnel-Dock Square exit. Park in any of the nearby garages. (The Government Center garage is the biggest, but smaller lots abound.) By subway: Take the Green Line to Government Center, one stop from Park Street. **Season:** All year. **Days:** Daily. **Allow** 1 to 4 hours. **Telephone:** (617) 523-2980.

New Bedford

You can tell you're coming into New Bedford's downtown historic area from Interstate 195 by the difference under your wheels as the asphalt becomes a bumpy cobblestone. And looking on either side, you can see the contrast as period street lights replace modern lamps. After parking the car and resorting to foot power, you can get a closer look at the Federal and Greek Revival styles of architecture, which are most commonly found in the district; you'll also note the liberal use of Victorian and Gothic modes, letting you know that this is a surviving remnant of a past era.

Basically, a few hours spent walking through the streets of this fourteen-block area, now designated by the Department of the Interior as a National Historic Landmark, will enable you not only to observe some nineteenth-century architecture but also to explore the worlds of the New Bedford whalemen, dine in some historic buildings, and shop in some attractive craft and gift emporiums. And despite the fact that this has been transformed from a neglected area to a revived historic district, it's still employed residentially and commercially as it was during the glory years of the whaling era a century and a half ago.

It was from the early 1820s to the late 1850s that whaling was the kingpin of New Bedford industry. Whale oil was the primary source of energy then and just about every penny that went into a New Bedford resident's pocket came directly or indirectly from the business of chasing after and capturing the huge marine mammals. New Bedford was a thriving city.

But history has shown that there's always an end to such seemingly endless good fortune. Ironically, what started New Bedford's fall from glory was a tremendously successful catch in 1857, which brought about a whale-oil glut that signaled the end of high prices. The supply continued to be cheap and plentiful after that, and when oil was discovered in Pennsylvania in 1859, New Bedford whalemen soon knew they no longer had a gold mine. Confederate raids on whaling ships during the Civil War hurt further. While whaling did continue into the 1880s, the once hearty numbers in the Atlantic had dwindled significantly and seafarers now had to venture thousands of miles away into the Pacific, Indian, and Arctic oceans. It was costly and dangerous (there were two major disasters in the Arctic in the 1870s) and this proved to be the final pin to burst the whaling bubble.

Finding adaptation the key to survival, New Bedford next became a hotbed for mills and factories; fabrics, copper, iron, silver, and glass were major products for a while. But the stock-market crash and the Depression, capping a period of mismanagement, drove most mills out of the region. New Bedford was a dying town for most of the next few decades, but an

New Bedford, once a thriving city, fell victim to hard economic times during much of this century. The historic area has since been revitalized into a city that's today as fresh and vibrant as spring flowers.

Cobblestoned Centre Street, with its beautifully refurbished old homes, is perhaps the most attractive avenue in the historic area. It's also the home of a popular annual festival.

influx of high technology added to a burgeoning fishing and tourist industry has helped bring it out of economic purgatory.

Today, the city of over ninety-nine thousand is the home of a WHALE that has done more to preserve its heritage than all the legends and stories about the great whaling era ever could. This WHALE, an acronym for Waterfront Historic Area League, is a nonprofit group devoted to revitalization and restoration of the historic area, and its products are the cobblestoned streets and sandblasted old buildings you see here. Organized in 1962, WHALE gained full strength in the 1970s. At times alone, and at times with the partnership of other local nonprofit groups or local government, WHALE has been responsible for purchasing, refurbishing, and usually reselling some of the gems of historic structures located in this special city by the sea.

The **Caleb Spooner House,** located at 22 Centre Street, just down the road from WHALE headquarters, is a perfect example of WHALE's works. It's an 1806 frame structure that was restored, then moved from another location to a vacant lot; it's now used as both a gift shop and a private, single-family residence. A Greek Revival structure, the refurbished **Double Bank Building,** situated on the corners of Water and William streets, is now the home of the Fishermen's Union; once the location of, as you might guess, two different banks, this pillared beauty was designed in the early

1830s by noted architect Russell Warren.

Another Greek Revival structure, the **U.S. Custom House,** at the corner of William and Second streets, is still employed as it was nearly one hundred fifty years ago, making it the oldest such office continuously used in the country. And on colorfully named Johnny Cake Hill, you'll find the **Mariners' Home** and the **Seamen's Bethel,** side by side. While the Mariners' Home, a place of lodging for those who earn their living by the ways of the sea, is closed to the general public, the bethel, a chapel for seamen, can still be inspected by all interested visitors. The gray clapboarded bethel, an 1832 creation, was originally constructed to afford moral guidance to sailors, who had a tendency, it can be safely understated, to be attracted to less wholesome diversions; immortalized in Herman Melville's *Moby Dick,* the Seamen's Bethel today is still used for services. The most notable feature is the pulpit shaped like a ship's bow, poking out toward the modest wooden pews. You can visit it daily during the summer and at other times by appointment.

The active use of this historic area as a place to live as well as do business, however, does not detract one bit from the experience a tourist will enjoy. For many visitors, browsing in all the specialty stores will fill a morning or afternoon; there are indeed many quality shops throughout this fourteen-block area. (Department, drug, and other more pedestrian stores are to be found in the central New Bedford shopping area to the east of the richly preserved waterfront historic district. County Street is regarded as the dividing line.) Additionally, restaurants serving lunch, brunch, and in-between meals are housed in an abundance of the vintage New Bedford structures.

A fine place to start your day is the **information center** at 48 North Water Street, operated by the Bristol County Development Council and open during the summer season. If you plan a trip here during another time of year, you might want to head straight to **WHALE** at 13 Centre Street. WHALE's home, the William Tallman Warehouse, deserves an inspection anyway — both inside and out. Dating from 1790, it's one of the oldest remaining buildings in the city; of brick and stone construction, it's actually two different buildings attached to each other. WHALE is located on the second floor; the personnel here are both friendly and helpful and are, needless to say, experts on this entire area.

Just about all the houses of interest, including those privately owned, are marked with plaques indicating their original uses and construction dates. You'll note that some, like the **Andrew Robeson House,** were moved from other locations in New Bedford in order to fill vacant holes in the historic district. This 550-ton home, which for all practical purposes had been cast aside like an old shoe and left to waste

The signs tell it all. Shoppers in New Bedford will find a variety of ways to spend their time.

The Seamen's Bethel was constructed in 1832 to afford moral guidance to sailors, who had a tendency, it can be safely understated, to be attracted to less wholesome diversions.

away in neglect for ninety years, was crated across a portion of a block to its current location, opposite the U.S. Custom House, at the southeast corner of William and Second streets. (It now houses offices and apartments.) Robeson, a wealthy whaling businessman, moved to New Bedford from Nantucket and built this Federal mansion in 1821; thanks to WHALE it's been saved, and fits so well in its current location that you'd never think this was the home's second home.

Probably the most striking example of adaptive reuse here is the **Rodman Candleworks.** Like Andrew Robeson, Samuel Rodman, Sr. came to New Bedford from Nantucket. He built the candle factory in 1810, emerging as the first producer of spermaceti candles in the city. After the closing of the factory in the late 1800s, the Federal structure became home, at different times, for occupants ranging from an antiques store to a mill workshop to insurance offices. Like that of so many other downtown New Bedford buildings, its appearance deteriorated over the years.

Today, thanks to Candleworks Associates, a corporation owned by both WHALE and the Architectural Conservation Trust (ACT), the Rodman Candleworks is a charming and attractive complex that combines a bank, a restaurant, and other businesses. When you step into the Candleworks, you will still see the old beams, worn wood posts, and native granite rubble walls that are testament to the years; on the outside, the two-foot-thick walls have been covered with pink stucco. Even if you don't plan on dining here, you might want to walk inside the historic building to look at a display in the basement that focuses on the Candleworks' original purpose: making spermaceti candles. These candles, you'll learn, were superior to others of the day because they consisted of waxes rather than fats and thereby lasted longer, caused a more brilliant flame, and generated no odors. A jar of unrefined sperm-whale oil, a bar of refined spermaceti, candle molds, and a sperm-whale-oil lamp that dates from the mid 1820s are some of the items you can examine. The display is free of charge.

If this little peek into the whaling industry that nurtured early New Bedford makes you want to see more, take a stroll into the highly respected **Whaling Museum,** located in the middle of the historic district at 18 Johnny Cake Hill. Here, for example, you'll see a much larger exhibit on early candle making with an explanation that this waxy oil called spermaceti came from a cavity in the forehead of the sperm whale. More exhibits, including other luminating fuels like tallow, bayberry, and beeswax, are also on view.

But the pride of the museum has to be what is claimed to be the largest ship's model in the world: a half-scale model of the bark *Lagoda,* made around 1916 and modeled after the original *Lagoda,* which sailed out of New Bedford in search of whale oil 140 years ago.

This thirty-foot-long whale boat was boarded by a crew of about a half dozen, lowered from the whaleship, and manipulated until it was close enough to the whale to harpoon it.

You are permitted to climb aboard this authentically reproduced model and investigate close up its riggings, masts, and inner workings. Next to the *Lagoda* is an actual thirty-foot-long cedar whale boat that was boarded by a crew of about a half dozen, lowered from the whaleship, and manipulated until it was close enough to the whale to harpoon it. Scrimshaw, ships' figureheads, sailmakers' gear, and paintings of boats and nautical scenes make up most of the other major exhibits here. And for those who would like to make a one-on-one comparison of New Bedford today to New Bedford of years gone by, a display to the rear of the building is of interest. On the sill of an open window looking toward Centre Street is a photograph of the same street in an earlier day.

You have a chance to admire examples of fine Pairpoint Glass, in addition to the works of other New Bedford glass manufacturers, at the **New Bedford Glass Museum** at 50 Second Street. The building, dating from 1820-21, is a Federal-style home still standing on its original foundation. Across the street in the Bourne Warehouse is the New Bedford Glass Works where glassblowing demonstrations are given. There is also a show room where you can buy some of their products.

Early August is one of the best times to visit the historic downtown area of New Bedford, but you'll have trouble taking a lone, relaxing walk down Centre Street then. For one weekend in this summer month, the narrow brick-lined road is blocked off and lined with New England craftsmen selling some of their hand-wrought creations, as the Centre Street Festival gets into full swing. Regardless of what year you go, you'll most likely find scrimshanders, weavers, potters, and woodworkers as well as those creating and selling a conglomeration of different items. Portuguese foods, street theater, and musical performances can also be expected. For up-to-date details, you can call the City of New Bedford, Office of Tourism at (617) 999-2931. The festival is a fitting way to glorify the rebirth of this grand old downtown, but with all the diversions here, it's hardly the only way to celebrate.

The signs tell it all. Shoppers in New Bedford will find a variety of ways to spend their time.

ACCESS

NEW BEDFORD WATERFRONT HISTORIC AREA.
Directions: From Interstate 195 exit 15, take Route 18 (Downtown Connector) to the Elm Street exit. **Season:** All year. **Days:** Most stores open Monday through Saturday; restaurants open daily. **Admission** charged for the Whaling Museum and New Bedford Glass Museum, not charged for the Seamen's Bethel. **Allow** 1 to 4 hours. **Note:** Street parking is severely limited; there is a municipal parking garage on the corner of Elm and Second streets, at the district's northern rim. **Telephone:** (617) 997-1776.

What better way to tour the Lowell of yesteryear than on a vehicle of yesteryear? This self-propelled rail car resembles the many trolleys that once clanged along the busy streets of the Spindle City.

Lowell National Historical Park

It was over 150 years ago that a site on the Merrimack River in northeastern Massachusetts was chosen as the location of a model city — America's first planned industrial city. It was named Lowell, after Francis Cabot Lowell, a Boston merchant who legend says had a photographic memory. Lowell visited industrial areas of England and Scotland, observing the latest in textile-mill technology; because he was not allowed to take plans out of those countries, he memorized the design of the most sophisticated power loom and with the aid of a mechanic "re-invented" it in America. The loom was to be one of the chief innovations in America's Industrial Revolution, and was used extensively in Lowell's textile factories.

It is most appropriate, with this history behind it, that Lowell is today the nation's model for another concept. Uniformed national park rangers may seem as out of place on the streets of downtown Lowell as a twelve-foot-high saguaro cactus. Yet, the rangers on duty are one result of the creation of Lowell National Historical Park, established in June, 1978; here is the country's first urban national park, so designated to preserve the relics not of one fleeting moment of history but instead of an entire historical period. Lowell National Historical Park, combined with Lowell Heritage State Park (since some of the waterways here are under the jurisdiction of the state of Massachusetts), is a recognition of the importance of the Industrial Revolution and the change in America from an agricultural to an industrial society. (The idea of national and state cooperation in the same park is in itself unique.)

Lowell's many canals have earned it the nickname "The Venice of America," but unlike those of the western Italian city, Lowell's canals are not the result of its setting being a natural archipelago. These canals

Because he was not allowed to take plans out of Britain, he memorized the design of the most sophisticated power loom and "re-invented" it in America.

were made by men for the famous Lowell textile industry; the mills were dependent on canals since the flow of water was integral in the distribution of power.

What is in effect Lowell's Grand Canal is not really a canal at all, but rather the Merrimack River, which originates in New Hampshire and flows for 110 miles. At an area called Pawtucket Falls in Lowell, there is a thirty-two-foot drop; this natural waterfall and its resultant power output were the main reasons for the founding of Lowell as an industrial center.

If the term national park brings forests and mountains to mind, you'll find that Lowell National Historical Park broadens the usual definition quite a bit. Instead of rocks or trees, you'll see a whole city of red textile mills, canals, and public buildings — all an urban preservation of the beginnings of America's Industrial Revolution and the heyday of New England's textile industry.

You'll want to begin your visit to this fascinating city at the **Visitor Center,** housed in a brick mill complex called Market Mills, at 246 Market Street in the heart of downtown Lowell. Here you'll find exhibits that tell the Lowell story, as well as those that explain the technology of water power and the textile industry itself. An early power loom, bolts of calico, and three-dimensional models of water wheels are just some of the items on display. In a small auditorium in the back, a 20-minute slide show entitled "Lowell: The Industrial Revelation" is shown continuously. This award-winning multi-image slide show is free, as are entrance to the park itself and all of its offerings.

There is more to the Market Mills complex than its Visitor Center. You'll want to check out both a group of food booths collectively called "The Melting Pot" and an area devoted to the arts, named "A Brush with History," where you'll find workshops with resident painters and craftspeople as well as a gallery for sales and exhibits.

Several types of tours, both guided and self-conducted, leave from the Visitor Center daily. Call ahead to make reservations and to check the schedule of tours, as many of them are seasonal. Special-interest tours vary throughout the year. The best known and most comprehensive overview tour, offered late May through early October, is called the **Mill and Canal Tour** and takes you through the fascinating history of Lowell by trolley, canal boat, and on foot.

The story of Lowell that you hear is one not of dry historical dates, facts, and figures, but of people. It is about Thomas Jefferson, who initially felt firmly that America's future was in agriculture and was repulsed by the shabby conditions of industrial Europe before finally deciding in favor of some industrial growth. It concerns the "Boston Associates," contemporaries of Francis Cabot Lowell, who were the first investors in America's leading industrial projects here and in

The story of Lowell that you hear is one not of dry historical dates, facts, and figures, but of people.

SEAN KARDON

Two sources of Lowell power: the Pawtucket Falls and a mill worker, portrayed by costumed guide Dorothy Zug.

Waltham, Massachusetts. It's about Lowell himself, who, believing that an industrial community could be conducive to both good health and high standards, incorporated here unheard of utopian ideas like a corporate structure, company-maintained and supported living quarters and social codes, and a heavily female work force. And it's about Kirk Boott, agent of the Boston Associates, a hard-driving man who helped turn Lowell's dreams into reality in the form of city streets, waterways, buildings, and company policies.

Much of the story regards the work force. Throughout the tour, you hear about the "mill girls," the unmarried farmers' daughters who worked for $2.25 to $4.25 (minus $1.25 for room and board) per seventy-two-hour week. You then hear about the immigrants — the Irish, French-Canadian, Portuguese, Polish, Hungarian, Greek, and Jewish — who replaced the original mill girls in the mid nineteenth century and worked in the mills through World War I.

You hear about the "mill girls," the unmarried farmers' daughters who worked for $2.25 to $4.25 per seventy-two-hour week.

It was about that time that more sophisticated steam-powered machinery, lower taxes, and a multitude of nonunion workers caused the textile companies to commence a slow but sure mass migration to the south. Lowell became a city of derelict factory buildings and mass unemployment; it remained that way until the 1970s, when many electronics and computer companies moved in to take advantage of the sizable labor pool. While unrelated for the most part to this latest industry, the park and its recognition of the former model textile industry are symbolic of the rebirth of Lowell and the uplifting spirit that accompanies it like fog to lowlands.

COURTESY
LOWELL NATIONAL HISTORICAL PARK

Another source of transportation for park visitors is the canal boats.

That feeling, combined with the many attractions of the park, creates almost an urban Disneyland atmosphere — except that all attractions were once elements of everyday life for thousand of workers. However, when you board **The Whistler,** the park's pseudo-trolley (a self-propelled rail car different from a trolley since there are no overhead wires, but a pleasant throwback nonetheless to the days when trolleys ran through the streets of Lowell), and when you sit in the red velveteen seats and take a peek at the potbellied stove and the conductor garbed in his realistic uniform, you'll find it difficult to believe that this was meant to be anything but fun. And if the small open **boat rides** are part of your tour, you'll be given as much time to enjoy the little canal cruises as you will to hear facts that may satisfy your curiosity. For instance, Merrimack Canal, the youngest and deepest, was built totally by hand in the 1860s by Irish immigrants; it is twenty feet deep in spots, twice as deep as the others. You may also hear that the canals are not used entirely as flowing museum exhibits or reminders of the past, since some computer companies are today employing waterpower from Boott Mill on the banks of the Merrimack River.

And then you get to see some of the manmade remnants of the past. We took a peek inside a few **gate houses,** looking about the same as they did when the Spindle City was feverishly churning out textiles. In the Northern Canal Gatehouse by the Pawtucket Falls, a mock nineteenth-century gatekeeper authentically decked out in white blouse, gray vest, black hat with yellow feather, and dirt on face climbed up a ladder from a room below to tell us about his busy day. A tree trunk, he stated, had floated into the water wheel, making it impossible to open the gates. After explaining to us the inner workings of the gate house, he excused himself and, we were told, went back to work.

At the Francis Gate, we were stunned to see the massive twenty-ton wooden gate that was dropped to stop floods in both 1856 and 1936. The ranger then informed us that this would be the only way to stop floods from entering downtown Lowell today, although flood-control efforts have made the chances of such a problem slim.

Although summer offers the most options in tours and activities, there are many year-round programs at the park. One special program, entitled "Tunes and Tales," is presented at the Visitor Center auditorium Tuesday through Thursday at 10:30 AM. This musical presentation includes folk songs and anecdotes of Lowell history. In addition to the overview Mill and Canal Tour, special-interest tours are offered during summer months, and many are offered throughout the year. Such tours last an hour and leave from the Visitor Center; topics include: "Lowell History," "Waterpower," and "Mill Girls and Immigrants." These are perfect for the visitor who just wants a small sampling of Lowell.

Whenever and however you decide to tour Lowell National Historical Park, you won't be able to help getting caught up in the exciting and colorful atmosphere of the place. Lowell is truly a piece of American history brought back to life.

When you sit in the red velveteen seats and take a peek at the potbellied stove and the conductor garbed in his realistic uniform, you'll find it difficult to believe that this was meant to be anything but fun.

ACCESS

LOWELL NATIONAL HISTORICAL PARK. Directions: From Interstate 495, take the Lowell Connector toward downtown Lowell and follow the signs to the visitors' parking area. **Season:** All year; limited schedule in fall, winter, and spring. **Days:** Daily. **Admission** free. **Allow** 3 to 5 hours. **Notes:** A reservation is recommended for guided tours, since there is a limit to the number of people allowed on any 1 tour. Self-guided tours are also available. Wear comfortable walking shoes and dress appropriately for the weather; tours are rarely canceled due to bad weather. Water coolers have thoughtfully been placed in some of the buildings you enter on a tour. **Telephone:** (617) 459-1000.

You'd have trouble walking through any of these front doors. They're all part of a mural painted on the back entrance of The Richardson, depicting a fictional turn-of-the-century Hartford.

The Richardson

Once upon a time in the bustling streets of downtown Hartford, there was a store called Brown Thomson & Co. It was a good-hearted store, and it tried to do its best, but its best just never seemed to be good enough. It sat between two even bigger stores called G. Fox & Company and Sage-Allen, and they always seemed to overshadow Brown Thomson's. Although the store had once been an outlet for high-quality merchandise, the goods that were sold there for the most part, well, they just weren't good enough. The material was gradually downgraded to that of — heaven forbid — a discount store.

Finally, Brown Thomson's fell victim to what seemed like a case of terminal suburbia-itis, standing as an obsolete structure in the middle of a city when everyone knew the suburbs were the place to be. The doors were permanently closed in the 1970s, and Brown Thomson's settled into a deep coma. Well-intended developers thought they could bring it back to life, but no one really knew how or in what form. Some feared that Brown Thomson's was doomed to be eternally darkened. And it is said by some that once in a while a veteran Hartford shopper could hear a sniffle and see a tear roll down the crusty exterior of the aged structure.

It is said by some that once in a while a veteran Hartford shopper could hear a sniffle and see a tear roll down the crusty exterior of the aged structure.

But as in all good stories, the ending here is happy. For it wasn't too long before people all over the country started to realize that old buildings were good after all. And as if from the effect of a fairy godmother's magic wand, in 1980 the Brown Thomson building was reopened, filled with shops and restaurants, and polished and decorated to be as good as new; it's now one splendid example of adaptive re-use, making for a fine way to spend a few hours browsing, shopping, feasting, and admiring some mighty impressive architecture.

The building today, along with a former warehouse and two infill buildings, forms The Richardson, named for the building's original designer. The bottom three floors in this complex (one section is five stories high, while another part is nine) are taken up by **stores and restaurants,** with the top floors entirely residential. What types of items are available for purchase or consumption? There's everything from shoes to bagels, books about New England to women's clothing from Mexico, croissants to pizza, and native plants to German nutcrackers. Altogether, there are four dozen-odd commercial establishments that occupy the million square feet of retail space, 75 per cent of which is devoted to stores, the rest to restaurants.

When the bone-biting chills of winter arrive, this enclosed shopping bonanza is as welcome as a down jacket. However, it does not serve as an overgrown, stuffy box in the spring, summer, and fall. **Temple Court,** for example, formerly Temple Street, is a half-enclosed, half-open passageway between The Richardson and neighboring department store Sage-Allen. The sloping, brick-lined walkway and the area immediately around it have been the showplace for vocal groups, Dixieland and other small bands, and outdoor vendors, at various times, drawing sightseers and lunch-hour strollers into the open in otherwise building-locked and car-congested downtown.

And while the interior of The Richardson is devoted to modern mall-ish design, the outside still exposes the general public to some truly classic **late-nineteenth-century architecture.** The building was designed by noted architect Henry Hobson Richardson, who also designed the famous Trinity Church in Boston's Copley Square and whose disciples included the renowned Stanford White.

The rounded arches on the Main Street side, which are so dominant, are a trademark of Richardson designs. His use of rough-textured, as opposed to smooth, masonry, and his incorporation of alternating colors of stone surrounding the arches, caused prominent architecture aficionados to label his style "Richardsonian Romanesque." Because of its elegant appeal and historic significance as the work of a major American architect, the building has been placed in the National Register of Historic Places and is now considered a national landmark.

The rear of The Richardson, which is actually the back of the warehouse building in the complex, also deserves an admiring glance. An oversized mural portraying a fictional turn-of-the-century Main Street

DIANE LEVY

The alternating colors of stone in The Richardson's arches were one trademark of the classic building's noted architect.

There's everything from shoes to bagels, croissants to pizza, and native plants to German nutcrackers.

DIANE LEVY

Who says pizza twirling is a lost art? There's plenty of it going on at the Richardson. And plenty of eating, too.

has been painted across the exterior that faces The Richardson parking lot. Painted by a New York City firm, it was completed over the course of five months and is absolutely charming. The storefronts depict the names of current retailers located in and around The Richardson, and the perspective is so fine that you'd think you could actually sit under an awning or walk inside one of the doorways.

One of the stores identified in this mural is, of course, Brown Thomson & Company. While this has always been a household phrase to most Hartfordites, not many realize that the building was originally called the Cheney Block and was built by the Cheney Brothers, who owned mills in nearby Manchester. It was never officially called the Brown Thomson building, although the company was the structure's first tenant. You may also be surprised to learn that it was not primarily a low-budget store and, instead, was mainly a silk importer as part of a cooperative operating out of New York City. It wasn't until some years later that Brown Thomson & Company developed into the department store that so many remember.

Stanley Schultz, principal of Metropolitan Properties, developer of The Richardson, says that it was an accepted thought that no one who has ever lived, worked, or had acquaintances or relatives in the Hartford metropolitan area could disassociate this majestic structure from the name Brown Thomson's. So a sticky problem emerged: how to keep alive the name of the distinguished architect who developed the landmark (which had already fallen neck deep into the ocean of oblivion) without tossing away the name by which most persons identified the structure? The solution: A restaurant, one of a handful inside The Richardson, has been named Brown Thomson & Co. Restaurant; the interior features a brick and stained-glass decor, with antiques ornamenting the floors and walls. It's a long way from the days when you'd walk up and down the aisles here looking for a cheap pair of trousers.

ACCESS

THE RICHARDSON. Directions: Eastbound: From Interstate 84 in downtown Hartford, take the Main Street exit and head south on Main Street. Westbound: From Interstate 84 in downtown Hartford, take the Ann Street exit; take a left onto Church Street, and then a right onto Main Street. Bus service is also available. **Season:** All year. **Days:** Most stores are open Monday through Saturday; most restaurants are open daily. **Allow** 1 to 3 hours. **Note:** Parking is available in lots at the rear of The Richardson; heading south on Main Street, take a left onto Kinsley Street and continue for 1 block to Market Street. Lots are immediately on both the right and the left. **Telephone:** (203) 525-9711.

LAURA J. REPOSA

The Arcade
& Westminster Mall

The Greek Revival Arcade was designed by two architects. One preferred this exterior. To see what the other had in mind, you'll have to voyage here and examine the other entrance.

Pity poor Providence! Long the butt of New Englanders' jokes, the capital of Rhode Island has for years tried to prove it is not only major league, but is worthy of visits by those interested in sightseeing, shopping, and dining. Although Providence has always boasted some underpublicized attractions and fine dining experiences, none has been as well received as two newly reborn downtown areas: one a formerly run-down complex once dubbed "Butler's Folly," the other a previously bland main thoroughfare.

The Arcade and Westminster Mall, within easy walking distance of each other, have both been cleaned and scrubbed recently and are open to all as prime examples of what can be done with New England's old downtowns. The **Arcade,** a three-level Greek Revival structure facing Westminster Street to the north and Weybosset Street to the south, was originally a century and a half ahead of its time: built in 1828 by Cyrus Butler and a group of investors called the Arcade Realty Company, the building is widely regarded as the country's oldest indoor shopping center.

However, you won't find inside the Arcade the sterile antiseptic atmosphere of modern-day suburban malls. From the iron railings to the curved door handles to the narrow passageways on the second and third floors, this shopping complex is a throwback to an earlier time.

Like today's malls, though, the Arcade was originally built in an outlying area and not in the center city. You wouldn't know it, but in 1828 the Arcade was plunked down in a corn field in a modest residential area; the heartbeat of Providence was a good carriage ride across town. The tag "Butler's Folly" reflected common opinion of the day that such a far-removed shopping area would never fare well.

From the iron railings to the curved door handles to the narrow passageways on the second and third floors, this shopping complex is a throwback to an earlier time.

From then on, the Arcade was like an aging songwriter: too out of step to be considered contemporary, and yet not ancient enough to be a classic.

Restaurants in the newly redesigned Arcade are on the first floor, stores on the second and third.

Wrong! It did take a couple of years for the shoppers of Providence to part with tradition and head out of town to buy their goods. But then the Arcade flourished, at one point becoming the busiest place in all Providence where you could buy fashionable ladies' hats and bonnets. In fact, it wasn't until 1911 that the Arcade closed its doors to shoppers for the first time, after a fire had gutted its lower portion.

From then on, the Arcade's life as a source of shoppers' bliss was like that of an aging songwriter: too out of step to be considered contemporary, and yet not ancient enough to be a classic. Though it went through a number of changes, it was always basically used as some form of marketplace. Not that this continuous usage was easy to pull off; in 1944, the Arcade was purchased by a local utility and was temporarily slated to be razed.

In 1976, the sad-looking Arcade was noticed by some Providence residents who had their eyes on an urban renovation program. In January, 1980, work on the $3 million-dollar project was started, and it was on October 9, 1980, that the reborn Arcade was opened. It was totally reorganized with new stores and outlets, and today the ground floor is primarily devoted to restaurants and food shops while the upper two levels are filled mostly with stores selling clothes and gifts. The exterior, except for a sandblasting, is unchanged. It's a masterpiece, and has been described by New York City's Metropolitan Museum of Art as one of the country's three best examples of nineteenth-century commercial architecture.

Try to catch a glimpse of the Arcade's exterior from both its Westminster and Weybosset street entrances. The original builders, Butler and the Arcade Realty Company, each hired a different architect to design the structure; you can see the effects of the architects' differences of opinion at the east and west entrances. Though both make use of six Ionic columns fronting the Arcade (the columns, incidentally, were transported to the building site by a team of oxen), the Westminster Street side is topped by a Greek pediment while the Weybosset Street doorway can be recognized by the stone panels overhead. The twenty-two-foot-high columns were hand-cut and, at the time, were the largest individual columns in the country. Despite other architectural wonders of the past 150 years, these are still impressive and are perhaps one reason why the Arcade has been included in the National Register of Historic Buildings.

The Arcade's late-night hours (most restaurants are open until midnight, and stores are open late one night per week) are one good reason for the return of life to downtown Providence. Many workers in the neighboring financial district and quite a few of those theater, concert, and sporting event attendees who used to head home on Interstate 195 as soon as they exited from the Providence Civic Center are now sticking around.

But while food and drink and shopping seem to be the Arcade's primary reasons for being, there are those who feel that any excuse for a party is a good one. From Saint Patrick's Day to Bastille Day to Halloween to Christmas, and all those other holidays in between, the Arcade is sure to have some sort of special events planned. During one recent Easter celebration, big hand-painted Easter eggs of every color in the rainbow were strung front to back from the ceiling; if you were lucky, the Arcade Easter bunny would honor you with free jelly beans or other candies. During the Christmas season, local choral groups serenade shoppers with carols while garlands of holly and Christmas lights drape the interior. And then there's a holiday celebrated only at the Arcade. It's Anniversary Day, held in October, and marking the day the Arcade reopened. It is the biggest pretext of all for a bash, usually including either a parade or a street fest.

The special events aren't the only times you'll see street entertainment, though. Throughout the summer months, chances are that whenever you come there will be some type of distraction to your buying and banqueting. Mimes, jugglers, and those adept with instruments like dulcimers and guitars are some of the appealing diversions, most often performing on the center stage downstairs or on the steps outside.

The revamping, reorganizing, and reopening of the Arcade was no doubt influenced somewhat by the tremendously successful Faneuil Hall Marketplace in Boston, but the Arcade is much smaller; with the possible exception of a long dinner, you will not be spending nearly as much time here as you would rambling in and out of the emporiums at Faneuil Hall Marketplace. So, to supplement your daytrip to downtown Providence, you may want to continue your shopping experiences by strolling along the close-at-hand **Westminster Mall.**

The stores lining the sides of this eight-block-long pedestrian mall complement the specialization of the Arcade's outlets. You won't find any surfeit of specialty or craft shops at this specimen of a reborn downtown. Instead, you'll be able to browse and buy in businesses dealing in general items not found in many stores designed for the single-minded. Many of these outlets have been around for decades — among them shoe, drug, clothes, and jewelry shops, and a department store.

The mall, formerly just another downtown thoroughfare, recently underwent its second rebirth. It was in 1965 that Westminster Street, a one-way side road, was cut off from traffic and made into a pedestrian walkway. During the ten prior years, downtowns in general had been suffering as more and more commerce headed toward the suburbs; the

It's a masterpiece, and has been described by New York City's Metropolitan Museum of Art as one of the country's three best examples of nineteenth-century commercial architecture.

LAURA J. REPOSA

Stores lining the eight-block-long Westminster Mall complement the specialization of the Arcade's shops.

prohibition of cars on this store-lined street was meant to make downtown Providence more attractive for shoppers. However, most of the available funding went for practicality, not cosmetics. The pedestrian passageway was made mainly of asphalt, and while there were some preform planters set about here and there, the mall was not known for its looks.

A little plastic surgery was planned in the late seventies, when the mall and some of the surrounding streets were slated for redesign. Of the entire area affected, which has been labeled Westminster Center, Westminster Mall is the nucleus. The fact that it continues to be closed to automobile traffic — and is therefore free from noise and exhaust fumes — makes it probably the most pleasant place in the area to take a morning or afternoon constitutional.

Pushcarts dot the pathway, along with hawkers of hot dogs, fruit salad, and chocolate chip cookies.

The asphalt, as you might guess, is no longer there, having been replaced by brick as well as by some cobblestone and granite paving. However, the intent here is not to simulate the old; modern but eye-pleasing lighting fixtures and pushcarts dot the pathway, along with hawkers offering edibles like hot dogs, fruit salad, and chocolate chip cookies. Street theater on the mall is also common. A public stage attached to a mall police booth and another in the front of Grace Church, at the corner of the mall and Mathewson Street, are settings for comedy, drama, mime, juggling, and other forms of downtown entertainment. Street furniture, which like the lighting is charming but not oldstyle, has been placed under and around shade trees; it's welcome when you want to do no more than rest your legs and people-watch.

Despite the extracurricular entertainment and the esthetic features of both reborn downtown attractions, they couldn't be more full of contrasts. One has many specialty shops; the other is made up of mostly traditional enterprises. One is inside an historic old building; the other sits in the open. One stresses old style, the other, more modern. And both are worth your looks, as evidence that downtown Providence is no longer a place to shun.

ACCESS

THE ARCADE AND WESTMINSTER MALL. Directions: From Interstate 95 in Providence, take Interstate 195 east. Take the first exit (Downtown) from Interstate 195, then the first left, onto Dyer Street, and the first right, onto Peck Street. **Season:** All year. **Days:** The Arcade: Daily. Westminster Mall: Most stores are open Monday through Saturday. **Allow** a total of 1 to 4 hours for both. **Note:** There is limited metered parking on the streets, and parking garages abound in the area. **Telephones:** The Arcade: (401) 456-5403. Greater Providence Chamber of Commerce: (401) 521-5000. For detailed information from the latter, ask to speak to an in-town representative.

MICHAEL QUAN

Don't believe your eyes. You can't enter this apothecary any more than you can cure a cold in one day. This storefront is part of a facade painted onto a building fronting Tommy's Park in Portland's Old Port Exchange.

The Old Port Exchange

Portland is Maine's equivalent of the Big Apple. Or, more appropriately, it's the Big Lobster. With a population of only sixty-five thousand, it's smaller than many suburban communities elsewhere. Yet its substantial downtown belies Portland's relatively minuscule population and there's never a lack of diversions for southwestern-Maine residents: a fine symphony, a brand-new library, a superb children's museum, and a modern civic center. And nearby, there's the Old Port Exchange, with an abundance of shops and restaurants and appealing jewels of architecture.

But it wasn't always that way. Although a vivid city, however small, Portland not too long ago also had its dying districts, the most notable being the waterfront, or port, area. In the late 1960s, it was filled with old, vacant buildings that could have been bought for almost obscenely low prices. Two local businessmen gifted with twenty-twenty foresight — Frank Akers, president of a company manufacturing brass items, and Henry Willette, whose background was in urban planning — joined forces with a few other area business operators to start the Old Port Exchange Association. After a few years, they had purchased over a dozen buildings that were soon occupied by young entrepreneurs, many of whom were selling their own handmade items. Within a decade, property values climbed higher than the space shuttle; Akers left his brass business behind and started a real-estate firm, and the Old Port Exchange, in an area once the pariah of Portland neighborhoods, became a fashionable place to shop and dine.

It's interesting to note that this was not the port district's first renaissance. On the contrary, this area is like the veteran elevator operator; to paraphrase the old joke, its life has been filled with ups and downs. Initially established as a port in 1632, it was destroyed

Stores rented space on the first floor to support the doings of the church, which was housed on the third floor.

MICHAEL QUAN

You won't go hungry while walking around the Old Port Exchange. Frozen yogurt is just one of many foods available for sampling here.

on two separate occasions by the Indians later that century and almost totally obliterated by the British during the early months of the American Revolution. Rebuilt following the war, the harbor bustled for a number of years as a base for the lumber-exporting business, only to be closed as a result of the Embargo Act of 1807.

More peaks and valleys followed. The area recovered from the depressed economy that resulted from the Embargo Act and the ensuing War of 1812. Mercantile and shipping companies based themselves in this district, and warehouses and other buildings soon took up locations on newly formed Commercial Street. And then the harbor-area balloon was burst again: a devastating fire blazed through much of the territory on Independence Day, 1866.

Rebuilding again was the rule, but because of the previous fires, it was decided to expand Portland's growth into another area, spreading out the proximity of important structures. Main and Congress streets, inland from the port area, were highly developed and today form the heartbeat of Portland's downtown.

By the 1920s, when the first skyscraper in Maine was erected in this inland area, neither the people of Portland nor their businesses had much reason to wander down to the waterfront. By the sixties and early seventies the port-area buildings had become homes for warehouses and light industry, and those who worked there recall frequent encounters with vagrants and derelicts who lived in this mini skid row.

It wasn't magic, but the transformation of this area into a fashionable and delightful district in a measly ten years may seem like it. Stories of buildings that sold for under one thousand dollars in the late sixties and now are worth one hundred thousand dollars are common. Though there's plenty for a visitor to see and do, lawyers' offices (the court is nearby) and other services in the same vicinity identify the Old Port Exchange as more than a dressed-up area for tourists. And while you browse in and out of the stores or grab a quick bite or a leisurely lunch, be sure to stop for a good look at the exteriors of some of the buildings, of which many are absolute beauties.

One of the most impressive is the **Mariner's Church,** at 366-376 Fore Street. It's a grayish Federal and Greek Revival structure from 1828 that was originally home for a group of shops and businesses. Back in the days when Portland served as the temporary residence of so many who lived by the catch of the sea, the church was as active as the shipping business; stores rented space on the first floor to support the doings of the church, which was housed on the third floor. Though there is no longer a church in the building, or even a warehouse, its unholy raison d'être for so many years, there are again retail outlets for your browsing or buying activity, many of which are marked by signs hanging from the windows.

The Mariner's Church was lucky to be located at an end of the port area that was unscathed by the fire of 1866. More common styles here, however, are Italianate and Mansard, both outgrowths of the mid-nineteenth-century Victorian period and representative of replacements for structures destroyed during the blaze. The pink and off-white Italianate **Merchants Bank Block** at 34 Exchange Street, built in 1866 and 1867, features arched recessed entrances that make it an attractive specimen of the era. Although the **Elias Thomas Block** at 102-132 Commercial Street was built six years before the fire, this low, long complex with brick facade and granite windowsills and lintels is another fine example of this same Italianate style. The **United States Customs House** at 312 Fore Street, however, looking a little more like the grand Victorian-period architecture you may be accustomed to, is representative of the Mansard style and was built in 1868-1871.

You'll probably find yourself doing a classic double take reminiscent of the best of comedy movie actors when you look at the **Trompe l'Oeil,** that faces the corner of Exchange and Middle streets and fronts a patch of greenery known as Tommy's Park. Though it looks as if it fits right in with the post-fire style, a closer gaze will indicate that its year of creation is later — 1976, to be exact. It's just a facade, with its doors, storefronts, and windows, as well as brick construction material, painted on an old building by a local artisan named Chris Denison along with a few assistants. It took twenty-five gallons of paint to arrive at the finished form of this eye teaser. The grass at **Tommy's Park,** or any of the picnic tables here, by the way, are among the best places to sit and enjoy a relaxing lunch if you don't dine in one of the Old Port restaurants.

MICHAEL QUAN

The Old Port Exchange has come a long way from the days when it was little more than a mini skid row.

Along with Down East seafood, other samples include French pastries, Irish coffee, Near Eastern baklava, and Italian pasta of all kinds.

And, ah yes, glorious **food.** You can expect to find about a dozen and a half eateries in the Exchange, and the cuisines go far beyond the borders of the state of Maine. Along with Down East seafood, other samples include French pastries, Irish coffee, Near Eastern baklava, and Italian pasta of all kinds. And you can savor a meal in whatever type of atmosphere strikes your mood, from formal to eat-and-run.

Those who often dine here are lured to this area by the many specialty **shops** that abound; you could easily spend a half day walking in and out of the doors of the myriad stores offering rattan chairs, imported cheeses, silk kimonos, hand-crafted silver jewelry, canoes and backpacks, gourmet kitchenware, and innumerable other esthetic, practical, and edible items for gifts or for your own cupboard, end table, or closet. Expect to find a good fifty or so such stores along the streets of this area.

You can plan on finding wall-to-wall entertainment during late June, when the Old Port Exchange annually celebrates itself with a festival. Basically described as a community cultural event, this includes an abundance of music and art for the listening, observing, or partaking; a special effort is made to include workshops or entertainment for children. An athletic event, usually a bicycle or foot race, often opens the festivities. If your schedule doesn't permit you to attend the big June bash, you might enjoy one of the live musical performances often scheduled during lunch time on summer weekdays. Jazz, Dixieland, and folk music are often heard emanating from Tommy's Park or Wharf Street. And often, spontaneous entertainment on street corners features musicians, jugglers, or any other performers that can please a sidewalk audience.

Myriad stores offer rattan chairs, imported cheeses, silk kimonos, hand-crafted silver jewelry, canoes and backpacks, and innumerable other items.

Of course, if you're not fortunate enough to catch some music in the open air, you can still revel in the atmosphere here. And even if you don't have a chance to tempt the taste buds in some of the quality restaurants, you can still look inside storefront windows, not neglecting to admire the entire buildings themselves. If you want to partake in urban amusements in the state of Maine, you're best off taking a crack at the Big Lobster.

ACCESS

THE OLD PORT EXCHANGE. Directions: From Interstate 95 exit 7, go south on the Franklin Street Arterial to the Old Port Exchange. **Season:** All year. **Days:** Stores are open Monday through Saturday; restaurants are open daily. **Allow** 1 to 4 hours. **Note:** There are parking lots throughout the district; coming from the Franklin Street Arterial, take a right onto either Middle or Fore Street for one of the handier ones. **Telephone:** (207) 772-6828 (Intown Portland Exchange).

Brattleboro

You may remember hearing The Temptations singing in the late 1960s about "the hippies moving to the hills." To many from Massachusetts, New York, and other populous states, that meant the hills of Vermont. And for those who went to Vermont, the closest sizable community was Brattleboro. Located in the southeast corner of the state on the Connecticut River, the town and surrounding area were big enough to provide basic services without having given way to the theories of unlimited growth and suburban sprawl that had been so prevalent in the fifties. And it was that countercultural influx, some feel, that was the seed of Brattleboro's downtown face-lift.

Back in the late sixties, there were many empty storefronts along Main Street. Elliot Street, a chief side street, was a run-down road on which were located a couple of bars that, it has been implied, even Clint Eastwood might have been hesitant to enter. At the base of Main Street, the Brattleboro Union Railroad Station was vacant and in a state of awful disrepair — destined, it seemed, to be a parking lot. Though just a town of twelve thousand in a pastoral state, downtown Brattleboro was in as much a condition of decay as central areas in much larger American cities.

Enter the "counterculture." Artists and craftspeople began to sell their goods in the formerly vacant shops on Main Street. Others opened health-food stores or emporiums featuring rare and exotic imports. Many of the novice entrepreneurs, unfamiliar with the operations of business management, didn't make it. But some did. And when the unsuccessful merchants departed, others were always there to take their places. Before too long, these recent immigrants to Vermont had filled in all the empty retail spaces on Main Street. And it was this success that spurred more interest in revitalizing downtown Brattleboro.

With the enthusiasm that grew in the next few years came some grants from the Office of Housing and Urban Development. And in the early and mid 1970s, that capital was put to use. Decrepit Elliot Street, a mixture of retail and low-income residential buildings in addition to the two tough taverns, was the prime challenge to the office of community development. Spit and grit were applied to the fullest, the HUD funds welcome. And once private industry saw that people really were serious about bringing Brattleboro back to life, they weren't hesitant about making donations here and there to do their fair share.

Meanwhile, a couple of civic-minded groups were bandying about the idea of permanent collections for displays concerning the area's cultural and historical contributions. They eyed the unused railroad station, which in the early 1970s had been purchased by the town and slated for demolition. The building, raised in

Imposing Wantastiquet Mountain forms a pleasant backdrop to the newly polished Elliot Street in Brattleboro.

It was the counter-cultural influx, some feel, that was the seed of Brattleboro's downtown face-lift.

The Main Street Gallery, formerly Grant's Department Store, and a prime example of Victorian architecture sit across from each other on Main Street — a grand showpiece for the fruits of adaptive reuse of America's downtowns.

Artists and craftspeople began to sell their goods in the formerly vacant shops on Main Street. Others opened health-food stores or emporiums featuring rare and exotic imports.

1916 (although it is not known why the year 1915 is engraved above the doorway) was a beautiful old structure with an exterior of native stone and an interior including dark mission-oak woodwork, red quarry-tile floors, and white marble stairs leading to the ticket windows. It seemed a shame to leave it to the fate of the merciless wrecking ball. And so the town, showing it had a heart, leased it to the concerned groups for a nominal fee.

Today, Main, Elliot, and High streets (the last is a side street parallel to Elliot) are attractive thoroughfares where one can easily spend a morning or afternoon browsing through specialty and other shops and, when it's time to satisfy the stomach, find a myriad of places to enjoy a good meal. Within the center of the downtown area, there are three indoor minimalls that have been carved out of old buildings whose original tenants are long gone; for such a small community, this is astounding.

One mall, the **Main Street Gallery** (located, appropriately enough, on Main Street), is in the former home of Grant's Department Store, which closed its doors when the corporation folded. Another, the **Midtown Mall,** which connects High Street with the Harmony Parking Lot, had been the Montgomery-Ward warehouse for a good number of years. The third example of center-of-town reincarnation is the **Brooks House Mall,** which in its former life had been a portion of the Brooks House Hotel. In all three of these small enclosed complexes (each harboring four to six establishments), you will find places to look for items as mundane as a new blouse or stereo equipment, or as exotic as a Peruvian rug, a Mexican tile, or an antique glass jar. The hungry will be able to ease growling stomachs with choices ranging from crêpes and quiches to freshly baked pastries. In one mall, a number of stores that once rented inside became so successful that the limited mall space just wasn't extensive enough, and they've moved on to bigger locations on Main Street; yet there has been no trouble filling vacated space in the mall itself.

That's not to imply that there is nothing else to this Green Mountain community but minimalls. Both Elliot and Main Streets, for instance, have **other stores** dealing in crafts, furniture, and imports, as well as a substantial number of cafés and restaurants; menu variety here includes Italian, Chinese, health foods, and sandwiches. And as with any good downtown, there is your basic hardware store, department store, and real-estate agent, proving that there is substance to go along with the frills.

After filling the vacuous retail spaces and ridding Elliot Street of the less desirable establishments, the office of community development decided it was time for the area to clean up its act. The store fronts on Elliot Street were given a thorough scrubbing; brick exteriors were sandblasted, and other facades were cleaned. Iron posts holding up buildings were also washed. What was once a seedy dark alley where you wouldn't want to meet the town bully was filled in with an attractive white frame structure that now houses a women's clothes shop. To spruce up the front of the shop, a small garden was planted. And all along the street, drab modern street lights were replaced by electrified reproductions of Victorian-era gaslights while, in some spots, concrete footpaths were replaced by brick.

The train station was a beautiful old structure with an exterior of native stone and an interior including dark mission-oak woodwork, red quarry-tile floors, and white marble stairs.

Today, if you'd like a more thorough look at an earlier Brattleboro, take a walk to the lower end of Main Street and the former railroad station, now **The Brattleboro Museum & Art Center.** It's most appropriate that this prime example of adaptive re-use lies at the base of this downtown, where that technique has been the keystone to successful urban renewal. Doors labeled "women's waiting room" and "men's waiting room," and the former ticket windows, also properly labeled, are still in place. A small collection of antique Estey organs, manufactured in Brattleboro for over a hundred years until the company went out of business a few decades back, is permanently displayed.

But it's the temporary exhibits addressing the historical side of the dual-purpose museum that serve to bring out the nostalgia in all of us. Since the

Once seemingly destined to be a parking lot, this early twentieth-century train station is now the Brattleboro Museum & Art Center.

MELINDA MACAULEY

museum reopened those heavy front doors in September, 1972, displays have included the following: "The Way It Was," featuring antiquated everyday equipment and papier mâché models that portrayed life in the last century; "They Left Their Mark," devoted to Brattleboro natives who went on to become prominent in the arts and sciences; and "Rudyard Kipling's Brattleboro," focusing upon the author's four years living just outside the town in the 1890s and including original editions and illustrations of some of the books he wrote during that time (like *Captains Courageous* and *The Jungle Book*).

The former baggage room, thanks to gritty and tedious work, was turned into a second gallery; because of its recently installed fine lighting, this will most likely be the home for the museum's changing art exhibits. And with many talented artisans living in the area, fine locally produced art is often represented.

A fourth room is named for Mary Sommer, who was an enthusiastic worker during the formative days of the museum and who died prematurely of cancer. This is the focal point for small and frequently changing exhibits running the gamut in subject from the works of a local photographer to a collection of antique toys during the early Christmas season.

This beauty of a building is a testament to the energetic spirit and intensive travail that have renewed the town; in a true example of justice, the former train station was, in 1973, declared Brattleboro's first National Historic Site.

Other parts of town on the fringes of the downtown area are scheduled to be cleansed and redone also. Brattleboro's night life, which has included two theatrical groups and a club featuring name pop and jazz performers, can only benefit from the continuing invigorating revival. The feeling in this town is strong.

To ease growling stomachs, choices range from crêpes and quiches to freshly baked pastries.

ACCESS

DOWNTOWN BRATTLEBORO. Directions: From Interstate 91 exit 2, head east on Western Avenue (Route 9) and continue going straight as it becomes High Street. Follow High Street to Main Street. Museum **season:** Mid-spring through early winter. Museum **days:** Tuesday through Sunday, afternoons. Most downtown stores are closed Sunday. **Donation** requested at museum. **Allow** 1 to 3 hours in town. **Notes:** Short-term parking is available on the streets and in the Harmony Parking Lot, between Elliot and High streets; long-term parking is available in the Hi-Grove Parking Lot, between High and Grove streets, and on Harris Place, just off Main Street at the northern end of downtown. Almost all parking is metered. Free parking for the museum is available at the museum parking lot. **Telephone** for the museum: (802) 257-0124.

CHAPTER V

New England the Beautiful

T ree-laden mountains that dominate every view from narrow country lanes, cliff-side ocean vistas that present crashing waves and rocky shorelines, and sand-lapping waters that gently brush low-lying beaches and marshlands. These are the kinds of eye-pleasing attractions that have made day-long drives and hiking or bicycling excursions in the hills or on the coastline favorite pastimes among New England scenery lovers. There's a lot to see in this relatively small six-state region, and New Englanders are not the type to sit back and let others do the exploring.

With the help of the federal government, two specimens of Atlantic Ocean coastline are now a national park and a national seashore, respectively, and are destined to be spared from the developers' bulldozers. A great portion of the White Mountains in New Hampshire is classified as a national forest, and throughout the region, other places of natural beauty are protected by state and local authorities. All of which makes it certain that you'll be able to benefit from some special sights that are as untouched by man as possible.

Please note that the time allotments mentioned for hikes and walks are the actual times it took us; you may finish them more quickly or more slowly, depending on your conditioning and your stops along the way. Also, please realize that while some of the locations discussed can be fully explored in a day or half day, others could take a week to be totally experienced. But we encourage you to go and get a taste of nature's glories even if you have only a day in these beautiful lands. With the many opportunities offered — scenic drives, nature walks, bike paths, hiking trails, and ranger talks — the only hard part about having fun in New England's scenic wonderlands is deciding what to do first.

Acadia National Park

If you traveled the entire fifteen hundred miles along the eastern seaboard, you'd be hard pressed to find any aquatic scenery that could compare in beauty with Maine's Acadia National Park. Verdant pines framing placid blue ocean waters make for such frequent picturesque views that the spectacular starts to seem commonplace. There's a combination of mountains and coastline here that's virtually nonexistent anywhere east of the Pacific Coast. Even the villages on the fringes of certain park points — Seal Harbor, Northeast Harbor, and Southwest Harbor — are appealing and unspoiled. And for those who'd like to park their motor vehicles and resort to foot or pedal power, the park is a treasury of footpaths and bicycle trails. Even in Maine, a state that boasts three thousand miles of coastline including many inlets and islands, Acadia National Park is perhaps the acme of oceanside esthetics.

Today, little of New England's shoreline is still wild; most has been settled and built up for years. Acadia, 215 miles north along the Maine coast from the New Hampshire border and located mostly on Mount Desert Island, was set aside by the federal government with intentions of preserving at least a remnant of the New England shoreline's natural beauty. It's interesting that, unlike many western national parks, Acadia was established primarily on land that was once privately owned and then sold or donated to the government; eleven thousand acres, for example, came from John D. Rockefeller, Jr., who also built many miles of carriage paths now used by pedestrians here. Because this land is now protected, you'll get to take drives by the ocean and alongside hills without the distraction of manmade commercial establishments or their advertising. In coastal New England, that is something to be savored.

As with most national parks, the best place to start is the **visitors' center,** located off Route 3 at Acadia's northern entrance, just a few miles north of Bar Harbor (the most settled and commercial town by Acadia, containing most of the restaurants and lodging in the immediate area). This is the place to pick up the standard free guide and map (a must), listen to information from an on-duty ranger, or buy more detailed books or pamphlets.

While the main objective of a daytrip at Acadia would seemingly be to thoroughly hit Park Loop Road first and then branch out and see any of the small fishing towns or less developed parts of the park with your remaining time, your mind may be made up for you by the weather. Each season here offers a special side of Acadia, so regardless of when you get a chance to motor between its boundaries, you will be able to see the park as it plays to nature's ways and colors.

The rocky coastline of Acadia National Park, probably the most beautiful scenery to be found along the Atlantic coastline of North America.

Sunny, clear, and warm: that forecast signals vacation weather anywhere. At Acadia, it means you should motor up to **Cadillac Summit;** at 1,530 feet above sea level, it's the highest point of land along the Atlantic Coast. The view is exquisite. There's a foot trail at the summit, a little under a mile long, that leads you to lookout points highlighting the forests, bays, and roads on Mount Desert Island. The town of Bar Harbor in the distance appears small enough to be stepped on and crushed by a careless hiker. It's up here, as you walk amid the rocks and brush, that you see a series of markers bearing information about the park. One of these explains the derivation of the name Mount Desert Island; it was originally tabbed "Isle des Monts Déserts," meaning "island of wilderness mountains," by explorer Samuel de Champlain. (You probably won't see any markers, or anything else, if the skies aren't at their sharpest. One time when we tried driving up Summit Road during a clearing period following a day of rain, we weren't more than half way up before the visibility became nil.)

The fury of the ocean, on the other hand, is at its raging best following a period of inclement weather. And this is the best time to stop off at **Thunder Hole,** just off Park Loop Road. (Don't miss this spot after a calm day either, but it's *not* the place to be at the height of a storm.) The name of this hollow in the ocean-facing rocks is most appropriate: when crushing waves move with full force into the hollow, the air at the rear is compressed and emits a sound resembling blaring thunder. You are encouraged to walk down rail-guarded steps to the adjacent rocks, where you can see the waves foam and hear the deafening pseudothunder up close. Be prepared to feel some of the spray, although chances are quite slim that you'll get soaked.

During any climatic conditions in any season, you'll want to halt at some of the numerous turnouts along **Ocean Drive,** the segment of Loop Road that hugs the rocky shoreline and that is open all year. Whether you see fog hovering over the islands of Frenchman Bay, sparkling sunlit waters on a pristine morning, or snow covering the ground on some of the closer islands, you'll be in for some wonderful scenery watching. A good overview of Frenchman Bay, with its inlets and islands (one of them, Bar Island, is an island only at high tide since a natural gravel bar connects it to Mount Desert Island during low tide), is the focus of your view from the first turnout past the visitors' center. This bay has been regarded by many as containing the most wild beauty of any in the state.

There are more turnouts along Ocean Drive that afford grand ocean views, one of the most lovely being Champlain Mountain Overlook, about seven miles farther from Frenchman Bay Overlook. This is a stop that should not be missed. Facing north, you'll see distant Gouldsboro Bay on the horizon, with the waters of

Sand Beach was created by the constant action of the ocean, and actually consists of tiny particles of sea shells.

CAROLYN J. CASEY

If you hear "thunder" on a clear, sunny day, you'll probably be near the crashing waves at Thunder Hole.

Blue, placid Eagle Lake was formed over a million years ago by an ice sheet. But to many boaters today, it's known as the source of smooth sailing.

Frenchman Bay close up. Egg Rock Light Station stands as sentinel by the doorway to Frenchman Bay, and to your right a mansion is a remnant of the time when Bar Harbor was a playground for the wealthy from New York and Philadelphia. There's a path at Scenic Overlook nearby that is definitely worth strolling upon. It will take you only about three minutes to reach its end and you'll be quite a bit closer to the sounds and smells of the ocean.

The highest headlands along the Atlantic Coast north of Brazil are a few more miles up from Champlain Mountain Overlook. Otter Cliffs, 140 feet high, are of a pinkish granite and certainly exemplify Acadia's catch phrase, "where the mountains meet the sea." If you're energetic, you can walk to the roadside vantage point from Sand Beach, a beautiful broad beach off another turnout. It was created by the constant action of the ocean, and actually consists of tiny particles of sea shells. Human polar bears may want to change in the lockers and brave the waters at this, the only saltwater beach in the park; summertime water temperature fluctuates between fifty and sixty degrees.

But Ocean Drive and Cadillac Mountain, while the sources of the most memorable and noteworthy scenery here, do not hold a monopoly on the park's attractions. Some of the bluest inland lakes you'll ever see are within eye range of Park Loop Road on its inland swing. **Eagle Lake,** the biggest freshwater body in the park, is typical of the lakes that were formed by ice sheets that moved through this region over a million years ago.

Human polar bears may want to brave the waters here; summertime water temperature fluctuates between fifty and sixty degrees.

You should also notice, as you motor your way through, the levels of floral growth at different areas in the park. A devastating fire in 1947, which lasted twenty-six days before finally being declared out, burned over seventeen thousand acres, about one third of the forest area in the park. As you drive along, a second-growth forest that includes small pines, birches, and aspens suddenly becomes larger and darker, with spruce, pine, birch, maple, and beech trees prevailing. If you maintain a keen interest in native plants, shrubs, and flowers, you'll want to stop by the nature center and garden at **Sieur de Monts Spring,** located on the Loop Road just prior to its ocean-side swing. The garden features labeled wildflowers that are native to the park, and makes for a pleasant walk, while the nature center exhibits mounted animals and birds that are native to this area. Also located here is the Abbe Museum of Stone Age Antiquities, a sort of small natural-history museum that displays artifacts associated with pre-Columbian Indians. The museums are open in late spring and summer.

Most people who only have a day to spend here stick to Park Loop Road. That doesn't mean there aren't alternatives, however. **Hiking trails** zigzag their way across the park. Around Eagle Lake and Jordan Pond (to the south of Eagle Lake), and around some of the park's mountains, there are fifty miles of graveled carriage paths perfect for bikers, joggers, and hikers; and in the winter, both the carriage paths and snow-covered paved roads turn into **snowmobile and cross-country ski trails.** Maps detailing all these routes are available at the visitors' center.

If you'd like to gain some deeper understanding as to what Acadia's all about, you can rent a cassette tape and player at the visitors' center. You are permitted to keep them for a twenty-four-hour period (deposit required), during which you can let the tape be your guide; in addition to being told where to stop and what to look for on the fifty-six-mile stretch through the park and bordering towns covered, you can pick up some answers to questions you have always wondered about. For example, the ice sheet that created the inland lakes on Mount Desert Island may have been as much as five thousand feet thick.

There are other parts of Acadia not as easily accessible as Park Loop Road. Off the beaten track is the western portion of Mount Desert Island, which incorporates some of the less developed parts of the park; Isle au Haut (known for its low mountains and isolation) and the Islesford Historical Museum on Little Cranberry Island, both under the jurisdiction of Acadia, are accessible only by ferry. Schoodic Peninsula, east of Mount Desert Island and the only part of the park on the mainland, features a rocky prominence over 400 feet high that is said to offer a wonderful view. However, your first daytrip won't allow time to see many of these other parts of the park. In a place of such widely varied scenic wonders as Acadia National Park, it's obvious that a few more daytrips are in order for those who want to see it all.

ACCESS

ACADIA NATIONAL PARK. Directions: From Route 1 in Ellsworth, follow Route 3 south to the park. **Season:** All year. The visitors' center is open May through October. **Days: Daily. Admission** free. **Allow** at least six hours. **Note:** Due to snow, much of the interior of the park is inaccessible in winter. **Telephone:** (207) 288-3338; (207) 288-4932.

Acadia is one Maine attraction that's not for summertime visitors only.

The ice sheet that created the inland lakes on Mount Desert Island may have been as much as five thousand feet thick.

Cape Cod National Seashore

To many who know Cape Cod, or who think they know it, a daytrip to this narrow, arm-shaped land mass of Massachusetts usually means an outing at the beach with a stop for a fast clam-roll dinner prior to heading home before bedtime. To all those who say there's no life off Route 6 — surprise! Hiking trails, bike paths, attractive modern museums, marshes, sand dunes, manmade monuments and, yes, beaches, are all to be found within minutes — literally — of Route 6. All are part of Cape Cod National Seashore.

Extending from the Cape's forearm to its fist, the national seashore land intertwines with pockets of land still privately owned. The Cape had been settled hundreds of years before the Department of the Interior established the national seashore from donated and purchased land in 1961. So unlike other preserved scenic areas that are part of the National Park Service, here there are stretches of motels, restaurants, cottages, and shops intermixed with undeveloped land from Nauset Marsh to the Highland Lighthouse. The key here is that you leave the commercial Cape behind as you take left or right turns off Route 6 into the protected wilderness of the national seashore. Those who have always just cruised down Route 6 all the way to Provincetown may be pleasantly astonished to discover the older, original, and most beautifully natural side of Cape Cod.

At the four major areas included in Cape Cod National Seashore — Nauset Area near Eastham, Marconi Station Area near South Wellfleet, Pilgrim Heights Area near North Truro, and Province Lands Area near Provincetown, in addition to patches of land located in between, you'll find much. Miles of footpaths snake their way around beaches and forests, perfect biking routes wind among the trees and the marshland, tables just beg for red-checkered tablecloths and picnic baskets, interpretive displays tell you what the Cape was about before the settlers, and some

Children caress the fanlike pinkish sea-scallop shell and gingerly brave the pointed horseshoe crab.

At the Cape Cod National Seashore Visitor Center at Salt Pond, you can see what a razor clam looks like or find out just who discovered Cape Cod.

RUSS KENDALL

fine stretches of sand and sun and ocean await, where you need do nothing more strenuous than turn over to avoid sunburn. Other more singular attractions: a couple of lighthouses still in use, the site of Marconi's first wireless transatlantic message, the exterior of a whaling captain's grand Victorian house, naturally formed sand dunes, and a partially cultivated cranberry bog.

How you spend your day in this park (while labeled a national seashore, it is for all practical purposes a national park) depends largely, of course, on your own personal tastes. However, there are some attractions that, like ice-cream cones on hot days, are loved by just about everybody. The dunes by Province Lands Area are one, as is the Highland Light (what's more "Cape Cod" than a lighthouse?); the modern audio-visual and charmingly touchable displays at the two visitors' centers are also admired by most, especially by those who don't even like museums. Here you won't be bored by facts and figures presented in pedantic displays, and you *will* gain a better understanding of what you are about to explore.

While the children at the **Salt Pond Visitor Center** are caressing the fan-like pinkish sea-scallop shell and gingerly braving the pointed horseshoe crab, you could be discovering little known Cape trivia like the fact that the Pilgrims anchored off the Cape for thirty days before sailing on to Plymouth and that whaling took place off the Cape in the sixteenth century, long before it became the pulse of New Bedford and Nantucket. Here's a brain teaser to stun your knowledgeable acquaintances with when you get back home: Who originally named this piece of land "Cape Cod"? The answer is the incomparable Bartholomew Gosnold, who is hardly a household name today, but who sailed by in 1602. Gabriel Archer, one of Gosnold's crewmen, wrote, ". . . we called it Shole-Hope. Neere this Cape, we came to anchor in fifteen fadome, where wee tooke great store of codfish for which we altered the name and called it Cape Cod."

The **Province Lands Visitor Center,** which you may want to visit after inspecting some of the Cape itself, allows you to sit and let an expert explain Cape history and geology to you. A well-made film features some of the most romantic photography this side of "The Love Boat": a lone lighthouse standing sentinel to the shore, the ocean enveloped by nightfall, a fishing trawler docked at the water's edge. Some tall trees are gone, it's stated as the film focuses on changes made by man, and there is now sand where grass once grew, but the ocean is still here. People, it continues, come today to sun and swim; they plunk themselves down and wonder where history is, and forget that they are themselves part of it.

If the twenty-minute film is not showing when you arrive, ask a ranger about it. While you're waiting, the youngsters can place their mitts on more shells at

The landscape is almost desert-like, and you'll probably see children mockingly trudging up the slopes begging for water.

another do-touch display. There's also a collection of fishing implements like a tub-trawl anchor, used for securing a backline and buoy, and a stick'n tom, which held candles while fishermen baited their hooks in the darkness. And don't leave without grabbing a peek at the almost beige vertebra of the right whale, which got its name because it was once thought that, because it floated, it was the right whale to hunt.

It's been estimated that before early Cape Codders hunted whales, and before Europeans even settled here, the land was 97 per cent forested, despite the fact that Wampanoag Indians had been living on the same land for centuries. When the settlers came, they quickly cut down trees to build homes, furniture, tools, and ships. And after homes were built, they had to be heated, which meant the chopping of more trees. By the late seventeenth century, most of the forests and the shallow soil covering over the land were gone; winds combining with the sand created dunes over the course of many years.

Though much dune reclamation has been achieved this century, the hills of wind-blown sand around Truro are as active as ever, steadily being shifted to the southeast. Work is currently being done to halt this mass migration of the dunes; in the meantime, you are permitted to park your car in a designated lot off Route 6, and to climb the **dunes** until sand pours out of the tops of your shoes. The landscape, especially from the parking-lot view, is almost desertlike, and you'll probably see children mockingly trudging up the slopes begging for water. Walking to the dune summit may be a little tougher than you think, sort of like making your way along an uphill beach. It's an eerie landscape for a while as you climb and see nothing but sand and sky. But don't expect the ocean to be lapping below your feet when you hit the top. After reaching the summit, people for some reason always seem to expect the ocean to be directly below them, and are disappointed to discover that it's about two miles away.

There's less toil involved in looking at the **Highland lighthouse,** the only one along the national seashore that you can really see close up. To see the interior, though, you need to make an appointment by calling the Province Lands Visitor Center at (617) 487-1256. This is the most popular tour offered, so to be assured of a spot, call at 9 AM the day you plan to take the tour. The third lighthouse on this location, it was built in 1857 and is still operating today; in fact, with more than six hundred thousand candlepower, its glow can be seen for more than thirty-two miles in clear weather, making it one of the most powerful on the Atlantic coast. For obvious reasons, this is a favorite photo stop.

Unless you're deeply interested in the history of radio or Guglielmo Marconi, inventor of the wireless

It's an eerie landscape for a while as you climb and see nothing but sand and sky.

transmitter, you may wish to bypass the **Marconi Site,** the spot where Marconi transmitted the first wireless transatlantic message. There is a scale model of the wireless station and some markers commemorating the event, but nothing remains of Marconi's actual station, save some insignificant ruins; the station was deemed obsolete following World War I, and was subsequently dismantled and abandoned.

You may, rather, depart on a short hike on a loop located near the site. The **Atlantic White Cedar Swamp Trail** is a mile and a fifth in length and we knocked it off in little over a half hour, walking briskly though stopping occasionally. Of the ten self-guiding trails, this one perhaps best illustrates both inland and swampside topography and vegetation. When you're tromping past the tall pines and young black and white oaks on the well-groomed path, it really may seem as if you're fifty miles in from the shore. And as the dirt-and-sand path becomes an elevated boardwalk, the Atlantic white cedar and mossy, stagnant water will signal that you're nearing the swamp, which is really a glacial depression that filled with fresh water about one thousand eight hundred years ago as the fresh-water table of land was lifted.

If you want to mix a manmade masterpiece with nature's noteworthy sights, try a walk along the mile-and-a-half-long **Fort Hill Trail.** It ultimately will take you up small grades to both Fort and Skiff hills, where you can overlook Nauset Marsh. At the beginning, though, is the isolated Edward Penniman House. In 1867, wealthy whaler Penniman built this Second

This is Cape Cod? Where are the beaches, the dunes, the lighthouses? There are all those, but much more as well — including lush forests just a short distance from the ocean's edge.

When you're tromping past the tall pines and young oaks on the well-groomed path, it may seem as if you're fifty miles in from the shore.

Buttonbush Trail includes markers with text in braille and urges patrons to "stop often to look, listen, smell, and feel."

You needn't be a hearty hiker to enjoy the walking trails at the national seashore. Most are short, level, and relatively easy.

French Empire style house, topped off with the typical Mansard roof. It was the most expensive house in the entire community at the time, and stands as a symbol of the long-lost grandeur of the age of whaling.

Other notable trails include: the mile-long Nauset Trail, which begins and ends at the Salt Pond Visitor Center and includes an impressive overlook of Nauset Marsh; the Buttonbush Trail, another .2-mile-long trail that starts at the Salt Pond Visitor Center but which also includes markers with text in braille and urges patrons to "stop often to look, listen, smell, and feel"; and the Beech Forest Trail, which starts at the Province Lands Visitor Center and brings you by a pond, a forest of beech trees, and a view of the sand dunes. Wise summertime hikers bring along insect repellent and sun-tan lotion. Also remember that poison ivy grows wild on the Cape in various locations; if you don't know what the plant looks like, play it safe by keeping to the center of the trail.

More ideas for daytrippers? A small cultivated cranberry bog in Truro (take Route 6 to North Pamet Road, park at the Environmental Education Center, and walk the half-mile trail) may be of interest to those who have always wondered what makes the tart red berry grow among all that swampy land. If you've brought your own bike you can resort to pedal power on either Nauset Trail in Eastham (1.6 miles of path); Head of the Meadow Trail, Truro (2 miles); or Province Lands Trail, Provincetown (7.5 miles). For those who have brought their own lunches as an alternative to hamburgers and shrimp plates, there are picnic areas in Eastham at Doane Rock Picnic Area, in Truro at Pilgrim Heights Area, and in Provincetown at Beech Forest. And for the individuals who would rather take a quick look at a visitors' center, walk a snappy beat down a short trail, and then catch some sun, there are the following beaches: Coast Guard Beach and Nauset Light Beach, Eastham; Marconi Beach, South Wellfleet; Head of the Meadow Beach, Truro; and Race Point Beach and Herring Cove Beach, both in Provincetown.

Quite a bit, as you can see, in this land not most often thought of as a nature and wilderness area.

ACCESS

CAPE COD NATIONAL SEASHORE. Directions: The Cape Cod National Seashore is located off Route 6 on the upper Cape; watch for signs indicating major national seashore areas. **Season:** All year, although midwinter hours vary greatly. **Days:** Daily. **Admission** free, except for charge for use of beaches from June through Labor Day. **Allow** at least 6 hours. **Note:** Pests, including deerflies in June, greenhead flies in July, and mosquitos, can be in profusion, especially around some of the swampier areas; bug repellent, therefore, is recommended. **Telephone:** (617) 255-3421.

The Ocean Drive
& The Cliff Walk

Imagine a stretch of pavement that you can walk for hours, where your view in one direction is of the crashing Atlantic Ocean and in the other direction is of the most sumptuously designed palaces of America's late Victorian-era commercial royalty. Then envision a ten-mile drive where motorists can enjoy looking at equally wonderful locales where concrete and brick meet coastline and brine. The two are the Cliff Walk and The Ocean Drive of Newport, at both of which manmade beauty competes with nature's best for the most admiring looks.

Though similar in nature, these two routes are different in scope. The Ocean Drive takes you past many more sights than the Cliff Walk; the Walk, on the other hand, brings you closer both to the ocean and to some mansions and their backyards than you could get driving. Cassette tape recordings, available as guides for each tour, tell you the inside stories and about the daily routines of some of the people who lived inside the mansions; you hear about everything from the elegant dinner once given for one hundred dogs to the ultimately proper manner in which members of high society called upon one another. Because of the many redundancies between the two tapes, you will probably be happy renting just one. We recommend the Ocean Drive cassette, both for the ease of not having to carry the tape player on the walk and for its value in preventing you from missing high points as you proceed at the more rapid pace of a car. And of course, if you explore **The Ocean Drive** with the tape first, you'll already be an expert when you take the Cliff Walk.

Tapes and players are rented at the Chamber of Commerce at 10 America's Cup Avenue; once you leave the parking lot, switch on the tape and let it direct you down Thames Street to your first stop, at Wellington Park. Since there are only a few places to stop on the drive, don't feel guilty about leaving your car and walking around, stretching out to get a few minutes of sun, or snapping a couple of photographs of boats in the harbor or of the statue of Comte de Rochambeau.

Bonniecrest, Beacon Rock, Edgehill, and Shamrock Cliff are the names of a few of the grand summer palaces you pass while motoring your way down Harrison Avenue and Ridge Road before entering the part of the road officially called The Ocean Drive. Many of these are still private residences or have been converted into hotels or restaurants, so the interiors cannot be seen on guided tours. Virtually the only information the general public can hear on these homes, therefore, is what is told on the tape. Shamrock Cliff, for instance, a red-stone and cut-granite "cottage"

About a hundred dogs were invited to this special occasion, most of them sporting formal doggie clothes, and they dined at a legless dinner table that had been placed on the veranda.

When the natives tore down the wall, Lawrence put up another one studded with glass and guarded not by a mere watchdog but by a live bull.

Look in one direction from the Cliff Walk and you see the backs of Newport's mansions. Look the other way and you see the Atlantic Ocean. What a way to take a walk down the street!

(and all these opulent houses are referred to as "cottages"), was built in 1894 and later became the home of Barbara Hutton, the actress and Woolworth heiress, and Doris Duke, who were together known as Newport's "poor little rich girls." Another "cottage," Beachmound, a typical Colonial Revival structure, was built in 1897 as the home of Mr. and Mrs. George Tyson, who made their money in the steel industry; Mrs. Tyson's sister was famed socialite Pearl Mesta.

The phrase "It's a dog's life" carried a special meaning at one point in Newport's gilded age, usually thought of as being between 1890 and 1914. Newport canines were as much a part of the upper echelon of society as their masters, and on the taped tour you hear about Mrs. Stuyvesant Fish's famed dinner for dogs. About a hundred dogs were invited, most of which sported formal doggie clothes, and they dined at a legless dinner table that had been placed on the veranda. The menu included stewed liver with rice, fricassee of bones, and stewed dog biscuits.

While the upper crust in Newport past went crazy in special cases like the dog party, they were anything but casual in their day-to-day lives. They would never knock on a neighbor's door and ask, "What's going on?" when they wanted to stop by for a visit. Such a gauche manner of acting would never have been accepted. Instead, a society woman would order a carriage and footman for the day she wished to visit her acquaintance. The footman would then, after arriving at the home to be visited, present the calling card to the butler, who in turn would place the card on a silver tray and present it to the madam of the home.

On your driving tour past these homes that are silent reminders of the grand past, you come across some stopping places for which no formalities are necessary beyond pulling over and giving right of way. Brenton Point Park, for instance, was once a private estate filled with butlers and coachmen and all other necessary helpers. It then, in a turn of 180 degrees, served as a World War II observation point, and today is open to the public as a wonderful place to picnic, take a walk, and enjoy a thoroughly splendid ocean view. In contrast, Fort Adams State Park was a military lifer before "retirement." It was built over 180 years ago and served through the end of World War II. Time has taken its toll of the granite walls and tunnels. Tours of the fort itself have been discontinued but the park grounds are still open to picnickers.

The final portion of the auto tour brings you by the most famous of the Newport mansions, including The Breakers, Marble House, and Rosecliff (all open to the public and all described on pages 10-15). It also takes you near the Cliff Walk, and you are given the chance to walk around a portion of it. But instead of starting the Cliff Walk in the middle here, why not simply sit in your car and listen to the classic melodrama of the man who tried taking the most famous walk in Rhode Island away from the people who had loved it for years?

The narrator on the tape tells the story of William Beech Lawrence, whom we can almost see smoothing a long, twirled mustache as he sneers in archetypal villainous form. Lawrence, who owned much of the waterfront property at Ochre Point, made the mistake of selling an acre to a friend, then almost immediately regretted the decision. To separate the properties, he constructed a stone wall that extended right to the water's edge, cutting off the Cliff Walk. The natives proceeded to tear the wall down, an action to which Lawrence responded by putting up another wall studded with glass and guarded not by a mere watchdog but by a live bull. The locals, refusing to put up with any bull, demolished this wall too, throwing it into the sea. (No one, the tape states, knows what happened to the bull.)

Fed up with the public taking this matter into their own hands, Lawrence took the situation to court and was disappointed to hear it rule that the public had a right to access to the shore whether for fishing or just collecting seaweed. Lawrence appealed, taking the problem to the Supreme Court, which also ruled in favor of the residents so long as they respected the private owners' rights by not leaving the public walkway.

Lawrence's story comes virtually at the end of the Ocean Drive tape. Once you've completed the drive, you'll have all the background information you could want for the **Cliff Walk;** all you'll need now is energy! The walk totals three miles one way, although a portion near the end has been eroded to a degree and is not recommended. On the whole, the walk is a pretty easy grind, with only a few steps here and there and a couple of small climbs; still, unlike a tree-shaded hiking trail through a state park, this sun-baked trail is totally exposed and the rays may sap your energy. So don't be surprised if you are prematurely exhausted and feel the need to head back.

The walk is overgrown with plants and shrubs at some points, and you may come across scattered litter or isolated graffiti; Newport veterans will tell you that the Cliff Walk is but a shadow of what it was in days past. For the most part, though, the path is clear and clean and you'll have no trouble maneuvering as you saunter past the backs and sprawling yards of The Breakers, Marble House, the Astors' Beechwood, and a handful of other sizable homes that once belonged to wealthy people. (The only problem you may have is making way for other pedestrians who have come to enjoy the same views.)

One mansion, Ochre Court, was once the home of Ogden Goulet, whose ancestor founded Chemical National Bank in New York in 1824. Goulet had Ochre Court designed by well-known nineteenth-century

Here you saunter past the backs and sprawling yards of The Breakers, Marble House, the Astors' Beechwood, and a handful of other sizable homes that once belonged to the wealthy.

COURTESY NEWPORT COUNTY
CHAMBER OF COMMERCE
JOHN T. HOPF

Fort Adams State Park, off the Ocean Drive, houses a fort that was built 180 years ago and was active through World War II.

architect Richard Morris Hunt in 1888; in 1946, the French-chateau-style home was donated by the family to the Catholic Church, and it now serves as the home for Salve Regina College. Some of the privately owned mansions you see include Fairholme, a Tudor structure with a half-timbered facade, and Seaview Terrace, a large stone building that claims forty bedrooms and twenty bathrooms. It's by Seaview Terrace, which lies just past the Cliff Walk's midpoint, that you get a panoramic view of just about all the mansions.

But the sights here that call for your attention are not just those that are manmade. Restless waters also beckon, and whether you're eyeing the wide sands of Newport Beach at the walk's beginning or the seemingly endless waters of Rhode Island Sound farther along, the aquatic view commands as much of your attention as the flamboyant homes. If you wish to inspect the waters close up, take a walk along the Forty Steps down to the rocks, located at the early part of the Cliff Walk; the rocks were originally a fishermen's hideout, then became known as the leisure-time gathering place for all the mansion employees.

By the time you reach Miramar, which is now a private home but was formerly on separate occasions a girls' school and the home of a wealthy Philadelphia family, you will have trekked along almost all of the maintained Cliff Walk.

It won't be the same as being invited to dinner, but back-to-back jaunts on The Ocean Drive and the Cliff Walk will introduce you to many of the grand homes of the past and present Newport wealthy, in addition to permitting you to inspect some of the wonderful ocean vistas they enjoyed. And you won't even have to hire a coachman and present a calling card.

Take a walk along the Forty Steps down to the rocks, originally a fishermen's hideout and later the leisure-time gathering place for all the mansion employees in the area.

COURTESY MOUNT WASHINGTON AUTO ROAD/DICK SMITH

ACCESS

THE OCEAN DRIVE AND THE CLIFF WALK. Directions: To get to the Newport Chamber of Commerce, take Route 138 to Farewell Street to America's Cup Avenue; the chamber is at 10 America's Cup Avenue, facing the road in a small shopping center. **Season:** Auto Road: All year. Cliff Walk: In good, warm weather. **Days:** Daily. **Admission** free to drive The Ocean Drive or to walk on Cliff Walk; charge for tape rental with deposit for cassette recorder. **Allow** 1½ hours for The Ocean Drive with recorded tour and stops, or substantially less time without the cassette; allow 3 hours for the entire Cliff Walk. **Notes:** Avoid the Cliff Walk in either strong winds or substantial rains. Parking for the Cliff Walk is available on any side streets off Memorial Boulevard. You can also park on any street that terminates at a point by the Cliff Walk, and then start your walk from that point. **Telephone:** (401) 847-1600 (Chamber of Commerce).

Pinkham Notch

You'd think that most people would rather spend a free day helping their neighbors clean their ovens or watching old reruns of "Camp Runamuck" than visiting a place that claims to have the worst weather in the world. If you were to hear that people risk damage to their cars or bodies while embarking on a brutal climb to see such a place, you'd possibly begin to wonder about the future of humanity. Yet, on a clear summer day, you'll find this place, Mount Washington, as popular with travelers as the most refreshing beach.

You will also find people on the significantly smaller but still impressive Wildcat Mountain, and the way up here is a less hairy amusement park-like gondola. And you will come across, too, those who have decided to keep both feet firmly on low-valley terra firma; at Glen Ellis Falls Scenic Area, near both the **Mount Washington Auto Road** and the Wildcat Mountain Gondola, you can see what visual beauties nature can concoct with mountain slopes and prehistoric avalanches. All three of these scenic attractions can be taken in on a daytrip to Pinkham Notch in the White Mountains.

People who work and reside atop Mount Washington (yes, some who work at permanent weather

Mount Washington is the highest peak north of the Smokies and the source of winds up to 231 miles per hour. If you drive to the top, keep your car in low gear all the way up and down.

People who work and reside atop Mount Washington wear their claim of having "The Worst Weather in the World" as proudly as they would don a crown.

and radio stations also live here for days at a time) wear their claim of having "The Worst Weather in the World" as proudly as they would don a crown. In fact, the only tag they seem to get more satisfaction out of is the "Top of New England." While the weather claim may be disputed in parts of Siberia or Antarctica (although no other place on the globe has ever experienced a wind greater than the bone-chilling 231 miles per hour recorded on the Mount Washington summit in 1934), the latter label is incontrovertible. At 6,288 feet above sea level, it's the rooftop not only of New England but of the entire Northeast. You'd have to head south to the Great Smokies in North Carolina to find higher land.

It's the thrill of conquering the biggest mountain, even by car, and of seeing just what it's like at the top, that draws the hordes of visitors to this cloud-piercing peak each summer.

It's the thrill of conquering the biggest mountain, even by car, and of seeing just what it's like at the top, that draws the hordes of visitors to this cloud-piercing peak each summer. And if you're fortunate, you'll be blessed with a superb view of the rest of the Presidential Range.

Compared with other great mountains of the world, even to many other American peaks, Mount Washington is a lilliput. You'll find numerous peaks in the Rockies, Sierras, and Tetons that rise thousands of feet higher than it; since the White Mountains are well over two hundred million years older than the Western ranges, they've had a healthy head start in weathering and settling. However, relative to the size of its neighbors, not to mention the valley floor about 4,600 feet below, this mountain is a monster. And that goes for its temperament, too; its peak sticks up into a prominent path for major weather systems, accounting for its nasty winter record.

Not that the summers up here would be conducive to the lifestyle of a nudist colony. On the mid-July day that we drove up the eight-mile auto road, it was seventy-odd degrees in Pinkham Notch in the morning and only forty-nine degrees on the summit. More uncomfortable than the low mercury, though, are the winds, which sometimes seem to be strong enough to blow Orson Welles around like an autumn leaf. Although the summit temperature is listed at the entrance to the toll road, when planning ahead it's safe to bet that you'll need long pants and a jacket or windbreaker on top.

Of course, nobody even thinks of venturing up to the summit without wondering about the view from the top. The most dependable panorama, with minimal cooperation from the weather, includes the other mountains to the north in the Presidential Range. To the south, you'll see some of the smaller White Mountains and possibly Lake Winnipesaukee. And on the clearest of days, you'll see towns like North Conway and Bartlett, and possibly even the Atlantic Ocean at the Maine coast.

Closer at hand are the rocks and stunted summit

brush that almost resemble a desert landscape; as you motor your way both up and down the auto road you'll note the gradual change from fully grown spruce and fir trees in the valley to the dwarfed trees just before timberline (four thousand feet) to the bleak surroundings at the top. But because of the extreme weather conditions, this is your chance to see a number of alpine flowers that can be found elsewhere only in arctic regions hundreds of miles to New Hampshire's north.

The new summit house is the latest in a series of four that have stood atop Mount Washington: the first was built in 1852; the second, which had carpeted floors and could hold 150 people, was constructed in 1873 to accommodate the already substantial tourist trade at the top; the third was completed in 1915. The current version offers, in addition to the museum, a snack bar; a large, open observation deck; and a ranger on duty to answer all your questions.

As you drive to and from all this, it's mandatory to keep the car in its lowest gear all the way both up and back, and to pump the brakes often on your way down. If you need to cool your engine or your brakes, pull off onto one of the many turnouts and enjoy the view for a few minutes, as we did. If you find you are having serious trouble with your car, signal one of the vans or trucks going by; they are equipped with radio communications and will get help for you. Above all, be sure to heed the instructions on the free packet you receive at the base: *Take it easy.*

And before you drive up at all, you may want to ask yourself a few questions. Is your car in top shape? Do you have enough water and oil in it? Can you see yourself panicking while traveling up or down a steep road (one third asphalt and two thirds gravel) on the side of a mountain? If you're uncertain about the answers to any of these questions, don't even think about driving up. Instead, take a ride up in one of the van stages that leave from the Glen House, across from the mountain-drive base on Route 16. Each van stage seats eight, but will leave on demand with only a couple of passengers if a full load isn't ready. And on the way up you have the added benefit of the driver's fascinating comments on the mountain and its history.

At 3,960 feet above sea level, **Wildcat Mountain** is quite small compared to the New England behemoth across the notch, and the 2,300-odd-foot difference in elevation manifests itself in a few different ways. For one thing, there is vegetation on top, as opposed to the barren landscape of Mount Washington's summit. You will find that most of the trees gradually start appearing smaller, thinner, or barer as the gondola brings you higher and higher; you'll also notice the birch, maple, and beech trees you saw in profusion at the base slowly disappear while spruce and fir become more common. Another difference between mountain

To get a good view of Mount Washington, take the gondola to the summit of Wildcat Mountain.

Not all notable natural features in this area are up on mountain tops. A stop at Glen Ellis Falls, back on the valley floor, is a most refreshing way to end the day.

Even on a hazy day, from the top of Wildcat you'll be able to pick out the town of Berlin.

tops concerns the temperature; while there will be a few degrees difference between the base and the summit here, it won't be substantial. (If you take the ride late in the day, however, it may be a little breezy on top, so a wrap is advised.) You will also find that, even on a hazy day, you'll be able to pick out the town of Berlin and other sights on the valley floor.

Some take the ride up just to see the view, grab a bite at the snack bar (there's also one at the base as well as some picnic tables), snap the camera shutter a couple of times, and hop the next gondola down. Others, who have more time to spare and want to get a bit of exercise as well as learn something about their surroundings, can take the nature trail that starts at the summit. It's a pretty short walk (a half hour or less depending on how often you stop to admire the scenery) and an explanatory brochure is available at its entrance. In addition to this nature trail, there's also a brief trail (it took us less than five minutes) up steps and stones to an observation point overlooking the notch and the mountains. If backpackers pass in front of you while you admire the distant scenery, chances are they are following the two thousand-mile-long Appalachian Trail, which crosses the Wildcat summit on its way from Maine to Georgia.

To many people, and that group is not limited to children, the ride itself is part of the thrill. It's not dangerous or a bit scary, although during a breeze, the gondola cars can be blown about a bit (the lift is closed if the winds are too strong). More than likely, the air will be calm and the ride will be the ultimate in peacefulness; although there are ninety-one gondolas that travel along sixty-eight hundred feet of cable to the summit, the cars are widely spaced; and except for the times when you pass one heading in the other direction, you can enjoy the trees, the crisp air, and the distant mountains without obstruction. As you might imagine, autumn is a splendid time to come here.

But nature's best doesn't come only in the form of heights. Back on the floor of the notch, a short distance south of the entrance to Wildcat, is a place where you can park and then take a short walk to see the refreshing effects that a mixture of cliffs, avalanches, and water can produce.

The trail from the parking area to the sixty-four-foot **Glen Ellis Falls** parallels a portion of the narrow and shallow Ellis River. The jaunt itself is pretty easy, level for the first part while finishing up with a few stone steps to climb as you approach the falls; it only took us about five minutes. If you're lucky enough to reach Glen Ellis Falls when there's nary a soul there, you're in for a special treat. But crowds aren't a problem. We were here for about thirty minutes on a hot July Saturday; during that period, there was a maximum of perhaps a half dozen others taking in nature's jewels at any one time.

Markers at the falls and on the way to them explain to you a little about the big attraction. At one, you're told that in the seconds it took you to read a few lines, over six hundred gallons have dropped and passed a certain distance down the river. It's believed the falls were created after a series of avalanches; the river, which had been flowing during preglacial times, was forced by the resulting land formations to plunge over the headwall of this hollow. Formed on the eastern slopes of Mount Washington, the Ellis joins the Saco River near Glen, New Hampshire, and then meanders through Maine before emptying into the Atlantic Ocean. Don't be shy about dipping your tired feet in the river (if you can brave the chill).

A trip that ends amid the refreshing trees and waters at Glen Ellis Falls Scenic Area and started at the place that boasts of the worst weather in the world: it's a testament to the diversity of Pinkham Notch in the White Mountains. Whether you live within driving distance, or are just passing through on your vacation, you'll find these three sights are one of the very best slices of New Hampshire.

If you're lucky enough to reach Glen Ellis Falls when there's nary a soul there, you're in for a special treat.

ACCESS

MOUNT WASHINGTON AUTO ROAD. Directions: From the junction of routes 302 and 16, head north about 15 miles on Route 16. **Season:** Mid-May through mid-October. **Days:** Daily. **Admission** charged for auto and driver, substantially less for passengers, in private car; charged per person in van stages. **Allow** 2 hours. **Notes:** It cannot be emphasized enough that your car must be in top condition before you drive on the road. If you take a van stage, you are allowed ½ hour on the summit. (You may stay longer and chance returning in a later van if there are empty seats; this is at your own risk, however.) **Telephone:** (603) 466-3988.

WILDCAT MOUNTAIN GONDOLA. Directions: From the junction of routes 302 and 16, head north about 13 miles on Route 16; or, from the base of the Mount Washington Auto Road, head south 2 miles on Route 16. **Season:** Memorial Day through mid-October, and during ski season. **Days:** Winter, summer, and fall, daily; Memorial Day through mid-June, weekends only. **Admission** charged. **Allow** 45 minutes. **Note:** Buy a ticket at the base lodge before heading to the gondola entrance. **Telephone:** (603) 466-3326.

GLEN ELLIS FALLS SCENIC AREA. Directions: From the junction of routes 302 and 16, head north 11½ miles on Route 16; or, from the Wildcat Mountain Gondola Ride parking lot, head south a little over 1½ miles on Route 16. **Season:** All year. **Days:** Daily. **Admission** free. **Allow** 20 to 30 minutes. **Telephone:** For information, call the White Mountain National Forest ranger station at (603) 466-2713.

Mount Mansfield

You start off at the Nose. Then, you can descend to the Forehead or climb up to the Upper Lip. And from there, you may want to ascend farther toward the Lower Lip, the Chin, and the Adam's Apple. Or you can detour to Wall Street.

It may sound like Jack climbing the beanstalk to the home of a giant stockbroker. But we're talking of a scene that can be viewed by any traveler in northern Vermont: the peaks atop Mount Mansfield. You need some imagination, but if you look at the peaks from the floor of Smugglers Notch below, they resemble a man's face looking up at the sky; thus their names relate to facial features. While this sight from the floor is impressive, though, the most fun is being at the top, standing at the base of either lip or the Chin, literally looking down the Nose at the city of Montreal, the village of Stowe, and Lake Champlain. The views, especially on clear days, are magnificent.

The most fun is being at the top, standing at the base of either lip or the Chin, literally looking down the Nose at Montreal, Stowe, and Lake Champlain.

To hardy hikers, leg power is the only way to ascend. For the rest of us, there are two other options, both of which are different and fun, and which lead to destinations a mile apart from each other on the top. The **Mount Mansfield Toll Road** is four and a half miles long, is made from gravel, is steep and winding, and is the source of some superb vistas you just can't get at ground level. The Gondola at Mount Mansfield, on the other hand, has room in each car for four passengers who need to do little more than simply sit back and enjoy the scenery. And if you'd like to get some closer views or different angles, remember that all major points on the mountain top are connected by trails.

But let's begin with one of the easy ways to reach the top. The drive, naturally, keeps you at eye level with the trees, plants, and animals all the way from the valley floor to the peak. And with the turnouts dotting the road, you're tempted to pull over whenever you see white blossoms on low-lying shrubs or a chipmunk scampering over some rocks; anything natural that grabs your attention is within easy reach.

Counting a few stops on the way up, the auto ride took us thirty minutes; if you don't halt, you should make it in little over half that time. It may be necessary to shift into a lower gear as you negotiate some of the steep and curvy turns while ascending, although for the most part, you can drive normally on your way up. However, your brakes can take a licking on the return trip, so keep your car in first gear all the way. The speed limit? Fifteen miles per hour, and while some sections of the road are level, on the whole you'd be hard pressed to top that speed on your way either up or down.

A small souvenir shop, called the Summit House, sits at the end of the road, but aside from this there are no frills. The show is the mountain view, both above and below you; from your vantage point here at 3,850 feet above sea level, you can look down and see Stowe and other communities in the distance. And a total of 543 feet above you is the Chin, the highest point in the entire state.

The **Gondola at Mount Mansfield** doesn't take you quite as high as the road: the Cliff House, debarkation point of the gondola, is 3,650 feet high (although an unofficial sign there lists it as 3,750 feet). But gliding along with almost a lighter-than-air feeling, you are constantly from twenty-five to thirty-two feet above the ground, and you have a bird's-eye view of the landscape as it gradually changes from a northern hardwood forest to a virtual arctic environment.

And this alteration occurs in the span of just a ten-minute ride, in which you climb 2,150 feet. At the Cliff House, where you may find it up to ten degrees cooler than on the valley floor, there are picnic tables, a sun deck, a restaurant, and some strategically placed observation platforms.

Although the air is chillier at the top than at the base, it hardly feels like arctic Canada. Yet, you'll hear from the rangers on duty that every one thousand feet ascended in elevation is equivalent to five hundred miles gained in latitude; so this climb in effect puts you in an area climatically similar to the Hudson Bay region of northern Canada. The summit of Mount Mansfield, which borders the timberline, is one of only two spots in Vermont that fit into the category of an arctic region (the peak of Camel's Hump to the south is the other), so be sure to take in all the unusual sights when you're up here.

Birds are rare in this elevation, but there are some hardy species like the white-throated sparrow, the dark-eyed junco (whose white coloring has led to its famed nickname, snowbird), and the raven that may fly by on occasion. More predictable sights are the alpine flowers that usually blossom in mid- to late June or July. One such rarity (except at this altitude) is the mountain sandwort, which grows in clumps and shows off its white flowers through midsummer. The mountain cranberry thrives at this altitude because of the plentiful supply of moisture; the blossoms it bears in June turn to berries in August or September. Then there's the diapensia, which grows like a weed in New Hampshire's White Mountains but can be found nowhere else in Vermont.

If you plan on hiking, you're requested to stay on the trails, of which there are two main ones. The lower of the two, which connects the Cliff and Summit houses, is known as the Cliff Trail. There are some tricky spots to watch out for — including two ladders, one tight squeeze through a narrow rock-bound passageway, and a rock with a cable you must hold to pass through. But as foreboding as it might sound, it's

A drive on the Mount Mansfield Toll Road will afford you close-up views of the plant and animal life on Vermont's highest mountain.

Gliding along on the gondola, you are constantly from twenty-five to thirty-two feet above the ground, and you have a bird's-eye view of the landscape.

Every one thousand feet ascended in elevation is equivalent to five hundred miles gained in latitude; Mansfield's summit is therefore climatically similar to the Hudson Bay region of northern Canada.

You're above the ground and away from cars when you take the Gondola at Mount Mansfield to the summit. Your reward is a ride in almost eerie quiet and a bird's-eye view.

not limited to George Willigs; according to a ranger, anyone in good health who is not an acrophobiac should make it. (Along the way, you can take a side trip to Wall Street and invest some time in a mildly adventurous walk through this split rock.) The trail can be covered in a half hour, one way.

The Long Trail — or rather the Mount Mansfield portion of the well-known trail that bisects Vermont from the Canadian to the Massachusetts borders — puts you face to face with the famous face. Here it stretches across the mountain summit, higher than the level of the Cliff Trail and totally exposed to all elements. The Summit House sits between the Nose and the Upper Lip. You can hike just under a mile through the Lower Lip to the Cliff House, or continue another .4 mile up to the Chin. Novices can conquer this lofty ramble, but they should be in good shape.

There are many other ways to see the peaks of Mount Mansfield, and two favorite variations include riding up the gondola and walking back down. Some visitors stroll down right underneath the gondola (which takes about an hour), while others take the Cliff Trail to the Summit House, walk a short connecting trail to the Nose, and then head down a third trail called Nosedive, which brings you back to the parking area. Expect that stretch to take about an hour and twenty minutes from the Cliff House, and about forty-five minutes from the Summit House.

Whether you climb to the Chin, stretch your legs, please your eyes, or just feed your stomach, the summit of Mount Mansfield is a place to make use of all your senses.

ACCESS

MOUNT MANSFIELD TOLL ROAD. Directions: From Interstate 89 exit 10, take Route 100 north to Stowe, then Route 108 north for 6 miles to the entrance for the toll road, on the left. **Season:** Mid-June to the first substantial snowfall. **Days:** Daily. **Admission** charged. **Allow** at least 45 minutes. **Note:** Check radiator, brakes, water, and oil before taking this drive. **Telephone:** (802) 253-7311.

GONDOLA AT MOUNT MANSFIELD. Directions: From Interstate 89 exit 10, take Route 100 north to Stowe, then Route 108 north for 7 miles to the entrance for the gondola, on the left. **Season:** Late May through mid-October and late November through the end of the ski season. **Days:** Late May through late June, weekends; all other times, daily. **Admission** charged. **Allow** at least 45 minutes. **Notes:** Because of exposure and elevation, bring a sweater or windbreaker if you plan on hiking the Long Trail. Wear hiking boots if you plan on hiking any trail. Avoid all hiking during thunderstorms; the ridge is hit by lightning an average of 400 times per year. **Telephone:** (802) 253-7311.

CHAPTER VI

Autumn Rambles

Autumn in New England. The words are almost as magic as "springtime in Paris." It's a special kind of romance here though — one that rings of natural beauty and nostalgia. Of crisp late afternoon walks with your best boyfriend or girlfriend. Of Saturday-night parties in old barns where you savored warm cider. And mostly, of relaxing drives along foliage-edged country roads where the leaves turned the colors of an artist's palette and even the least appreciative city dweller got caught up in it all.

Your high-school sweetheart may now be married to an accountant from Cleveland, and the location of your Saturday-night parties could just as easily be a condominium complex. But the country roads are still here. And every fall, like clockwork, nature still puts on its phenomenal autumn spectacle. For the price of gassing up the car and heading to the hills, this fall show can still be the source of some of the best fun today and your warmest memories tomorrow.

A few of the foliage trips described in this chapter take you on well-traveled routes that are widely regarded as the zeniths of fall scenery. Others bring you on less trafficked but equally colorful highways. Regardless of where you direct your motor vehicle, you are urged to park it occasionally, stretch, take in some deep breaths, and stroll among the variegated leaves. The vivid colors and autumn air may not take you back to your younger days, but they will offer evidence that the best of New England in the autumn is still around.

Are you looking for the charm of old New England as well as the beauty of nature's color show? If so, you'll enjoy a drive through Brattleboro's 1879 Creamery Bridge, located just off the Molly Stark Trail.

MELINDA MACAULEY

The Molly Stark Trail

The first question that many Vermont foliage seekers ask concerning the Green Mountain State's color-packed Molly Stark Trail does not regard routing information. On the contrary, the initial query refers to the road's unusual moniker. Who was Molly Stark and why did they name a trail after her?

Actually, it was Molly's husband who initially put her name into the local limelight and inadvertently eternized it. In August of 1777, General John Stark, a hero of the French and Indian War and of the Battle of Bunker Hill, was called upon to lead the American troops against General John Burgoyne's soldiers during the Battle of Bennington, an important engagement of the American Revolution. On the morning prior to the battle (which the colonists won), Stark exclaimed, "There stand the redcoats, and they are ours, or this night, Molly Stark sleeps a widow."

The Molly Stark Trail is, indeed, a main road. Though it is only two lanes, aside from an occasional passing lane now and then, it is the primary thoroughfare across southern Vermont and even during the off season can be congested with traffic on the way to Albany or New Hampshire. Still, the thirty-nine-mile route that connects Brattleboro to Bennington has more than its share of charm, quaint villages, and dramatic and vivid fall scenery. Bisecting Vermont's southern tier, it's close to most parts of New England (closer than you may think to highly populated areas in the south) and certainly warrants a daytrip during late September or early October.

"There stand the redcoats, and they are ours, or this night, Molly Stark sleeps a widow."

Traveling on this relatively short trail, you might want to allow time to see some of the interesting towns along the route. Wilmington has the only town center that is actually traversed by the Molly Stark Trail (which, by the way, is also Vermont Route 9), but Brattleboro and Bennington, just off the main road, are also primary stops for shopping, dining, and sightseeing. Portions of the last two towns are described in other sections of this book.

Commencing in the east, you get on the trail by taking exit 2 off Interstate 91 and heading west. Before you even have time to fold the map, you arrive at one of the trail's more notable sights. The **Creamery Bridge,** well kept and brightly painted in a way that belies its 1879 construction date, is the only covered bridge that sits within eyeshot of the route.

Soon after passing the bridge, you enter the center of West Brattleboro, where the speed limit suddenly dips to twenty-five miles per hour. The speed limit increases as you pass through a few more miles of "civilization," and it's about two miles from the West Brattleboro midpoint that you begin to penetrate the real countryside you came here for. After ascending a small grade on a somewhat winding section of the road, you see on the sides fewer buildings and more of Mother Nature's works. For the next half dozen miles or so, you have the picturesque Whetstone Brook keeping you company off and on at your left, as you cross from Brattleboro into Marlboro.

You continue to climb at this point, and you may find some wonderful potential photographs amid the trees, brook, hills in the distance, and old small buildings. There are spaces where the colors are brilliant, and even if you don't have a camera, you may not be satisfied with fleeting glimpses through the windows of a car moving at fifty miles per hour. Stops by the roadside are permitted; however, it is emphasized that for the safety of everyone concerned, your car should be pulled off the road and out of the way of oncoming traffic. For the most part, the trail is equipped with small shoulders, but choose your stops with care.

One stop you might consider is the **Hundred Mile View,** located about fourteen miles from the eastern start of the trail. You'll find it after you wind and ascend for a few miles. This isn't the location of the best view from the trail — because it's well known, you may have to fight with a few tour buses for a place to park, and the view doesn't include specific landmarks or the close-up vibrant colors you see elsewhere on this route — but it's the type of place that's hard to avoid and that you could very well find to your liking. By the way, one of the best times to whip out your camera here is if there's fog in the distance; the fog hovering over the trees can really look captivating.

If you're now starting to experience a growling stomach, keep in mind that **Molly Stark State Park** is on the left side only about a mile and a half from the Hundred Mile View. You have to pay to picnic here, though; a nominal fee is charged for all but children. There's also a hiking trail — a mile-and-a-half-long round trip. The park closes the Tuesday following Columbus Day.

Back on the trail with the park entrance in your rear-view mirror, you continue driving downhill as you start noticing signs welcoming you to the Mount Snow Region; long regarded as a ski haven, this area teems with visitors throughout the year, and the heart of autumn is hardly an exception. The center of

The Creamery Bridge, well kept and brightly painted in a way that belies its 1879 construction date, is the only covered bridge that sits within eyeshot of this route.

Wilmington, marked by the only traffic light on the trail (at the junction of routes 9 and 100 north) is right in the middle of the trail. If you haven't brought your own lunch, good restaurants are waiting for your indulgence both just south of and up to a few miles north of the traffic light. You may have trouble finding a street-side place to park around here, though. And you might have to wait up to fifteen or twenty minutes at the traffic light due to the many other foliage seekers. Patience can indeed be a virtue.

A couple of miles after entering Searsburg, you find yourself in the midst of some of the most extraordinary scenery on the trail.

Between Wilmington and Searsburg, about three miles past the traffic light, you find the small Deerfield River alongside the road; it accompanies you for a good portion of the rest of the trip and, with the hilly and colorful backdrop, affords some remarkable photo possibilities. A couple of miles after entering Searsburg, you find yourself in the midst of some of the most extraordinary scenery on the trail. The road curves repeatedly, but there are some turnouts scattered about, all the better to help you savor the exquisite panorama on your left side.

But the beauty doesn't stop here. You cross the Deerfield, which now flows to the right of the road. As you continue onward, you can't help taking in the wondrous views on both sides, which include both some faraway hills and the close-up Red Mill Pond. And just over ten miles past the traffic light in Wilmington is **Woodford State Park.** Like Molly Stark State Park, it closes the Tuesday after Columbus Day.

Some think the scenery around this part of the trail is the nicest on the entire route. You certainly see more evergreens here than at earlier points, and the greens intermix well with the fall colors for some different kinds of autumn views. Foliage-packed hills are off in the distance, and the blue waters of Lake Woodford are to your right for a short while.

You go by some of the sights of Woodford, including a few buildings with classic white frame New England architecture, as you motor along. The natural scenery, including water and trees, continues to refresh as well, serving as additional inspiration for photographers and other foliage fans. Again, don't hesitate to pull over on some of the wider shoulders to get out of the car and take in some of nature's finest.

About six miles past the information booth, you see signs announcing the end of the thruway and welcoming you to Bennington. While you may want to continue and see some of the attractions of this historic Vermont town, you've by now seen some of the loveliest foliage in all of New England.

ACCESS _____

MOLLY STARK TRAIL. Directions to the beginning of the trail: From Interstate 91 exit 2, head west on Route 9. **Allow** 2 hours.

Smugglers Notch

Stowe, Vermont, is one of those New England resort towns that claim to be year-round playgrounds. Skiers head here en masse from November through March, while weekend swimmers, golfers, tennis players, and Alpine-slide enthusiasts make use of the facilities during the warmer months. In the middle are the fall-foliage fans, to whom there is no place other than northern Vermont to be during peak colors. And the area around Stowe is the best place to start.

From the junction of routes 100 and 108 in Stowe, head north out of town on Route 108 toward Smugglers Notch. Your initial vista will be of trees on hills, fronted by many signs of the ever-healthy ski industry. From the Alpine architecture of the lodges to the Austrian and German cuisine of some of the restaurants, you'll have everything but the Matterhorn to make you think you're in central Europe (there is a bit of Austrian history here, too, in the Trapp Family Lodge owned by Maria von Trapp). As the skiers' shelters and eateries become less clustered, you will encounter colorful trees hugging both sides of the road. About six and a half miles along, you'll pass the entrance to the Mount Mansfield Toll Road and about a mile farther ahead, you'll see the road to the Mount Mansfield Ski Area with its gondola ride. Both are also popular in times other than foliage season, and on clear days, the view from the top can make you wish you never had to leave. (These attractions are described in detail on pages 128 through 130.)

If you've brought your own lunch, a good place to stop for a pleasant picnic is **Smugglers Notch State Park,** the entrance to which is located on the right side of the road almost directly across from Mount Mansfield Ski Area. There are about two dozen tables, and the best news for hungry, budget-minded travelers is that there is no entrance fee for picnickers. The same goes for hikers; you can walk to your feet's content on any of the thirty-two trails in the adjacent state forest for free.

But some of the most spectacular scenery in Vermont awaits, and the anxious among you may find the drive through Smugglers Notch too exciting to put off. Before you motor even a mile from the state-park entrance, you see some significant specimens of Vermont's Green Mountains looming in the distance. Within another mile, you're maneuvering your way around the hairpin turns on this narrow road as it winds its way through the famous notch, source of ski areas, sheer cliffs, leaves, and legend.

The name "Smugglers Notch" is not an untruth. Nor was the use of the notch by smugglers one isolated incident. At least three times over the course of a century, this pass was actively used by those unlawfully transporting goods or people from the United States

You'll have everything but the Matterhorn to make you think you're in central Europe.

SEAN KARDON

There are other ways to see the leaves than through the window of your car. Here a father and son get a close-at-hand view in Jericho Center.

into Canada.

Because of the notch's cloud-piercing elevation — 2,162 feet above sea level at its highest point — it's often barricaded with snow during winter. Only the hardiest, or the most brave, would venture here, making it easy for smugglers to pass through undetected. After Congress passed embargo acts in 1807 and 1808, making it illegal for America to trade with Great Britain and Canada, Montreal was the most convenient market for northern Vermonters, and nothing would stop them from reaching it. They drove cattle through the notch to Canada and smuggled goods back down through it. Officials must have been a little slow to pick up on things, since the notch was used on other occasions later on: prior to the Civil War, when fugitive slaves were shown the way to Canada, and then when thirsty Vermonters performed some quarterback sneaks with Canadian potent potables during Prohibition.

Prior to the Civil War, fugitive slaves were shown the way to Canada along this route.

The only thing you might want to sneak in is a thirty-seventh photograph on your roll of thirty-six, and this is one of the finest places to do so. The peak scenery (pun intended) lasts a good three miles before you start coasting on a downgrade out of the actual notch. Drivers will want to keep their eyes to the road though; it's not for stunt drivers only, but it *is* for the attentive. There are some turnouts by the roadside if you want to pause for closer looks. Have a windbreaker or sweater handy, though, since it's estimated that temperatures here can be ten degrees lower than in Stowe.

From the time you start descending, you travel about five miles through open and flatter land (with hills in the distance and multicolored trees, of course, surrounding you on all sides) before entering the village of **Jeffersonville** (which is a part of the town of Cambridge). In the village center, take a left onto Route 15 west. You'll pass the Second Congregational Church, a white wood frame building with an interesting clock tower and green steeple, on your right. (It's not as old as you might think; it recently celebrated its ninetieth anniversary, so it's just a youngster among New England churches.) Turn your head quickly, and on the left, you'll get a look at the Old Town Hall, a brick structure with white cupola that dates from 1826. It originally was built as an interdenominational church by Baptists, Methodists, and Universalists, a notable fact in itself since different religious denominations haven't always lived as brethen in Vermont. In 1901 the church was made into a town hall, then in 1958, converted into a playhouse. Though it's on the National Register of Historic Buildings, the aged landmark sat vacant from 1970 to 1981; a restoration process was underway as we went to press.

Crossing the Lamoille River, you leave Jeffersonville behind as you pass corn fields, barns, cows, and trees and make your way two miles to **Cambridge** itself. (If the names and boundaries of towns and villages confuse you, you're hardly alone; even Vermont newcomers — residents for less than thirty years — are baffled on this matter.) Before entering the center of Cambridge, you take a left and cross a bridge at two markers denoting "West 15" and "To Route 104." Two tenths of a mile away, just past the brick Cambridge Inn Motel, take a left onto Pleasant Valley Road. (The sign indicates only the direction of the town, but if you should need to ask directions, refer to this as Lower Valley Road and you'll pass as a native.)

Pleasant Valley is four miles away, and the name is highly appropriate. It was a settlement about one hundred fifty years ago and is now part of rural Cambridge. And because of the burgeoning ski business making its way into other parts of this town, Pleasant Valley is the only totally agricultural part of Cambridge remaining, locals report with a sigh.

The road narrows as you climb gradually, driving toward your view of the western and more gently sloping side of Mount Mansfield. The scattered farms dotting the green hillsides are as typical of classic pastoral New England as you might ever see. Add the birch, maple, and beech trees radiant in their fall colors and you've got scenes that could have jumped right out of calendar pages. Rows of corn, barn silos, and old homesteads on the fringes of the road add to the images of pastoralism.

On the way out of the valley to the junction with Route 15 in Underhill, Pleasant Valley Road becomes The River Road although nobody can single out just the spot where the change takes place. But by the time the hills on your left have diminished in size and the trees start to border the road in plenitude, you're on The River Road approaching Underhill. If you passed up the opportunity for a picnic before, or if you'd like to take a walk on some hiking trails for close-up foliage views, you may want to take a detour to **Underhill State Park;** the entrance is marked by a sign about five miles out of Pleasant Valley. Don't plan on going if you're in a hurry, though, since the park is four miles away on a steep gravel road. There is a small charge for adults and teenagers for park usage.

Back on our foliage tour, you pass through **Underhill Center,** marked by its white wood frame two-story town hall, built as a church in 1850 and 1851, and then travel four miles to the junction with Route 15. The road parallels the little Brown's River through some of Vermont's dairyland. Cows and corn, fences and farmland are on either side of you before you reach **Jericho,** home of the world-renowned Snowflake Bentley.

Yes, he is world renowned. In an exemplary case of town pride, the people of Jericho honor Bentley with a marker in the center of their little green and boast that anyone who knows snowflakes, from Vermont to

The Old Red Mill in Jericho, a National Historic Site, is an architectural gem that sits just off the trail.

If names and boundaries of towns and villages confuse you, you're hardly alone; even Vermont newcomers — residents for less than thirty years — are baffled on this matter.

Vladivostok, knows Bentley. Wilson A. Bentley, a Jericho farmer, is credited with being the first person in the world to photograph individual snowflakes and to discover that no two are alike. Bentley (1865-1931) made his finding at age twenty while taking photo micrographs (photographs taken through a microscope): the findings were to affect meteorologists throughout the world. In the world of snowflakes, when you've said "Bentley," you've said a blizzard.

In the world of snow-flakes, when you've said "Bentley," you've said a blizzard.

Before leaving Jericho, you might want to bear right at the green and head a few hundred feet straight into the center of town, where the Old Red Mill sits on the shores of Brown's River. This mill, dating from the 1850s, was the first in New England to use a roller process for milling flour; today it's a National Historic Site, and guided tours may be scheduled on weekends. For more information, call (802) 899-3225.

Now backtrack, passing the green on your left (or, if you don't stop at the mill, bearing left at the green), and follow the sign toward Jericho Center, heading southeast on Lee River Road. (There are no street signs, so it takes a careful navigator to avoid getting lost.) You parallel the Lee River for two miles on a narrow farm-lined road; then Lee River Road ends at Brown's Trace Road, and you turn right toward Jericho Center.

Less than a mile away, the town green of **Jericho Center** beckons the weary traveler. Benches make for a nice respite and the white-steepled, brick-fronted Congregational Church (built in 1835, renovated in 1877 and 1878) is the centerpiece for a picturesque New England village scene. The gray two-story general store, according to locals, is one of the oldest continuously run stores in the entire state, dating from the early 1800s.

Continue on this road, through more farm country of rolling hills and colorful trees, about five miles to **Richmond,** located just south of the Interstate 89 overpass. Then turn right on Route 2 and drive for a mile to the junction with Interstate 89, final point on this jaunt through some of northern Vermont's most attractive landscapes.

ACCESS _____

SMUGGLERS NOTCH FOLIAGE TOUR. Directions to the beginning of the tour: From Interstate 89 exit 10, take Route 100 north to Stowe, then turn left onto Route 108. **Allow** 2 hours.

The Mohawk Trail

If you have never traveled the Mohawk Trail in autumn, don't be put off by the critics who tell you that you can't see the forest for the cars. On weekends, it is true that Route 2 from Greenfield to North Adams is heavily trafficked and you may have to plod along behind a row of automobiles and buses that can seem as long as Macy's Parade. That's the bad news. The good news is that the Mohawk Trail is the source of probably the most eye-pleasing vistas of fall colors in the entire state. Whether you're looking across fifty miles from a mountain summit or examining the leaves just inches from your car, you'll see the best of autumn. So damn the tour buses and full steam ahead.

You might want to begin your scenery scrutiny by following the path of a poet who is known more for his favorite seat than for his poems. Although the name Frederick Tuckerman is most likely as obscure to you as that of the inventor of dental floss, he remains a legend in the environs of Greenfield, Massachusetts. In 1911, Tuckerman built a tower atop a nearby hill where he could be left alone to look out over a magnificent vista, contemplate the universe, and put his thoughts into verse. While his poems have been lost in oblivion, his tower, the **Poet's Seat,** lives on. You can contemplate in the same location, and while you're at it enjoy the view as well. To get to the Poet's Seat, take the Route 2 east exit off Interstate 91 and follow Route 2 through town, where it becomes Main Street. At the end of Main Street, take a right onto Crescent Street and continue until it ends. Take a right onto Parkway, and after about fifty yards turn left onto the access road to the tower.

Follow Route 2 back to the trail, which is well marked by signs once you leave the center of Greenfield. Then it's off to retrace the path of the Mohawk Indians who first cleared this route, and the colonial travelers who made it the country's first interstate toll-free avenue, today referred to as a "shunpike."

After crossing under the Interstate 91 overpass, you immediately encounter a hotel-motel-gasoline-station strip. But that disappears within a mile and your view is soon taken up with pines, maples, elms, and birches. There are viewpoints at various spots off to the right, and although some have been commercially exploited, others are free for the parking, as there are turnouts dotting the length of the trail.

Though your heart may belong to the fall colors this time of year (and rightly so), a short jaunt off the trail about eight miles past the Interstate 91 overpass (well-placed signs show the way) will take you to another kind of foliage display. The **Bridge of Flowers** in Shelburne Falls is a monument to small-town ingenuity: it's a vintage 1908 trolley bridge, long abandoned and turned from a public eyesore to a public

The Bridge of Flowers is a vintage 1908 trolley bridge, long abandoned and now turned into a public pathway enveloped with shrubs and colorful flowers — a virtual floral bonanza.

RUSS KENDALL

A rolling panorama like this is quite typical of the scenes you'll see while traveling on the Mohawk Trail, especially on the western half.

Old looking but relatively new, this covered bridge lies just off the Mohawk Trail in Charlemont.

Would you believe that Shelburne Falls residents are also proud of their potholes?

pathway enveloped with shrubs and colorful flowers — a virtual floral bonanza. (It's scheduled to undergo repair soon, however, so we suggest you call the Mohawk Trail Association at (413) 664-6256 for up-to-date information before you visit.)

Shelburne Falls residents are also proud of their **potholes,** especially the really old ones. We laughed too; but these fifty-odd potholes are ground out of granite and date back some fourteen thousand years. One is thirty-nine feet in diameter, the largest on record in the world. (Well, not everyone can have the Grand Canyon.) They're located by the New England Power Company dam on Deerfield Avenue, off Bridge Street in the center of town.

But bridges, shrubs, and potholes are supplementary for fall-foliage fans, and it's less than a mile back to the Mohawk Trail itself. Take a left onto the trail and as you head west you're back under nature's esthetic domination. The Deerfield River is your roadside companion for the next seven or so miles as it flows on your left; on the right, some of man's appealing additions to natural settings appear. The symbols of America's rurality — barns, farms, tractors, and wagons — seem right in place as adjuncts to the domesticated, but not desecrated, landscape.

The small town of **Charlemont,** which straddles the Mohawk Trail, also fits right in. The narrow, two-lane road that leads you into Charlemont is what one would expect to find in the heart of the country, and the highlights of Charlemont itself — an inn, some old gas stations, a few stores, and the combination town office and historical-society museum — are most appropriate for a town of just over a thousand directly in the middle of this famous trail. The museum, a big brick structure dating from 1892, keeps limited hours, but if you would like to see some of the nineteenth-century memorabilia like sleighs, pottery, bottles, and even bathtubs, you can make an appointment by calling (413) 339-4335 at least a day in advance.

A detour in town will take you to the old looking but relatively new (1951) covered bridge. Back on the trail, you'll notice a conventional *un*covered bridge and then see, on the left side, an eight-foot-high bronze statue, symbol of the road's official eponym. **Hail to the Sunrise** is a Mohawk Indian garbed in loincloth and headdress with his arms outstretched as he faces east and lovingly greets the morning sun. He was erected in 1932 in memory of the Mohawks who first settled this area in the late sixteenth century. In the address at the unveiling it was stated, *"Hail to the Sunrise* symbolizes the hopefulness of humanity through the ages. This is an occasion when we commemorate the Red Man — not only the organization that has kept alive the great fundamental traditions of Freedom, Friendship, and Charity, but for the race of the Red Man from whom we have taken and inherited the boundless territory of this great republic." A memorial pool eighteen feet in diameter sits in front of the statue and serves as a wishing well while evergreens immediately behind the statue and the blue outline of hills in the distance make a suitably picturesque tableau.

As you continue westward, the river emerges on your right now and follows alongside you for a few miles. Just after the river breaks away from the side of the road, you find the entrance to the **Mohawk Trail State Forest,** which is perhaps the best place on the road to stop to consume the contents of your picnic basket or to take a walk. Facilities here include a three-mile hiking trail and seventy-five picnic tables. But if frugality is next to cleanliness, you should be forewarned that there is a charge for park usage.

The unclogged air and woodsy grounds of the Mohawk Trail State Forest can draw you into a longer stay than you had planned. But keep in mind that the most spectacular scenery on this route is awaiting. The refreshing views of the first few miles soon become more and more dynamic as the legendary Berkshire Hills start dominating the vistas like a basketball team over a kindergarten class, surrounding you on all sides and leaving you with no doubt that you're driving through a valley. The rolling mounds that had been so far off in the distance are now considerably closer as you head toward the afternoon sun and the road is girded by evergreens and maples.

Then the climbing begins and for all but the driver, who should have his eyes peeled to the road under all circumstances, the views are magnificent. From Florida (the "Welcome to Florida" sign is a favorite of photographers) to North Adams, a distance of about four miles, you'll be ascending, winding, and swerving. From Eastern, Western, and Whitcomb summits (the latter, at twenty-two hundred feet above sea level, being the highest point on the trail), you can see for miles.

The harried driver doesn't get much opportunity to relax on the descent, either. There's a sign that forewarns you of steep downhill curves. And woe to the motorist who ignores admonitions about the infamous hairpin turn. It's not as bad as some people would have you think, but it is sharp and does sneak up on you. Just take it slowly and there should be no problem.

The Mohawk Trail itself continues to the New York State border, but the beginning of the small industrial city of North Adams is regarded by many as the end of the most scenic part.

ACCESS

MOHAWK TRAIL FOLIAGE TOUR. Directions to the beginning of the tour: From Interstate 91 exit 26, follow the signs to Route 2 west. **Allow** 2 hours.

Arms outstretched to greet the morning sun, Hail to the Sunrise *is dedicated to the Mohawk Indians, for whom the trail was named.*

The Mohawk Trail State Forest is perhaps the best place on the road to stop to consume the contents of your picnic basket.

One of the most photographed churches in New England is the Litchfield Congregational Church, which you can see (and photograph) at the start of this Connecticut foliage trip.

DIANE LEVY

The Litchfield Hills

Litchfield, Connecticut, the starting point of a fifty-mile foliage trip through the hills of the north-western part of the state, was snubbed by the railroad in the nineteenth century, and that may have been the town's biggest blessing in its three centuries of history. The railroad placed its tracks in the Naugatuck and Housatonic valleys instead. Industry followed the railroad like cats to cream, and Litchfield was left on its own, not growing and prospering like neighboring communities. The result is that today, according to a survey done by the National Park Service of the Department of the Interior, "Litchfield is probably New England's finest surviving example of a typical late-eighteenth-century New England town."

"Litchfield is probably New England's finest surviving example of a typical late-eighteenth-century New England town."

You may need an entire day to explore all that **Litchfield** has to offer, but that is best saved for another time when the Litchfield Hills aren't glowing in their autumn best. It's better during the fantastic fall show to stay outdoors, focusing your eyes on the combination of manmade and natural sights that fully complement each other. Instead of gray industry in the center of Litchfield, there are handsome Colonial buildings surrounding an immaculately manicured village green. The Congregational Church, with its white skyline-dominating steeple, is one of the most photographed in New England — and is about as striking as any you will ever see.

As you depart from the green, heading north on Route 63 (North Street) through the village, you'll notice that the buildings are reminiscent of the early days of television — everything is in black and white. Not to say it is bland. Hardly! The well-kept eighteenth-century homes, all white with black shutters, make impressive eye-catchers. Some are still privately owned while others are open to the public as historic museums. Notable houses are the Beecher Homestead (family of author Harriet Beecher Stowe) and the site of the Pierce Academy (first academy for girls in America, dating from 1792). This street, along with other parts of Litchfield, has been declared a National Historic Site.

You just have a chance to start enjoying the scenery when the village of **Goshen** sneaks up on you. At first you may think Goshen is getting in the way of your view. On the contrary, Goshen is a part of the view. Just over six miles from the green in Litchfield, this village of about seventeen hundred is smaller and less polished than Litchfield, and therefore a little more typical of rural northwestern Connecticut. And another thing: it's not all black and white. One of the first buildings of note you'll come across is the white and blue Goshen Historical Society on the right side of the street. You'll next likely notice the oversized gold eagle sitting atop the 1824 Federal-style society building. But put your eyes back in your head; the eagle is actually a woodcarving covered with gold leaf. No one knows exactly who carved the big bird, but it is believed to have been done by an itinerant worker years and years ago in honor of the Eagle Academy, which was the structure's original tenant. The society's weather vane, also done in gold leaf, was created in the early 1970s as an exact replica of the 1824 original. Although the society museum keeps no regular hours in the fall, you can call (203) 491-2665 a couple of days in advance to be given a special appointment to examine the old clocks, furniture, tools, and paintings inside.

At the junction of routes 63 and 4 in the center of Goshen, you may notice the Old Town Hall and the Congregational Church, located across the street from each other. Although the Old Town Hall, bedecked in white with green trim, *looks* impressive, it was actually

At first you may think Goshen is getting in the way of your view. On the contrary, Goshen is a part of the view.

DIANE LEVY

No one knows who actually made that gold eagle, a wood carving covered by gold leaf, that's mounted on the pediment of the Goshen Historical Society.

built in 1895 — which makes it seem almost new in this town. But the church, an 1835 creation, is the pride of Goshen, as it was the site of the ordination of the missionaries who set out to preach in what is now the state of Hawaii.

Taking a left onto Route 4, heading toward West Goshen, enables you to admire some of Mother Nature's landmarks as well as those built by man. The placid **Tyler Lake** is just a few miles past the center of Goshen, and the **Mohawk State Forest** is not far beyond the lake. All the while, there are foliage-smothered rolling hills on your left as you motor westward; on your right side, thick clusters of trees cling to the roadside.

Horses and red barns pick up where the trunks and branches recede, dotting the face of the landscape now and then like freckles. Indeed, there seems to be a sort of irregular pattern emerging as you drive past the bucolic sights; hills thickly laden with trees give way to a small group of white clapboarded homes that yield to equestrian settings. Then, once again, there are the maples and elms and birches.

About the only interruption one could put up with along this route of pastoral pulchritude emerges soon, but not without a few hints. The first sign you see for the **covered bridge,** which is one of Connecticut's few, is at the junction of routes 4 and 128, about five miles from Goshen. Pick up Route 128 and stay on it for three and a half more miles. After descending a formidable decline, you see the red bridge in the distance, with a sizable hilly backdrop.

Though the recipient of some cosmetic surgery now and then, the bridge essentially appears the same as it did when it was constructed back in 1837. It was last touched up in 1973, when it was raised about two and a half feet to prevent damage caused by ice jams, known to clog the Housatonic River during brutal winters. The bridge is picturesque in its own right, but it becomes even more of an attraction when you consider that it's one of just four covered bridges in the state, and is the only one of the four that's on a state highway.

After crossing the bridge (be careful — it's only one lane), take a right onto Route 7 and head north. On this stretch, known as the Ethan Allen Highway, you will find some of the most colorful and scenic vistas on this trip. As you make your way north, hills surround you on all sides, and verdant pines and other evergreens add even more hues to the scenery.

Continue on Route 7 for a little over twelve miles until you reach the junction with Route 44 in **Canaan.** Take a right and be patient. In a little under a mile, the drive-ins and shops you see give way to another panorama of hills, barns, horses, and autumn colors. An attractive Congregational church with the Litchfield Hills in the background appears shortly on

You'll notice that the buildings are reminiscent of the early days of television — everything is in black and white.

the right side as you cross into **East Canaan.** Then you approach the village of Norfolk.

At the junction with Route 272, you may want to continue on Route 44 into the attractive center of Norfolk. But a pleasant side trip, especially if it is a clear day, is to **Haystack Mountain State Park.** The entrance is on Route 272, just two tenths of a mile from Route 44. After driving one and a third miles up a narrow but good road, you can enjoy the view right from your car in a small parking area or you can hike a switchback trail to the stone tower at the mountain top, a little under a half mile from the parking area. Looking north, you can see into Massachusetts. Picnic tables are located by the roadside.

Back on Route 44, the center of **Norfolk** is less than a mile away. One of the younger towns in the state, relatively speaking (it wasn't incorporated until 1758), Norfolk boasts a richly verdant triangular village green framed by some dazzling buildings. Whitehouse, a mansion bathed in glorious colonial white with black trim, sits at the northwest corner of the green and serves as the main building of the Yale University Summer School of Music and Art. The cranberry-red gabled structure with the fluted Spanish tile roof at the northeast end of the green is the Norfolk library, while the blanched Church of Christ was built next to Whitehouse in 1814. Facing the green at its southeastern point is the Historical Society, which has formerly been an academy, a town hall, a jail, and a court. On the green's southern tip you'll find the Eldridge Fountain, designed by famed architect Stanford White.

Before leaving the center of this former bustling summer resort, take a look at the signpost located on the green directly across from Whitehouse. Without a doubt, it's the most picturesque mileage marker on the route. The names of the nearby communities as well as the likenesses of the wild rabbit and deer next to them are of a distinct nineteenth-century style. This enchanting sign is a recently reproduced copy of a sign in the Historical Society Museum. If you're interested, you can set up an appointment to tour the museum by calling (203) 542-5178 at least three days in advance.

The road becomes a little wider as you motor on Route 44 (now called the Albany Turnpike), heading east toward Winsted, ten miles away and the ending point on this foliage tour.

ACCESS

LITCHFIELD HILLS FOLIAGE TOUR. Directions to the beginning of the tour: Eastbound: From Interstate 84 in Waterbury, take Route 8 north to exit 42; follow Route 118 west to the green. Westbound: From Interstate 84 exit 39 in Farmington, follow Route 4 west; continue until Route 4 becomes Route 118, and then follow the road west to the green. **Allow** 2½ hours.

The only thing Norfolk, Connecticut's Whitehouse has in common with the more famous building of the same name is the color. But this one, property of Yale University's School of Music and Art, has more beautiful surroundings.

On the Ethan Allen Highway, you will find some of the most colorful and scenic views on this trip.

An original Revere bell sits inside this 1834 First Congregational Church in Alfred, a picturesque town you reach at the end of the trip.

In the early part of this century, the local schoolhouse straddled the state line; the children sat in New Hampshire while the teacher instructed them from Maine.

Foliage in the Pine Tree State

The official nickname of Maine is the Pine Tree State and the reasoning behind the naming is wholly evident, even during the peak fall colors of autumn. Along this eighty-odd-mile foliage route through southwestern Maine and a sliver of New Hampshire, a substantial number of dark-green pines form a picturesque mix with the typical reds and yellows and golds you expect. And certainly, you'd be hard pressed to travel any great distance in New England without passing through cozy villages, seeing historic buildings, and inspecting noteworthy examples of architecture; there's plenty of all here.

Sanford, a town of a little over ten thousand inhabitants, is the starting point for the trip; from the junction of routes 109, 11, and 202, head north on Route 11 past a few miles of commercial and residential buildings. Sanford suddenly becomes **Springvale,** which becomes **Shapleigh** as you continue on Route 11. About one and eight tenths miles after the Shapleigh town line, make a sharp right turn to stay on Route 11; if you went straight ahead, you'd be on Route 109.

Route 11 bends to the left in Shapleigh, and upon your exodus from that area, the abundance of pines may cause you to forget just what time of year it is. The road continues for about four miles, in which you'll see few fall colors and many green or brown pine needles on branches and ground before you again see the brighter colors intermixed. Note the many birch trees that seem to take over when the pines disappear.

Turn left onto Route 110 toward Wakefield, New Hampshire, and continue on this narrow, tree-shaded, two-lane road for three and a half miles as it crosses the border into New Hampshire. At the junction with Route 153, turn right toward Effingham and Province Lake for some of both man and nature's most appealing allurements. You're then immersed in golds and yellows that are close at hand as the vista of **Province Lake** and its hilly backdrop soon come into view. The road makes a sharp right turn as you approach the lake — the arrows on well-placed signs show you where — and then you can enjoy both the inspiring view close up and the distant bluish peaks poking up beyond the nearby mounds. There are some sandy shoulders on the right if you'd like to pull over and luxuriate in the surroundings for a bit. But watch where you wander, since much of the land nearby is private property.

You're back in Maine before you realize it as you continue up Route 153; the state line crosses over the eastern side of the lake, which the road parallels. Barely two miles later, though, the road snakes its way back into New Hampshire as you motor into **South Effing-**

ham. The border-hugging location of this town has led to more than its share of peculiar situations. School spirit with a split personality existed in the early part of this century when the local schoolhouse straddled the state line; the children sat in New Hampshire while the teacher instructed them from Maine. Recently, the post office in South Effingham (known locally as Taylor City for a family of long-time residence) was moved to another building since locals had unknowingly been posting New Hampshire letters from Maine land!

As you enter South Effingham, observe the South Effingham Union Church. With its noticeably angled windows and doors, this white wooden church looks more complex than some of the more basic white-steepled meeting houses and churches that sit at the heads of many New England town squares; one reason may be that this church was built in 1891, quite late compared to many others. The church is recognized for its original interior stencil work, done in an obviously religious motif. If you're interested in taking a peek inside, ask somebody in the Taylor City Store across the street to open it for you. It's free, but there is a donation box in case you feel inclined to contribute.

The colors of the leaves along Route 153 are rivaled only by the colorful local history of the area along this route. The schoolhouse and post office tales are lusterless compared to the stories of the village rivalries between Center Effingham (or Drakes Corner, to area residents) and Effingham proper (known throughout as Lords Hill). Name calling and accusations reached their peaks in the great church-bell stealing incident of the early 1830s. Members of the Drakes Corner Baptist Church, who claimed ownership of the Paul Revere bell that was hanging in the Lords Hill Meeting House, stole into the village one night, maneuvered their way into the church, and brought the bell back to their own church, two miles down the road. The Lords Hill folk, who were not the type to take such violations lying down, stood their ground, stated that they rightfully owned the bell, and made quite an issue of it. It wound up in the state legislature, which ruled that Lords Hill had more of a claim to the bell than did Drakes Corner.

The original Baptist church, which had been built in 1822, no longer exists, but its replacement, sitting on the same spot as the infamous place of worship, dates from 1844. And the **Lords Hill** Meeting House, which was constructed in 1798 as the first meeting house in Effingham (and later remodeled twice in the nineteenth century), still stands proudly across from the village green. Features include green shutters, white belfry, weather vane, and Paul Revere & Sons bell.

More than historic churches exists in these two lore-laden villages, however. What was once Drakes Store in **Drakes Corner,** a building that dates back to

Members of the Drakes Corner Baptist Church stole into the Lords Hill Meeting House one night, and brought the Paul Revere bell back to their own church, two miles down the road.

MICHAEL QUAN

Something to take stock of at the Effingham Historical Society, just across the Maine border in New Hampshire.

In 1981, Alfred was selected by Newsweek *magazine as one of the country's ten most perfect small towns.*

MICHAEL QUAN

The town library has a close brush with a nearby tree in Limerick, located north of Ossipee Mills.

1820 and that also housed one of the state's first photographers' studios (tintypes from the 1840s have been found here) is now the Effingham Historical Society. Old tools, harnesses, photographs, a loom, and a flax wheel are some of the items displayed inside. For an appointment to see tangible records of old Effingham, write (at least a week before you visit) to the Historical Society at P.O. Box 33, South Effingham, NH 03882. By the way, the weathered pillory and stocks sitting in front of the building have no historical significance; they were made by a local artist for the Bicentennial.

The Masonic Charitable Institute, which you can see from Route 153 and can reach by taking a left just past the historical society, has more of a past. It was built between 1858 and 1860, was at one time an academy, and is now the town hall (on the first floor) and the Masonic Hall (second floor). The privately owned farm across the road once was a dormitory for students and was, at a later point, an inn.

Up the road a bit and back in Effingham proper — er, excuse me, Lords Hill — the square, century-old bandstand on the village green is the site of summertime concerts but sits empty in the fall. That white building with the attached barns across from the bandstand on Route 153 dates from 1785, and through its nearly two centuries has been a tavern and inn; it's now privately owned. The first normal school in New Hampshire is found a bit out of town, farther up Route 153; it's the roughly square, two-and-a-half-story, white wooden building identified by an historic marker. The naming of the first normal school does not mean that other schools were a little out of kilter. The name comes from the French *école normale*, an original model school after which other teacher-training schools were patterned; any school that trained teachers, especially those who instruct young children, was referred to as a "normal school."

Leaving Effingham behind, continue on Route 153 for another three miles to the junction with Route 25. Turn right toward Kezar Falls, Maine, and cross the Ossipee River; you then parallel the river for about one and a half miles. As you enter Maine again you'll start noticing the many pines that once more mix fittingly with the trees of many colors. A little over two miles past the grand sign welcoming you to Maine, you'll see another sign informing you of a covered bridge ahead — a rare entity in Maine, with only ten covered bridges remaining in the state. Turn right onto Route 160 and after a half mile, you'll see the worn gray **Parsonfield-Porter Historical Bridge** on your left, spanning the Ossipee River. It's no longer passable by car, although you can walk through it. To reach it, take a left onto a narrow unnamed road reached after crossing the river, then take another quick left to the bridge.

Next, backtrack on Route 160 to Route 25 and turn

right, continuing through the village of **Porter.** After leaving Porter and passing through **Kezar Falls** (Route 25 twists and turns, but is well marked), you'll find a pine-shaded rest area on your right. There are about ten picnic tables, including some with grills, in addition to a small walking trail and public rest rooms.

Until the junction with Route 5, about two and a half miles ahead, Route 25 is a relatively wide main road with some pretty trees. After taking a right onto Route 5 heading south, however, you'll have the pleasure of taking in some of the most beautiful scenery on the route. Trees of all shades — including, of course, many pines — embrace the road, and foliage-packed hills are to your sides and in front of you. You'll find some overviews here that you won't find on other portions of the trip; one particularly beautiful vista lies on your left, just outside the town of Limerick. Continue through the villages of **Ossipee Mills** and **Waterboro Center,** where the land gradually flattens. After Waterboro Center, turn right at a sign that indicates the way to Route 202. From this connector, take routes 202 west and 4 south toward Alfred.

As you approach **Alfred,** you'll notice a bit more loftiness in the landscape as there are some hills to your right. Alfred itself is an attractive town of just under nineteen hundred that in 1981 was selected by *Newsweek* magazine as one of the country's ten most perfect small towns. A well-groomed town green sits directly in the center, while throughout the town are fine examples of nineteenth-century architecture.

A sparkling white church with a black shingled roof sits across from the green. It dates from 1834 and the bell you see is, like the one in Lords Hill, an original Revere bell. The history behind the bell suggests that one of Revere's sons must have created it on an early Monday morning or late Friday afternoon; it apparently did not emit a proper sound while tolling and was sent back to Boston to be recast. It no longer tolls, but is hooked to a striker and is struck every hour. The Thomas clock on the church was in disrepair for many years, but is now wound regularly and keeps an accurate count of minutes and hours.

So if a quick glance up there tells you that time is marching, you may want to finish up this foliage trip. About one mile out of Alfred on routes 202 and 4, there's a rest area with picnic tables where you might stop for a lunch that you missed before. Otherwise it's back, on the same road, to your starting point.

ACCESS

WESTERN MAINE FOLIAGE TOUR. Directions to the beginning of the tour: From Interstate 95 exit 2, turn left onto Route 109 and continue to the junction of routes 109, 11, and 202 in Sanford. **Allow** 2½ hours.

MICHAEL QUAN

Closed to cars but not to pedestrians, the Parsonfield-Porter Historical Bridge is one of the few remaining covered bridges in Maine.

The history behind the bell suggests that one of Revere's sons must have created it on an early Monday morning or late Friday afternoon.

The Currier & Ives Corner

The state of New Hampshire likes to refer to the Monadnock Region, tucked into the state's southwestern section, as its Currier and Ives Corner. If you associate the nineteenth-century duo's famed lithographs with visions of white steepled churches, town squares, still ponds, and old meeting houses, you'll find enough such scenes along this seventy-odd-mile foliage trip to convince you the tag is fitting. The narrow country roads and small villages represent, to many, perfect storybook New England.

Starting at the junction of routes 101 and 202 in **Peterborough,** head north on Route 202 for two and a third miles, then turn right onto Route 136 toward Greenfield. This tree-lined road takes you by the entrance to **Greenfield State Park,** a good place for a picnic; there are over two hundred tables here, about half of which are accompanied with fireplaces. After Labor Day, there is no charge to enter the park, but after Columbus Day, the facilities — including rest rooms and water — are shut down and fires are not permitted. You still can use the picnic tables, though, as well as a few walking paths, each about a half mile in length.

Back on Route 136, head toward **Greenfield,** whose historic combination town meeting house and Union Congregational Church sits about one and a half miles away. It's the oldest of the few meeting houses still used for both religious and secular town gatherings; meetings take place on the building's first floor, while the church is one floor above. Built in 1795, it has been altered on a number of occasions and once, in 1867, the whole edifice was turned ninety degrees to its present situation so it would face the then-planned Main Street.

Turn left at the town center, continuing on Route 136 north. You get a good look at the meeting house's clock, installed during Greenfield's centennial celebration in 1891, and weather vane. (A 1975 referendum suggesting the clock be electrified was voted down in favor of repairing the original works.) You pass by the old church cemetery, and then through some of residential Greenfield. But after a couple of miles, the only manmade touches amid the roadside trees are some stone fences a few feet from your car. (Study one closely — you'll see that there is no mortar holding the stones together.)

Continue straight on Route 136 through the junction with Route 47 and into the center of **Francestown,** which is one of the region's most picturesque villages. There aren't many towns that can claim main streets filled exclusively with houses built in the nineteenth century. That's the case here, however, with the majority of these residences put up between 1800 and 1830; construction dates are posted by many of the

The Union Congregational Church in Greenfield dates from 1795 and is one of the few New England meeting houses still used for both religious and secular town gatherings.

There aren't many towns that, like Francestown, can claim main streets filled exclusively with houses built in the nineteenth century.

The town of Hancock epitomizes, to many, small-town New England. The meeting house and bandstand are two of the reasons.

front doors. Expect to find Georgian- and Federal-style homes predominating, with a few Capes thrown in to remind you that this is New England.

This town, in another reflection of its regional heritage, is not without its meeting house. The Unitarian Meeting House, in the town center, was built in 1801. Across the street is the town hall, constructed in 1847 and originally the home of Francestown Academy. This academy didn't begin here, though — it started in another building, and locals will proudly point out that a New Hampshire favorite son and the fourteenth President of the United States, Franklin Pierce, attended school there.

Another illustrious figure in state political history, Levi Woodbury, is honored by a marker in front of the town hall. For those of you to whom this is not a household name, Woodbury (1789-1851) served at various points as United States Senator, United States Supreme Court Justice, Secretary of the Navy, and Secretary of War. The big, yellow house directly across from the meeting house was his home for many years and is now privately owned. Titus Brown, another local boy who made good by serving in the United States House of Representatives, lived in the interesting Georgian brick building that now is the town library.

Route 47 takes you past the Crotched Mountain Ski Area, where you get some appealing views of distant color-filled hills on your way to **Bennington;** in the center of Bennington take a quick right, then a quick left, following the signs for Route 31. After you cross a small brook, you're on routes 47 and 31, which you follow for about two tenths of a mile. Turn left onto Route 202 and after a mile, take a right onto Route 137 in the direction of Hancock. Continue for just over three miles and then take a right onto routes 123 and 137. The center of the lovely town of **Hancock** is just one tenth of a mile away.

If you've been itching for an opportunity to raise yourself from your upholstered seat and take a relaxing stroll, this is one fine place to do so. The buildings in Hancock are wonderful to look at, and there's just so much you can see from the window of a fleeting car. A few hundred feet from the town center, the gray-and-white John Hancock Inn, with its distinctive Greek Revival entrance, is the oldest operating inn in the state; it was constructed in 1789, but has been altered since. Hancock's version of the town meeting house, built in 1820 to replace one destroyed by fire one year earlier, was constructed on the town green. It was moved across the street in 1851. On the green now is a brown-and-white bandstand that, while dating only from 1909, still forms a picturesque vision of what many feel is an archetypal New England village center. Because Hancock residents donated labor, the bandstand was raised for an entire cost of $120.60.

Turn left at the green, head down Route 137 south toward Dublin, and you'll see a few more stone fences and a lot of foliage-covered maples. About three and a half miles from the center of Hancock, turn right off Route 137 toward Harrisville. (A sign points the way.) A narrow thoroughfare, this unnamed road takes you past **Skatutakee Lake,** where for a little over a mile you'll have a water-filled foreground to a colorful background. Just after you pass the lake, turn right at the stop sign and drive toward Nelson. Your destination here, however, is not the town of Nelson (found farther up), but **Harrisville,** an old mill town one third mile from the turn. The center of Harrisville looks distinctly different from most of this part of New Hampshire because the prevalent building material here is industrial red brick and not the homey white wood you've been seeing. The mill has left, but the building that housed it, as well as those that housed workers, are now used as both commercial and residential space. It's an interesting place to walk around.

Off your feet and back in your car, backtrack next for the one third mile, then continue straight toward Dublin. This road, also unmarked, but known as New Harrisville Road by those who want to be official, meets with Route 101 in a little under three miles. At the junction with Route 101, you can detour to the left for a short jaunt into the center of **Dublin.** (The highest town in New England, at 1,493 feet above sea level, Dublin is also the home of *Yankee* Magazine.) Then do an about-face and head west toward Marlborough.

Route 101 is the main highway bisecting the entire

The gray-and-white John Hancock Inn, with its distinctive Greek Revival entrance, is the oldest operating inn in the state.

southern tier of the state, so expect it to be substantially more crowded than the earlier, ribbon-like back roads. This is not to say that it's not esthetically pleasing; within a mile, you'll be curving around **Dublin Lake,** a quiet, blue body of water girded by trees and backed by Mount Monadnock. There are shoulders alongside and across from the pond, but the angle of the curve on this heavily trafficked road is sharp. Be careful if you pull over to enjoy the classic view.

Stay on Route 101 for a little under seven miles after you leave the lakeside. Just over three miles after the sign marking the entrance into **Marlborough,** take a left onto Route 124, heading south. After about a half mile of residential Marlborough's buildings, you'll be immersed in a wooded landscape with magnificent fall colors. The road curves and winds amid the trees, and about seven miles past Marlborough on the left side is the quintessential view of the southern slope of Mount Monadnock. This close-up perspective makes it appear even more commanding than it does from the many distant vantage points.

Route 124 becomes Main Street in **Jaffrey Center** before three miles pass under your tires. This is another small-town main thoroughfare that you might want to take the time to explore with leg power. About five hundred yards from the street are the old meeting house (built between 1775 and 1780) and the old schoolhouse (built in the early 1800s). The cemetery behind the meeting house may be more historic than the building itself; author Willa Cather and local heroes Hannah Davis and Amos Fortune are buried there. (Davis made and sold the country's first wooden bandboxes, while Fortune was a slave who purchased his freedom, established a tannery, and at his death left money behind for the church and schools of this town.) An interesting variation on the local New England church is Saint Patrick's, located a little farther up on Route 124; it's made entirely of stone.

Follow Route 124 through Jaffrey Center into **Jaffrey;** at the junction with Route 137 in the center of Jaffrey (as opposed to the center of Jaffrey Center, not to be confusing by any means) turn left and head north, back to Dublin. Follow this pleasurable six-odd-mile road to the junction with Route 101; then turn right toward Peterborough and the end of this circular trip through the Monadnock Region.

ACCESS

MONADNOCK REGION FOLIAGE TOUR. Directions to the beginning of the tour: Eastbound: From Interstate 91 exit 3, follow Route 9 east to Keene, where the road becomes Route 101; continue to the junction of routes 101 and 202, in Peterborough. Westbound: From Route 3 exit 7W, take Route 101A west to Route 101, and follow Route 101 to the junction with Route 202 in Peterborough. **Allow** 2½ hours.

Amos Fortune was a slave who purchased his freedom, established a tannery, and at his death left money behind for the church and schools of this town.

CHAPTER VII

Serendipity

And then there are those attractions in New England that won't fit neatly into any concise category, yet are the kinds of amusements that represent other facets of work and play in this area.

Some of these pay tribute to past and present industrial and agricultural greatness. You can have the chance once again (or, for many of us, for the first time), to let the familiar clang, clang, clang jog your aural nerves as you ride along the once daily used trolley tracks. Or you can look at pretty faces all day in a museum offering homage to a once resounding local clock industry. Or finally get the opportunity to see the work that goes into the making of all that savory Vermont maple syrup we matter-of-factly pour over waffles and French toast on Sunday mornings.

In the same vein, diversity has also always been a hallmark of our leisure-time activities. In fact, there's always been a ludicrous sort of juxtaposition of possibilities: one weekend, you can be studiously analyzing the subtle colorings of a Franz Hals portrait in a formal art gallery, while just a week later you can be donning old jeans and a flannel shirt and tromping through an orchard picking Baldwins and Macouns from overhanging apple-tree branches. Perhaps New Englanders enjoy their free hours so much because there are always more things to do than there is time to do them.

This chapter is called Serendipity, which, according to *The American Heritage Dictionary*, is defined as "the faculty of making fortunate and unexpected discoveries by accident." We'll go that two better: the unexpected and accidental factors have been removed, while the fortunate discoveries remain.

There are all sorts of places you can stumble upon in New England that don't fit neatly into any one category — like the Anheuser-Busch, Inc. Brewery in Merrimack, New Hampshire.

There are plenty more where these came from: Applecrest Farm Orchards in Hampton Falls.

Applecrest

Eve didn't chomp on a peach in the Garden of Eden, Sir Isaac Newton wasn't clunked on the head by an orange, and New York City isn't known as the Big Pear. Apples are the stuff of which legends and nicknames are made, and at Applecrest Farm Orchards in the seacoast town of Hampton Falls, New Hampshire, the famed fruit is celebrated. There is always some excuse for a preplanned celebration here, and even when no festive ode to the apple is on tap, there's a hefty acreage of pick-your-owns waiting for your pull.

Applecrest Farm is a family-run operation; Ben Wagner, who manages the enterprise with his mother, Jean, and brother, Peter, emphasizes that his goal is to make Applecrest a fun place for a family to spend an afternoon. Although Wagner says there will most likely be no major price difference between apples bought here and those from the grocery store, the local supermarket is no place to ride a pony, enjoy a picnic, or indulge in an apple-pie-eating contest. Besides, by its very name, a pick-your-own offers a chance to choose what you feel are the prime models of apple pulchritude. The freshest and juiciest are within your reach.

Those who are as green as unripe apples when it comes to hand-to-stem labor will be afforded whatever information they need.

Strawberries (in late June), blueberries (in early August), and pumpkins (starting Labor Day weekend), are also pickable here, but apples are the *raison d'être* for Applecrest Farm. **Apple-picking** season commences on Labor Day weekend and extends into mid-October, although there is always the chance that climate and demand will alter the schedule a bit. For a couple of weeks following the end of pick-your-own season, you're invited to scurry around under the trees and fill your container with those apples that have fallen from trees and are now scattered about the ground. It is during this drop season that, according to

Wagner, there will most likely be some kind of price break as compared to paying retail.

Driving along Route 88 within a few miles of the Applecrest Farm store, you're likely to view what seem like more apple trees alongside the road than there are clam bars on the coastline. You're welcome to park by the roadside anywhere that you see workers stationed by gates in front of the orchards. You'll be given a bag and then directed (or, on weekends, transported by a trailer) to a spot where the heavy pickings are going on. Here another employee will offer all the answers to your how-to's. Those who are as green as unripe apples when it comes to hand-to-stem labor will be afforded whatever information they need regarding where to start, how to pick, and what varieties are on which trees. McIntosh, Red and Golden Delicious, and Cortland are the most commonly picked. As you exit, your harvest is weighed and you pay by the pound.

Horsing around by the orchards may not seem to be the wisest of ideas, but the Wagners make a special exception where kids are concerned. Picking one's own produce being as popular a pastime as it is, there can be a short wait at the entrance gate while the trailer is transporting other pickers to the trees. Knowing how children can lose patience standing in one spot waiting for something to happen, and how parents can be exasperated by whiny cries of "When do we go?" the Wagners have been offering **pony rides** to the youngsters for quite some time. The rides are free of charge and are offered on weekends during all pick-your-own seasons.

With five hundred acres of land (about seventy-five of which are allotted for pick your owns), there's always plenty of space for picnics and, says Ben Wagner, you're most welcome to bring your basket and savor the tree-studded outdoors. Want a more active form of recreation? Horseback riders and joggers are also invited to use the grounds. The Wagners ask only that you check in with personnel at the market or on the grounds in advance. Here, you'll be told of a place where you can picnic, ride, or jog without tripping over somebody else's dishes, hoofs, or sneakers.

The appeal of apples stems not only from their taste but also from the variety of things you can do with them. Pies and cider are eternal favorites that conjure up thoughts, even among the most unfeeling grouches, of crisp autumn days when the leaves are as picturesque as the air is piquing. Both delectables are sold in the **Applecrest Farm Orchards shop** and are made by Applecrest employees. Russet cider, a blend of 50 per cent Russet apples and 50 per cent other varieties, is one of the Wagners' special offerings; another one that should please cider insiders is the cider doughnuts made right here. Nonapple goodies from the bakery? Blueberry and cherry pies as well as

Knowing how children can lose patience standing in one spot and waiting, the Wagners offer free pony rides to the youngsters.

On Miracle Mac Day there's free apple pie and ice cream for the taking.

At Applecrest, special events such as this wagon ride are meant to be especially exciting for youngsters, but don't tell that to all the grown-ups who have as much fun as their children.

cookies, along with the apple pies, cider, and doughnuts, are sold year round.

As are the apples. Bags and bags of them stock the store, even in the dead of winter. And the list of varieties extends beyond those available as pick-your-owns. Russets, Baldwins, Macouns, and Rhode Island Greenings supplement the varieties that you can hand-pick. (All the varieties available to those who pick their own, by the way, are also sold here for the benefit of those who can't come during pick-your-own season or would simply rather have others do the picking.) Like a proud father, Ben Wagner beams as he discusses the extensive storage units at Applecrest, which enable the Wagners to sell apples during any season. But apples are not the limit. Other seasonal produce you can buy (but not pick) includes pears, peaches, plums, nectarines, corn, and acorn, butternut, and buttercup squash. And what would a northern New England delectables shop be without its full share of maple syrup, cheeses, and jams and jellies stocking the shelves?

Although with all this abundance Applecrest Farm Orchards may itself seem like a virtual celebration of the apple, the management feels that free **special occasions** should be set aside for praising its favorite fruit. Stuffing yourself to the gills with apple pie while trying to out-gorge your neighbor is but one of the regular events at the annual Harvest Festival, held the last Sunday in September. Prizes like apples or T-shirts are given to winners of the apple-pie-eating contest, while if you prefer not to indulge you can observe square-dancing demonstrations (or join in, if you wish) or simply grab a pitcher (of cider, of course), sit back amid the leaves, and listen to a bluegrass or other live band picking away. Want to learn just what goes into making cider or what's involved in harvesting apples? The New Hampshire Farm Museum

NEAL HAMBERG

always presents exhibits for the occasion.

Though the Harvest Festival may be the core of the apple events here, it's by no means the only special day. A tractor takes the place of Donner and Blitzen as Santa Claus drives it onto the grounds of Applecrest for the annual Christmas Festival, held the first Sunday in December. And though apples are not traditionally a Christmas food, don't tell that to anyone here; they decorate the farm Christmas tree. Well, they do come in red and green, don't they? Hot mulled cider is offered in addition to the old fashioned holiday treat of roasted chestnuts, and this is a fine time to look for your Christmas tree or wreath. The sounds of carolers, meanwhile, make wonderful background music for your cider sipping or tree searching.

Other yearly special days? Miracle Mac Day, held in late March or early April, gives the Wagners a chance to promote their apples, picked some months earlier and kept in controlled-atmosphere storage over the course of the winter. Displays explaining the process are shown while, on the lighter side, apples are sold at a reduced price and there's free apple pie and ice cream for the taking. (There's usually a limit of one helping per person; who wants to waddle back to his car anyway?) Depending on Mother Nature's moods, apple-blossom time often peaks around Mother's Day. The orchards look like a sea of cotton balls, and picnickers are, of course, welcome.

On Mother's Day itself, a free apple tree is given to anyone who makes a purchase of ten dollars or more. Ben Wagner talks about the families that have been coming back on this day for the past few years and have a half dozen trees in their backyards that are continually bearing fruit (although he also cautions prospective apple growers that there is know-how, care, and luck involved in growing anything).

There won't be any picnics or picking in the heart of winter, but in conjunction with a local sporting goods store, Applecrest offers cross-country skiing through the orchards. There are about a dozen Appletour Trails groomed for your skiing pleasure, with names like "Easy as Apple Pie," "Cortland Cruise," and "Jonathan's Jaunt." Trail maps are supplied, lessons are available, and equipment can be rented. All skiers over twelve years of age are charged for use of the trails.

ACCESS

APPLECREST FARM ORCHARDS. Directions: From the junction of routes 1 and 88, follow Route 88 north 2½ miles. **Season:** Open for pick-your-owns late June through mid autumn, subject to availability of produce. Store open all year. **Days:** Daily. **Allow** 2 to 3 hours for picking, browsing, and partaking in other scheduled activities. **Telephone:** (603) 926-3721.

During drop season in late October, you will probably get some kind of price break. But that's not the main interest of this young man, who cares more how they'll taste in a warm apple pie.

Trail maps are supplied to skiers, lessons are available, and equipment can be rented.

While they don't actually perform at the hamlet in Merrimack, Baldy, Prince, Major, and the rest of the Clydesdales do live here. You can see them after your tour of the brewery.

Even if you're not an equestrian, you should still walk the quarter mile to the stables; the Clydesdales are big and sturdy, yet graceful.

The Busch Brewery & America's Stonehenge

"It's a beer drinker's paradise," our guide said as visitors on the Anheuser-Busch, Inc., Merrimack Brewery Tour and Clydesdale Hamlet gaped in awe at three stories of beer-storage tanks. Beer guzzlers in the crowd overwhelmingly nodded agreement. It was the end of the tour, however, that spelled wonder for those who take pleasure in less potent thrills as they gazed admiringly at the famous Clydesdale horses.

Meanwhile, over in North Salem, New Hampshire, about twenty miles away, some onlookers stared in awe while others skeptically shook their heads as they strolled among stone ruins of foundations and structures labeled "oracle chamber," "tomb of lost souls," and "sacrificial table." Nobody really knows the when, how, what, or why of America's Stonehenge, formerly Mystery Hill, but there is evidence to date these ruins before the time of the Pilgrims — three to four thousand years before the Pilgrims.

To start out your day with something less cerebral and dwell on some of the heavier stuff later, motor your way over to the **Anheuser-Busch, Inc. Brewery** in Merrimack, between Nashua and Manchester. Tours are not given at regularly scheduled intervals here, but instead are offered whenever a crowd forms. Things were hopping at the brewery on the midwinter Sunday afternoon we visited, and tours were led through the facility on the average of every twenty minutes.

Everyone having different tastes, individual highlights are hard to pinpoint. Licking one's chops while eyeballing those gargantuan tanks is certainly up there as one of the more astounding features on the twenty- to thirty-minute guided tour; and those who view the experience as an educational process are pleased simply to walk away from the escorted tour with an understanding of just what is done to transform barley, hops, rice, and whatever else into that sudsy amber liquid. And how can anyone forget the complimentary beer served in the relaxing Hospitality Room at the conclusion of the tour? Finally, for those who have ever watched the Clydesdales perform in public, or have seen them on some of television's better sixty-second advertisements, the walk over to their hamlet is well worth the jaunt.

Something's always brewing in this room on the Busch tour. But the highlight to many is the Hospitality Room, where free samples are given out.

The twenty-five-foot-deep brewing kettles in the brewing room, which you see a few minutes into the tour, mark the first time you get to see and sniff what is on the way to becoming beer. If you had been wondering why your guide is carrying a microphone, this is where you see why; the background hum of machinery, while not loud to the extent of breaking one's eardrum, could drown out anyone's voice. In spite of the microphone, it's a good idea here, and throughout this journey to the center of beer creation, to stand close to the guide when he speaks.

By following the verbal routine, you can easily understand the brewing technique. Once the beer has become fully fermented, it is moved to lager cellars to age gracefully. Does the term "Beechwood aging" ring a bell? Here, you're told that there really is such a thing; Beechwood chips cover the lower portion of the tanks to aid the clarification process. Finally, you're led to an upstairs hallway where you look through windows into the bottling and packaging room. (For protection from the ear-shattering noise and the possibility of flying glass, you're not allowed into the room.) Here you watch conveyer belts moving boxes and bottles faster than bartenders push beer at a crowded Texas truck-stop.

The wood-paneled, cozy Hospitality Room marks the end of the tour; this is the place many have been waiting for. It's the neighborhood bar without the rowdiness, and best of all, all drinks are on the house. (For obvious reasons, there's a limit of three beers per patron.) To promote all three beers brewed here (Busch, Budweiser, and Michelob), each is rotated at the tap. When the Busch runs dry, Budweiser replaces it, and when they're out of Bud, you get to try Michelob. Then it's back to Busch.

Sitting back and nursing a glass of beer while talking to your friends isn't a bad way to end a tour. But unlike other brewery tours, this one has the additional attraction of the Clydesdale Hamlet. Even if you're not an equestrian, you should still walk the quarter mile from the brewery to the stables; the horses, with names like Prince, Baldy, Major, and Peter, are big and

There is evidence to date these ruins before the time of the Pilgrims — three to four thousand years before the Pilgrims.

It's called America's Stonehenge because of its theorized use as an ancient astronomical calendar. Above is the main site.

sturdy, yet graceful. They stand in side-by-side stalls and are impressive to look at. In an adjacent room, you can see some classic carriages and wagons associated with them. A staff member is on duty to answer all questions; the most common queries, we were told, concern the horses' size (six feet to the shoulder and eight feet to the head) and weight (a hearty two thousand pounds).

There are no such pat answers at **America's Stonehenge,** however. Experts say it's been there for at least a millennium and discoveries about it are still being constantly made. In spite of its catchy name, America's Stonehenge in no way physically resembles the mammoth group of stones standing on Salisbury Plain. Here on a small hill you'll see foundations of structures built from slabs of stone. Surrounding this collection of ruins is a series of stones theorized to be an astronomical calendar; hence arises the comparison to England's famous Stonehenge.

There is no guided tour here; you buy an admission ticket in the lodge and are given a complete guide/map to help make something out of your wanderings among the stones. Any questions? The guides (human, not printed) at the lodge or at the top of the complex will provide you with answers. A small entrance trail leads you to the main site, where there are over thirty points of interest that are identified and explained on your map.

Our initial question was, "If America's Stonehenge is so old and mysterious, how come I've never heard about it, especially when Stonehenge is a household word?" The answer, according to a guide, is the newness of the site. Though that may seem a contradiction, America's Stonehenge is only in its early days of being researched; it's been open to the public since 1958 and is still yielding new facts and findings. For instance, it wasn't determined until 1974 and 1975 that one oversized stone in the outside circle lines up perfectly with sunset at the winter solstice; on that day, the sun sets directly over the pointed top of the stone, as seen from the viewing point of the main site at a spot called the "sacrificial table."

The sacrificial table is perhaps the most important and controversial feature here. It's a slab of rock that weighs four and a half tons, is marked with a carved rectangular shape, and rests on stone legs. Its location also adds to the mystery. It's situated above the "speaking tube," a cylindrical hollow space between the stones that stretches from the "sacrificial table" to the "oracle chamber," a semi-subterranean room encased by built-up stone slabs. From inside the oracle chamber, one could talk into the "speaking tube," emitting a voice that would sound like it was coming from under the "table." At least, that's the theory. The real purpose for the structures, markings, and arrangement of all this is shrouded in mystery.

At first, there seems to be nothing very spectacular about it all, and it appears that America's Stonehenge could be forty as opposed to four thousand years old. But the background information from your printed guide as well as from personnel will dispel some "phenomenal hoax" thoughts immediately.

The mysteries of the site have been intensified in its relatively recent past, beginning when a fellow named Jonathan Pattee built his farmhouse (later destroyed by fire) over the ruins and lived in it from 1823 to 1849. During and following those years, many of the stones then here were crated off to become curbstones in Lawrence, Massachusetts. Some of what doesn't guard Lawrence's roadsides was destroyed by William Goodwin, who lived on the site in the 1930s. Goodwin, who thought Irish monks built America's Stonehenge about one thousand years ago, dug his way through many of the remains while orienting the ruins to fit his lifestyle here. Much of what could have answered questions is now gone.

So what proof is there that America's Stonehenge really does date from prehistoric times? Well, according to America's Stonehenge officials, neither colonial settlers nor Indians could have built these structures, since the architecture and materials are quite dissimilar to anything those two groups would have utilized. On the contrary, the stone site has similarities to structures existing on the Iberian Peninsula (Spain and Portugal) and on the island of Malta, and some of the pottery and stone tools unearthed here have a great resemblance to those used in Europe three millennia ago.

Other support for the theory of prehistoric usage? Radiocarbon testing, a scientific process wherein charcoal is examined and the age of the subject determined, has dated some pieces back one thousand to four thousand years. Long-worn inscriptions on some stones have been attributed by researchers, including a Harvard professor, to tribes of ancient Celts who lived on the Iberian Peninsula centuries before they went to Ireland. But the most fascinating argument is the astronomical-calendar idea. In addition to the winter solstice monolith, the stone that lines up with sunset on December 21, there is the summer solstice monolith, over which the sun sets directly on June 21. And there is the North Pole Star Stone; in the mid 1970s, it was discovered that the oversized rock lined up with the pole star, Thuban, around 2000 B.C.

Despite the wonder of this complex of ruins and the unanswered questions about its age and reason for existence, America's Stonehenge is not for everyone. There is nothing especially scenic about the main site (although you do walk from the lodge along a wooded path to get there) and while there are some displays in the lodge, there is no extensive visitors' center. As a guide at the main site said to us, "What you see is what you get." And what you get is a look at the ruins and an aware-

"If America's Stonehenge is so old and mysterious, how come I've never heard about it?"

Did ancient peoples use these four and a half tons of flat rock as part of religious ceremonies? That's one of the mysteries at America's Stonehenge.

NEAL HAMBERG

According to America's Stonehenge officials, neither colonial settlers nor Indians could have built these structures.

ness that there are indeed great mysteries around us today, including those right here in New England. Once you contemplate the theory behind the central America's Stonehenge site, it can really boggle your senses.

There are two other caveats you should consider before planning a visit here. Admission is not cheap, although it probably won't be any more expensive than admission to a first-run movie at your local theater. Second, you'll think that mosquitos and other bugs are as interested in prehistoric ruins as you are; either wear arm and leg coverings, bring some repellent, or do your best in the battle of the bugs.

There is one amenity here, though: a group of picnic tables by the parking lot outside of the main wooded area. It's a good place to discuss over a mid-afternoon repast your own theories of what ancient Celts were doing in this part of the world with their sacrificial table two thousand or so years ago.

Foam and stones. Modern industry and a possibly ancient discovery. Proof that New Hampshire offers more to locals and visitors than even its famed scenic wonders, with this pair of fun places to see and explore within the heart of the state's populous southern tier.

ACCESS

ANHEUSER-BUSCH, INC., MERRIMACK BREWERY TOUR AND CLYDESDALE HAMLET. Directions: From the Everett Turnpike exit 8, take Route 3 south to the brewery and hamlet. **Season:** All year. **Days:** May through October, daily; rest of the year, limited days. **Admission** free. **Allow** 1 hour to take the tour and to visit the Clydesdale Hamlet. **Note:** Children must be accompanied by an adult at least 18 years of age. The tour goes up and down many steps and through several temperature variations. The Clydesdales don't perform right at the brewery, but do tour now and then: you can call in advance to hear how many will be in the hamlet when you plan on visiting. **Telephone:** (603) 889-6631.

AMERICA'S STONEHENGE. Directions: From Interstate 93 exit 3, head east on Route 111, then follow signs. **Season:** April through November. **Days:** May through October, daily; April and November, weekends. **Admission** charged. **Allow** 45 minutes. **Telephone:** (603) 893-8300.

MELINDA MACAULEY

The flows of the robes and the curves of the faces belie the fact that this reproduction of da Vinci's Last Supper, *displayed at the Vermont Marble Exhibit, was carved out of one block of the hard rock.*

Marble & Maple

It's no mistake that the frequently held stereotype of the tough-skinned but friendly native-Vermont Yankee refers to one who is hard as marble on the outside but sweet as maple syrup inside. The naturally formed smooth rock, which creates so many of Vermont's hills, is as typical a state product as the syrup made from the sap of the sugar maple. And tributes to both marble and maple syrup in the form of museums can be visited in Proctor and Pittsford, just a few miles from each other in central Vermont.

It's no accident that these products have become state trademarks. Vermont is the undisputed United States leader in total production of both marble and maple goods. In a recent year, Vermont produced five hundred forty-five thousand gallons of maple syrup, a rate of more than a gallon per state resident; second place New York was well over two hundred thousand gallons behind. The marble industry has also been stable as a rock; one hundred eighty thousand tons valued at a little over twenty-three thousand dollars were quarried and processed in a year recently passed. Little wonder these products are the symbols of proud Vermont!

Actually, the **Vermont Marble Exhibit** in Proctor, in a nonchauvinistic way, pays homage to marble from all over the world and just subtly tips its hat to locally found rock. Located in an upstairs wing of the Vermont Marble Company, an actual factory where marble products are manufactured (you can tell you're entering a factory when you walk to the exhibit by crossing railroad tracks and passing through an opening in a wire fence labeled "Gate 6"), the exhibit initially introduces you to the innumerable varieties of the four-hundred-million-year-old metamorphic rock.

In the first display you see, which also happens to be the biggest, panels of different kinds of marble from all over the world are on view. Colors and shades represent what seems like every degree of the spectrum. Of course, there's the typically whitish mar-

You can see the involved process as workers cut, transport, and polish marble slabs in various stages of completion.

The marble-laden stone boat pulled by oxen looks ancient compared to the diesel-powered, rubber-tired fork-lift pulling a block of marble that weighs about the same as a few African elephants.

ble, such as Colorado's Yule Statuary. But then there's the reddish Rosora and the dark-green Verde Issorie, both from Italy, as well as Golden Vein from Peru, containing flashes of beige, tan, and gold. And Vermont's own Champlain Black is about as coal-like in color as you'll come across.

But those who would come to look at a marble museum usually have more in mind to see than simply panels. Since the days of ancient Greece, this rock has been the stuff of creativity for builders and artists; visitors are often interested in seeing some examples of both practical and esthetic uses. Of course, you get a sample of the former in about two dozen marble steps that take you upstairs to the exhibit area. The graceful curves and lines produced by artists can be viewed in the chapel, where a copy of Michelangelo's *Pietà* and a sculpture based on da Vinci's *Last Supper* are exhibited. Though both were carved out of solid blocks of marble, the delicate flow of the disciples' robes in *The Last Supper* and Jesus' slumped body in the *Pietà* belie the hardness of the material. Everything in the chapel, by the way, including the candlesticks, the altar, the steps, and the vases, are made of — what else — solid marble. As another example of marble as art, and for a chance to brief yourself in a little history, a bas-relief plaque of each American President is on display in a room next to the chapel. State loyalty hasn't been tossed by the wayside here; these are all made from Vermont white statuary marble.

As you may already know, the beautifully polished marble you see on the panels and finished products does not look so glossy when it's quarried. Through displays, photographs, an approximately fifteen-minute-long film, a sculptor in residence, and a factory viewing site, you can get an understanding of the process of creating with marble from inside the mountain to inside the living room.

Rough, dulled marble comes from the ground in the form of large blocks, many weighing in the vicinity of fifteen tons; these are then shipped to the factory to be sawed and polished. (Incidentally, nearby Dorset Mountain contains the largest underground marble quarry in the world.) From your bird's-eye vantage point looking into the enormous factory, you can see the involved process as workers cut, transport, and polish marble slabs in various stages of completion. For a closer but more static view, you can see in one display room the production of a marble table top in five stages, starting with the small, rough block just as it comes from the quarry and finishing with a smooth table top with polished face and edges. And don't leave without looking at some of the photos comparing marble-production methods of today with those of a century ago. The marble-laden stone boat pulled by oxen looks ancient compared to the diesel-powered, rubber-tired fork-lift pulling a block of marble that weighs about the same as a few African elephants.

Similarly, the old wooden sap buckets on display at Pittsford's **New England Maple Museum** appear to be relics next to the galvanized pails often seen dotting trees in late winter and also a part of the museum collection. Like the methods in the marble industry, those in the maple sugaring field have remained basically the same; only the modernity of the equipment has changed.

This is emphasized throughout the museum, arranged in chronological order. The first displays you'll see are crude wooden troughs used hundreds of years ago by Iroquois Indians as a means of catching sap. You then gradually approach the late twentieth century, represented by six-barrel gathering tanks and plastic hosing. Hosing, the only major exception to the rule of unchanging methods, has been received with mixed reviews from sugarers. It was developed to be used on trees in inconvenient locations and works by funneling sap to a central gathering station; however, some have found it clumsy and hard to maintain.

In addition to the displays of antique equipment (an ox cart, an ox-drawn wooden sap sled, wooden buckets, tin maple molds, and a cast-iron kettle, to name only a few), the story of sugaring is told in a well-organized and entertaining manner through murals. The initial mural relates the story of the Iroquois squaw who gathered what she thought was rainwater from beneath the broken limb of a maple tree only to discover the sweet aroma and taste when she used it as part of a meal. Capping the tale of the history of sugaring is a ten-minute slide presentation (narrated professionally by NBC News' Peter Hackes) that focuses on the operation run by a specific Vermont sugarmaking family. The slide show reveals that while many modern sugarers use gasoline or battery-powered tappers to tap trees, this family still uses those pounded by hand; on their property are approximately four thousand taps. The gathering, as you might guess,

According to legend, an Iroquois squaw gathered what she thought was rainwater from beneath the broken limb of a maple tree only to discover the sweet aroma and taste when she used it as part of a meal.

Wooden troughs like this, once used by Indians to catch maple sap, represent the many years the New England institution of sugaring has been around.

MELINDA MACAULEY

You can see what's good enough for your pancakes when you taste the different grades of syrup in the museum.

How long does it take to fill a bucket with sap? Which types of trees are best to tap? What is the prime time for sugaring?

is stated to be the most difficult part of the process.

There are answers to other questions here too, many of which you've doubtless wondered about while driving past bucket-laden trees on February and March days. How long does it take to fill a bucket with sap? Which types of trees are the best to tap? What is the prime time for sugaring in your section of New England? Find out as you wander through the museum.

Proud of this product, Vermonters don't mind making comparisons. An exhibit near the end of the museum showcases nearly two dozen containers of supermarket name-brand syrups with their percentages of maple purity labeled for all to see. Many of the competitors are revealed to be totally artificial; others contain only two or three per cent real maple syrup. Vermont maple, with its whopping 100 per cent rating, shines like sugar frosting.

But the proof is in the judging and visitors are encouraged to sample all four grades of Vermont maple syrup after finishing the self-guided tour. Fancy grade, with its translucent amber color and delicate flavor, is the acme; grades A and B are progressively darker, heavier, and stronger in flavor, while Grade C, the darkest, heaviest, and strongest, is used predominantly in cooking. But it's really a matter of taste: you decide what is good enough for your pancakes.

While the marble exhibit is housed right in a section of an operating factory, the maple museum was not the beneficiary of such an appropriate location. So museum managers Tom and Dona Olson did the next best thing; Tom constructed the museum building from scratch and designed it to look like a nineteenth-century New England sugarhouse. While the locale, therefore, is not a bona fide sugar house, it's about as close as they could get. And it is, like the marble exhibit, a fitting showing of a Vermont trademark.

ACCESS

TO GET TO THE RUTLAND AREA. From Interstate 91 north exit 9, take Route 12 north to Route 4 west to Rutland. From Interstate 91 south exit 10, take Interstate 89 north to exit 1 onto Route 4 west; follow Route 4 to Rutland.

VERMONT MARBLE EXHIBIT. Directions: From the center of Rutland, follow Route 4 west, then take Route 3 north and follow signs to the exhibit. **Season:** Late May through mid-October. **Days:** Daily. **Admission** charged. **Allow** 1 hour to 90 minutes. **Note:** Wear good walking shoes. **Telephone:** (802) 459-3311.

NEW ENGLAND MAPLE MUSEUM. Directions: From Route 4, take Route 7 north to the museum. **Season:** Mid-March through late December. **Days:** Daily; shorter hours during spring, fall, and winter. **Admission** charged. **Allow** 30 minutes to 1 hour. **Telephone:** (802) 483-9414.

Old-Time Transportation

Many of us who grew up thinking that you could always zip down Interstate 95 at fifty-five miles per hour to reach a destination or that the quickest way to get to New York has always been to catch the next jet owe ourselves a trip to two museums on Maine's southwestern coast. And the same goes for those of us who remember cranking up the old Ford to take a spin down the newest paved road or waiting on a corner to take the next trolley. In Kennebunkport and Wells, the Seashore Trolley Museum and the Wells Auto Museum both offer the chance to look at and try out these two antique methods of transportation. This trip will let you savor the charm of the old and praise, or curse, the conveniences of today.

In 1921, the electric railway industry was the fifth largest in the nation, and trolleys were common transportation to the countryside or the seacoast. While a handful of cities today keep these cars in use as a means of mass transit, routes are fairly limited. However, at the **Seashore Trolley Museum** in Kennebunkport, you can take a ride on one of many beautifully restored cars; the twenty-minute-long, two-and-a-quarter-mile round trip along the old Atlantic Shoreline trolley right of way is a taste of the time when OPEC and rush-hour traffic jams were decades away.

From the old car cards extolling the virtues of B.T. Babbitts 1776 Soap Powder to the appropriate uniforms worn by the conductors (some of whom actually did this same job in their younger years), the era when the trolley ride was an everyday event is re-enacted. About four dozen of the substantial collection of cars are actually operable, and those used for rides are rotated daily. Three were in use when we visited, two to provide rides down the old trolley tracks and one to serve as a shuttle down the one third mile-long path to the main exhibit barn. Boarding takes place outside the gift shop in a mock station setup; then bells clang and the conductor punches your ticket. ("We don't have to punch them y'know. Just adds a little flavor.") The conductor is usually silent during the ride itself, when you can admire the varnished wood and polished brass or simply delight in this diet of sweet nostalgia. At midpoint when you're turned around for the ride back, you hear a little about the museum and trolleys in general. A trolley, you hear, once raced an airplane and beat it. Now, would a Maine trolley conductor lie to you?

The first horse-drawn cars for mass transportation, it's generally agreed, were introduced in New York City in 1832 and traversed a one-mile stretch along Fourth Avenue between Prince and Fourteenth streets; it wasn't until about twenty years later that street railways began to catch on as a serious method of

A trolley, you hear, once raced an airplane and beat it. Now, would a Maine trolley conductor lie to you?

DON RICHESON

The "City of Manchester," with its grilled front, leather seats, and velvet drapes, is one of the Seashore Trolley Museum's most elaborate cars.

moving people around, and it was in 1872 that the city of New Bedford, Massachusetts, joined in the new mass-transit movement. It was from this city that the museum got its oldest exhibit — a closed horsecar that was made in 1873 by the Fiegel Car Company of New Utrecht, New York, and was electrified in 1894, then used as a postal car.

By the turn of the century, the idea of using electric power from overhead wires along streets had fully manifested itself. Very few horsecars remained, although many of the early electric cars resembled horsecars in many ways. There are about a half dozen cars here from this early period, most from New England. There's one, however, that dates from 1897 and is quite atypical: the "City of Manchester," with its dark blue color and lovely grille work outside and leather seats and blue-velvet drapes inside. A real dazzler, it served as a private car that carried Manchester, New Hampshire's VIPs around for a number of years.

Do you remember the Snowmobile, the Grout Steamer, and the Orient Buckboard?

The collection, though, doesn't stop at domestic models. If you have ever vacationed in Rome and ridden on the sardine can-like buses there, you'll probably smile when you see the two-axle streetcar that came here straight from the Eternal City. This dark green specimen has only six tiny wooden seats inside, allowing the maximum possible room to pack in standees. By contrast, the streamlined double-decker tram from Glasgow, Scotland, with its leather and plush seats and both smoking and nonsmoking sections, maintains a sign that states there's a limit of ten standees. Other foreign representatives here come from such places as Germany, England, New Zealand, and Canada.

The Seashore Trolley Museum is constantly obtaining new cars, most of which need some refurbishing work. To help you appreciate the tedious, detailed work that goes into making a trolley look brand spanking new, you're invited to walk past the two exhibit barns and up some stairs into the visitors' gallery. From here you can look down onto the main floor of the railway shop.

If you venture into this part of the Maine seacoast on a Sunday during the off-season you can take advantage of some special events the museum schedules. Snowfighting Day in midwinter gives you a chance to look at the old-time snow removal equipment in action and ride on heated city cars, while a bit later, Interurban Extravaganza lets you enjoy riding and looking at some of the high-speed interurbans (which connected cities substantial distances apart and which are rarely run otherwise). Along the same line, on Old Timers Day, held in the spring, you can ride and examine some of the museum's oldest cars; and late in the year, City Trolley Car Day exhibits and lets you ride on city cars from throughout the world.

Ironically, the villains that ended the heyday of

the trolley are grandly displayed just a few miles down Route 1. However, the antique automobiles can hardly be viewed in anybody's eyes as bad guys. Most of the time, they're talked of in terms that one would use to describe Gary Coleman: cute, adorable, lovable. You'd almost want to go up and pinch their cheeks. There are upwards of sixty antique gems at the **Wells Auto Museum** and although cars are the main attraction, you can also enjoy other treats such as nickelodeons, picture machines (which you may call "peep shows"), license plates, and bicycles that are displayed here.

The museum is housed in a modern warehouse-style structure, but you can get an initial taste of the early atmosphere just by listening to the music machine or peeking at the automotive Methuselahs kept in the parking lot. You'll also likely hear more sounds of the era as you enter the huge display room where many of the nickelodeons still work for just one twentieth of a dollar. A warning, though — your idealization of sweet-sounding music may be crushed. One scratchy number with a weak distant voice that we played could best be described as "ear-ritating." We couldn't deny, however, that there was a charm in dropping in a nickel to hear this old recording.

Another diversion is the antique picture machines that you probably would have found in 1920s speakeasies. Each still works for a nickel or a dime, and you'll be happy to know that one of them has been "approved by New York Censors." Whether you see Rhonda do her balloon dance or the show (entitled "Double Your Pleasure") that features one stripper following another, you'll find these more laughable than anything else.

Of course, the bodies that most people stop here to see are bodies by Fisher. While there are some foreign cars, the collection here emphasizes American-made automobiles. There are representatives of makes that you'll still find today: Chrysler, Ford, Oldsmobile, and Cadillac. You'll also see former classics to which fate dealt a harsh blow — Pierce Arrow, Stanley Steamer, Packard, and Maxwell. And do you remember oldies like the Snowmobile (no relation to today's vehicle of the same name), the Grout Steamer, and the Orient Buckboard?

It's the names of these early automotive specimens that underline much of the fascination of this museum. The 1923 Snowmobile, for instance, made by the Snowmobile Manufacturing Corporation (natch!) of West Ossipee, New Hampshire, was basically a Model T Roadster with a lengthened frame, a pick-up bed, chain tires in the rear, and orange ski runners in front. This classic example of Yankee ingenuity was killed later that decade when snowplowing started. The barrel-hooded Grout Steamer, made in 1905 (its last year of production) was designed to look like a locomotive. The advertising campaign for the Grout stated that the

As you watch, the frantic driver cranks the car in the front, then attempts to rush back and push a knob on the steering wheel.

COURTESY WELLS AUTO MUSEUM

The 1912 Pathfinder, like many of the other old autos you'll see at the Wells Auto Museum, has long since passed on to the great highway in the sky. In fact, this is believed to be the only 1912 model in existence.

car had "locomotive power." Probably the most unusual car is the 1901 Orient Buckboard, which was manufactured in Waltham, Massachusetts. It looks like an overgrown skateboard and is equipped with no reverse gear; so to change direction it had to be picked up and turned around.

For the sake of the youngsters, to whom riding in an antique vehicle may mean riding in Dad's '73 Duster, and for the rest of us, who may have faint memories of an old Nash Rambler, rides are offered in a 1911 Model T Ford Depot Hack for an extra charge. Though very brief, the ride brings you up and down hills and around curves in a neighboring housing development. Actually, the entertainment starts just after you climb on board. As you watch, the frantic driver cranks the car in the front to turn the engine over, then attempts to rush back and push a knob on the steering wheel to advance the sparks and throttle while the engine is still running. Don't attempt to help him out; it's all part of the show. The car, originally used as a taxi, can seat as many as six. The driver will explain whatever you wish to know about the vehicle, probably including the use of the three pedals on the floor: the one on the right is the brake, the middle is reverse, and the left is low (pressed down) and high (let up) gears.

If listening to the put-put of these old-time modes of transportation makes you wax nostalgic, you're catching on to the whole idea. Even if you don't take the opportunity to hop in the old Model T or get the chance to ride in your favorite trolley, just the sight of these old vehicles can bring out the sentimentalist in anyone. Unless you're careful, you'll find yourself cruising back home down Route 1 or Interstate 95 at a bruising twenty-six miles per hour.

Just the sight of these old vehicles can bring out the sentimentalist in anyone.

ACCESS

SEASHORE TROLLEY MUSEUM. Directions: From Interstate 95 exit 3, go south on Route 35 to Route 1, then north on Route 1 for 2.8 miles to Log Cabin Road; turn right onto Log Cabin Road and continue for 1.7 miles. **Season:** Late April through late October. **Days:** Daily in summer, limited hours in spring and fall. **Admission** charged. **Allow** 1 hour to 90 minutes. **Note:** There is much walking involved along and over tracks and dirt pathways, so sturdy walking shoes are recommended. **Telephone:** (207) 967-2712.

WELLS AUTO MUSEUM. Directions: From Interstate 95 exit 2, turn left onto Route 109, then go right onto Route 1 and continue 1 mile to the museum. Or, from the junction of Route 1 and Log Cabin Road in Kennebunkport, head south about 8½ miles. **Season:** Late May through mid-September. **Days:** Daily in summer, weekends in spring. **Admission** charged. **Allow** 30 minutes to 1 hour. **Telephone:** (207) 646-9064.

The Bay Queen

We had been afloat on the 120-foot-long M/V *Bay Queen* no more than a half hour when we passed dozens of quahoggers in small boats, pressing on poles in attempts to scrape up as many of those hard-shelled clams as they could from the floor of Narragansett Bay. As soon as the clamdigging workhorses were in close view, Andy, the *Bay Queen's* captain, and Lou, one of two naturalists on board, explained that at the base of the thirty-foot-long aluminum poles are heavy rakes; the quahogs are raked up into sections of these. However, nothing stops heavy rocks, sand, and water from also landing at the base of the poles that have to be lifted up and back onto boats. So the men who ply this trade make muscles as well as money. The captive audience of about 250 passengers on board the excursion boat also learned that when you eat a quahog right out of the shell, he's alive, and the liquid you might feel in your mouth is the quahog's blood. But we were then told not to let that discourage us. "I'll put ketchup, horseradish, anything on it. I don't care how alive he is," offered Lou.

Off-the-cuff remarks and spontaneous discussion regarding anything that seems appropriate are typical of an experience cruising the waters of Narragansett Bay on this triple-decker boat. The day-long ride on the *Bay Queen* is for active as well as passive types. Lou or another **naturalist** offers morning and afternoon talks on quahogs, lobstering, or another appropriate topic, and Andy explains the meaning of the flag with the diagonal white line that's posted on a small boat you pass by. You will also be given the opportunity to

You can learn all about clams and quahogs, sun yourself while reading that new paperback, or get out and explore the islands on a day trip aboard the M/V Bay Queen.

"I'll put ketchup, horse-radish, anything on it. I don't care how alive he is."

step off the boat for a nature walk or shopping spree at the two scheduled hour-long stops. If you just want to read that paperback you've been putting off all summer or watch the bay and island scenery without taking part in extracurriculars, you'll find that no passenger is forced to take part in anything. The options are there for you to choose from.

During the 9:30 to 5:00 trip, you miss no corner of Narragansett Bay. The *Bay Queen* departs from Warren, may stop very briefly at Rocky Point (a major amusement park located by Warwick) to pick up passengers, and then cruises south, to the west shores of Prudence and Conanicut islands, before stopping for an hour at the former military installation on Dutch Island. A loop around Conanicut Island brings you briefly out into the Atlantic Ocean, and by the time you stop at Newport (either at Fort Adams or at the harbor in the center of town), you're back in the peaceful waters of the bay. You then cruise past the west shore of Aquidneck Island (and the east shores of Conanicut and Prudence islands), before heading back to Warren. In the interim, you will have passed numerous bantam isles like Hope Island, Fox Island, and Rose Island, and will have crossed under both the Jamestown and Newport bridges. All the while, you'll have been witness to buoys bobbing and clanging, seagulls brazenly hovering over the boat's deck, and all sorts of vessels, from sailboats to freighters, passing by in all directions.

And no matter what you see or hear, the captain, naturalist, or some other *Bay Queen* staffer will be able to afford some interesting factual explanations culled from a mental file of seafaring information acquired over the years. The seagulls floating above after getting a whiff of the food being cooked up on board are herring gulls; you hear that you can tell them by their grayish rings. An immature herring gull is recognized by his brown coloring. You'll see colored markings of another sort on brightly painted buoys, some of them simply old milk or other bottles, all color-coded to identify the owners. And that big freighter that was outpacing us on our way back in the late afternoon was

During the 9:30 to 5:00 trip, you miss no corner of Narragansett Bay.

Bay Queen *passengers disembark onto uninhabited Dutch Island, where they have the chance to investigate the old military ruins, either with a guide or on their own.*

MICHAEL SCHUMAN

COURTESY NEWPORT COUNTY CHAMBER OF COMMERCE/JOHN T. HOPF

Twelve-meter yachts, sheets to the wind, are a frequent sight in Narragansett Bay.

bringing Datsuns to be unloaded in Providence. If whatever you see and wonder about isn't automatically discussed, be sure to ask. Someone on board will most likely have an answer.

And while the appearances of birds, buoys, and boats can change day by day, the islands are as constant as the rippling waves of the bay. *Bay Queen* personnel are experts on all the islands you sail by. Hope Island, they'll mention, is a nesting ground for some birds, like long-legged egrets and ibises, not usually seen in populated areas; the birds feed on small fish and shrimp and on the island are undisturbed by man and other mainland predators. An unusually large herd of white-tailed deer survives by living off the tender shoots of shrubs and trees that grow on Prudence Island, while Rose Island was a popular stopping ground for late nineteenth-century excursion boats. And then there's your own stopping point, **Dutch Island.**

This, along with many of the islands in Narragansett Bay, was once a military installation; it is now a state park. The installation was used mainly during the Spanish-American War and World War I; by World War II it had already been abandoned and had deteriorated. You stop here for about an hour and are

You witness buoys bobbing and clanging, seagulls brazenly hovering over the boat's deck, and all sorts of vessels, from sailboats to freighters, passing by.

allowed to walk about on the trails on your own or on a guided tour with a naturalist; trails are narrow, overgrown, and littered in spots with broken brick or bits of seashells, although authorities state that when the budget permits, the trails will be cleaned and widened. In the meantime, their not-so-pristine condition combined with the empty shell of an old brick barracks adds to the feeling of exploring an island ghost town.

Depending on the schedule, your other stop may be in Providence or at the Newport Yachting Center; here you'll have about an hour and fifteen minutes to browse in the gift and craft shops or grab a bite to eat in Newport's center. If you've got your heart set on one stop or the other, it would be best to call or write in advance for scheduling information.

The current *Bay Queen* is the third in a line of excursion boats that have carried water lovers along the far reaches of Narragansett Bay. It's also the biggest, with a capacity of 572 passengers. Day cruises are informal, and you should dress in whatever you feel comfortable wearing; T-shirts, jeans, shorts, and sundresses were the rule when we sailed on a comfortably warm July day. Food — coffee and doughnuts in the morning and hot dogs and sandwiches for most of the rest of the day — is for sale, as are alcoholic beverages; you are also permitted to bring your own food — but no alcohol — on board. Other *Bay Queen* rides? There are regularly scheduled dinner-dance cruises during many weekday evenings and Newport Brunch and other special event cruises slated for certain weekends.

ACCESS

THE BAY QUEEN. Directions: From Interstate 195 exit 1, take Route 114 south into the center of Warren, then turn right onto Campbell Street and continue to the dock. **Season:** Late May through late September. **Days:** Call for current schedule. **Admission** charged. **Allow** 6½ hours. **Notes:** The new *Bay Queen* is big enough that a reservation is not necessary and there is rarely any problem buying a ticket on the morning you want to sail; you can make a reservation, however, if you are driving a distance or simply want to assure yourself of a seat. If you wish to board the *Bay Queen* at Rocky Point, be sure to call in advance. Women may want to wear kerchiefs, but hats are not recommended due to possible winds. Sneakers or other rubber-soled shoes are advised. **Telephone:** From within Rhode Island: (401) 245-1350; from outside the state: (800) 556-7450.

You can stare at some 850 different faces at the American Clock & Watch Museum in Bristol, Connecticut.

Clocks & Locks

"A clock museum and a lock museum?" questioned an acquaintance when told of these two specialty museums located within five miles of each other in central Connecticut. "Soon," he added, "they'll have a museum museum." Museums for the single minded have become very popular with many who come to one conclusion: until a visit to such a museum, it is impossible to realize there are so many varieties, shapes, and sizes of such household items. That resolution can certainly be reached by anyone paying a visit to the American Clock & Watch Museum in Bristol and the Lock Museum of America in Terryville. Within a matter of a few hours spent viewing these two collections, you can see some 850 clocks and about 18,000 locks.

The initial question that popped into our head when planning this daytrip was why Bristol and Terryville, of all places? Neither is a population center or a tourist magnet. But the answer is evident as soon as you enter either and read the displays or listen to the museum personnel; the general Bristol area may have produced more clocks than the Black Forest and, with the Eagle Lock Company in the center of town, nobody in Terryville ever had to go far to find a way to bolt his door.

A fifteen-minute slide presentation is the way many visitors begin their stay at the **American Clock & Watch Museum,** and it is here that you learn of the magnitude of the American clock industry of long ago, especially that based around this city of fifty-seven thousand inhabitants. Although the Europeans admittedly made, on the whole, clocks of better quality, it was the American clock makers who mass produced them on such a wide scale that any citizen, regardless of personal wealth, could afford them. E. Ingraham Company of Bristol and Eli Terry & Sons of Terryville were two of the local manufacturers whose names you'll see on identification tags placed on clocks and watches throughout the vintage 1801 house built by

You'll see everything from a 1790s Harland grandfather clock to a Buck Rogers pocket watch that's classic 1940s.

and named for Miles Lewis.

Terry was a kingpin of the local clock-making industry; he started making clocks by hand in the late 1700s and continued until 1806, when he became involved in the beginnings of mass production. By the 1830s, clocks were being mass produced with cheap labor in such great numbers that it became impractical to continue making them by hand. When Terry retired in 1833, he passed the company on to his sons (the town of Terryville, formerly a part of Plymouth, Connecticut, was named after one of the sons). As a result of retirement, death, and in the case of one son, bankruptcy, the maverick clock-making company went out of business in the mid 1800s.

Here you're on your own, with all the time in the world.

Ingraham's company, on the other hand, while not an important early fixture in the industry, evolved into one of New England's seven major manufacturers; it remained in that position until the corporation was bought out by a conglomerate in the mid 1960s and the local plant ceased production. Ingraham himself was originally a case maker, heavily influenced by the Empire style of furnishings, and was credited with many original designs. The Ingraham business, started in 1860, grew steadily until approximately the time of World War II, when pendulum-clock manufacture ceased. Electric clocks were made locally until the 1960s. No clocks are made right in Bristol today, but in the nearby communities of Thomaston and Farmington, the Seth Thomas and New England Clock companies design the cases in which foreign-made movements are enclosed.

From a Harland grandfather clock dating from the 1790s to a Buck Rogers pocket watch that's classic 1940s, you can see the fruits of both hand and machine production on two floors and in a separate wing. There are no guided tours here; you walk around at your leisure, skipping over the clocks that don't interest you while stopping to scrutinize those that you find worth a second or third glance. If the museum isn't busy, a hostess may take a few minutes to explain a little about some of the more interesting specimens. Otherwise, you're on your own, with all the time in the world.

Most of the timepieces on the upper story of this museum are domestically made, many in the immediate area. You may be amazed by the multitude of clocks with attractive, elaborate designs under the faces, especially when keeping in mind that these were run-of-the-mill, mass-produced clocks in their day. Some of these beauties are decorated with likenesses of parks, a church, and even a stately place like Buckingham Palace. You may recognize on the other hand the shelf clocks from the 1930s and 1940s with more plain faces and the lack of fancy decoration.

Attached to the Lewis House is a wing built from parts of the first house in Bristol, constructed by Ebenezer Barnes in 1728 and now named the Barnes

Wing. Appropriately enough, here is where you'll find the oldest clock in the museum: a lantern clock made in England in approximately 1680 and brought to the colonies. It's a primitive-looking piece of machinery, with one hand, a brass face marked by Roman numerals, and weights and pendulum hanging uncovered. Yet, if you're here at the right instant, you can still hear it strike.

The Barnes Wing contains the widest scope of items in the museum. There are as many sizes and varieties of grandfather clocks as there are grandfathers. Most are local products, created by the likes of Isaac Doolittle of New Haven or Seth Thomas of Thomaston, but there is also one that, though cased in Pennsylvania, has movements made in 1795 in Germany. Did you know, however, that back then there was no such term as "grandfather clock"? At that time they were commonly known as "hall" or "tall" clocks and weren't referred to as grandfather clocks until an 1876 song about "my grandfather's clock" made the name popular.

Clocks in the shapes of pumpkins and pies, a clock with a bisque doll acting as a pendulum and perpetually bobbing up and down, another with a German beer drinker with constantly rolling eyes attached, and an 1863 globe clock that tells the time around the world are all collectively referred to as "novelty clocks," and there's a bunch of others on display here as well. In one corner of this room is a re-created clock maker's workshop, looking just as it did in 1825 with period tools and clock faces lying about. On your way out of the Barnes Wing and into the Miles Lewis House, take a peek into the courtyard and period garden, where a sundial marks the shadows as these devices did centuries ago.

And then there are locks, certainly not picturesque as many clocks are, but hardly nondescript or strictly modern household items either. At the **Lock Museum of America,** wood stock locks from the colonial era appear almost laughable compared to some of the more recent all-metal locks, while oddities such as the monstrous twenty-nine-pound padlock originally used in the 1700s in Connecticut's New-gate Prison, and the 1918 vintage Studebaker car lock, are attention grabbers. In addition, the museum features displays of related items like doorknobs and escutcheons (also not as mundane as you might think) and handcuffs.

Unlike the historic structure that houses the American Clock & Watch Museum, it's a contemporary brick building, dedicated in 1980, that houses this collective ode to American lock making. However, this is a case where the museum building does not actually mirror the topic that's represented. On the contrary, locks are by no stretch of the imagination a modern development; they have a history that's almost ageless. Elaborate locks made of iron were used by the Romans,

They were commonly known as "hall" or "tall" clocks and weren't referred to as grandfather clocks until an 1876 song about "my grandfather's clock" made the name popular.

Locks for front doors, old Studebakers, and prison cells are on view at Terryville's Lock Museum of America.

and doorlocks, padlocks, and keys were found in abundance amid the ruins of Pompeii. But it was the ancient Egyptians who, four thousand years ago, used a lock based on the pin-tumbler principle that has been the model for locks manufactured through modern times. These tumblers (small wooden pins attached to the upper part of the lock) fit inside concordant holes drilled in the main body (called the bolt) of the lock. The key had pegs on one side, which corresponded with the tumblers and would push them from their resting spots, allowing the door to be opened. A large replica of this ancient wooden lock is on display at the museum, as well as an oversized model of its descendant used so often today. If you're visiting at a time when the museum is not too busy, chances are a volunteer will be able to demonstrate them for you.

But despite the grand history of the lock, it's America's influence on locks and lock-making that is the key to this museum's reason for being. So the initial display that you see, the one devoted to the development of the lock, dates only from colonial times. The first bunch are odd; primitive appearing, totally wood except for some metal movable parts, these wood stock locks were used throughout the colonial period and later, then gradually disappeared from use until becoming extinct around the mid 1830s. French-style models dating from the 1600s are the earliest; the most modern are those being used today.

Of course, being located within eyesight of the old Eagle Lock Company buildings, the museum exhibits a hearty representation of five thousand Eagle locks that the company donated. (Incidentally, locks are still made on the site of the defunct Eagle Lock Company, on a part-time basis by the Colonial Lock Company.) And if you've ever checked your car keys or the knob on your front door and have seen the name Yale or Russwin, you're already familiar with two other major lock companies represented here that got started in Connecticut (Russwin is now part of the Farmington-based Emhart Corporation while Yale, which was the first modern company to patent the old Egyptian pin tumbler principle, is today part of Eaton Security Products & Systems of Charlotte, North Carolina). And, happy to accept a few of the more unusual locks that abound throughout the world, museum personnel are pleased with the purposely small collection of samples from other parts of the world. Representatives from England, Russia, Germany, Japan, and India are here to be inspected and compared.

You can see doorknobs made for the Waldorf Astoria Hotel, the city of Richmond, and the Masons, all worthy of admiration.

A few dozen or so old prison locks and handcuffs on display here may sound more fascinating offhand than doorknobs and escutcheons, but the latter two pieces of hardware are certainly more appealing to the eye. The doorknobs on view here are more intricate and decorative than those you'll have protruding from your bedroom doors at home, for all came from some very famous or important places and all have been imprinted with interesting symbols or logos. You can see those made for places like the San Francisco Public Library, the Waldorf Astoria Hotel, the Bell System, the city of Richmond, and the Masons, all worthy of an admiring examination. Many of the knobs are company samples, never used, and in mint condition. Then there are the escutcheons and hinges, used for years in buildings but still specimens of dedicated workmanship.

Admittedly, clocks are a bit more eye-pleasing than locks, but if you're interested in mechanical things, you'll certainly find both museums worth your while. And at the same time, you'll be able to see some of the major products that were Connecticut's contributions to Yankee ingenuity.

ACCESS

AMERICAN CLOCK & WATCH MUSEUM. Directions: Westbound: From Interstate 84 exit 38, take Route 6 west 8 miles to Maple Street, and turn left onto Maple Street; the museum is at 100 Maple Street. Eastbound: From Interstate 84 exit 31, take Route 229 north 6 miles to the junction with Route 6; head east on Route 6, then take a right onto Maple Street; the museum is at 100 Maple Street, 2 blocks ahead. **Season:** April through October. **Days:** Daily. **Admission** charged. **Allow** 1 hour to 90 minutes. **Telephone:** (203) 583-6070.

LOCK MUSEUM OF AMERICA. Directions: From Interstate 84 exit 20, take Route 8 north 10 miles, then take Route 6 east to the center of Terryville; the museum is at 130 Main Street. **Season:** May through October, and by appointment. **Days:** Tuesday through Sunday, afternoon. **Admission** charged. **Allow** 30 to 45 minutes. **Telephone:** (203) 589-6359.

The Yale Collections

Where in Connecticut can you see works of art produced by the greatest masters like Rubens, van Gogh, and Constable, skeletons of some of the biggest dinosaurs ever to roam the planet, and a violin made by the great Stradivari? The answer is at Yale University, home of the Yale University Art Gallery, the Yale Center for British Art, the Peabody Museum of Natural History, and the Yale University Collection of Musical Instruments. There's more than enough for a day's outing here (the art gallery is particularly extensive), so you're invited to pick two or three favorites as the focus for your day's outing.

The century-and-a-half-old **Yale University Art Gallery,** oldest such college or university museum in North America, is the home of priceless works and the closest thing to paradise for art enthusiasts in the state. Five floors of paintings, sculptures, furniture, antiquities, and other forms of art can keep one spellbound for hours. Instead of trying to tackle this collection of creative classics in order from top floor to bottom or vice versa, you may prefer to pick out the area that interests you most and begin there. Ancient art is found on the ground floor, sculpture and special exhibitions on the first, and African, pre-Columbian, nineteenth-century European, and early modern are among the areas to be seen on the second floor. On the third floor, you'll come across thirteenth- to sixteenth-century Italian art, sixteenth to nineteenth-century European art, and American art. The fourth floor is the location of the often changing Oriental displays as well as other special exhibitions.

Then again, there are those who have no favorite areas, who just like to look at all media, modes, and styles and who make special efforts to see the prized possessions. If you're the type who would consider it a tragedy to be inside the Louvre and miss the *Mona Lisa,* or to neglect to see Rembrandt's *Night Watch* in the Rijkmuseum, you probably should start your visit on the second floor. That's where you'll see van Gogh's *Night Cafe,* one of the museum's best known paintings. The setting is a café in Arles, France; objects of pleasure — a billiard table, wine bottles, and glasses — are bathed in the glare of natural gaslight while the people, slumping at tables, are portrayed as despondent figures. Van Gogh, the son of a pastor, wrote the following of his painting: "In my picture of the *Night Cafe,* I have tried to express the idea that the cafe is a place where one can ruin one's self, go mad, or commit a crime."

Picasso, Gauguin, Cézanne, and Pollock are also among the many well-known artists represented here. Picasso's *First Steps,* a forceful painting depicting the moving scene of a child learning to walk under his own power, is a favorite of many. Pollock's *Number 4*

Van Gogh's Night Cafe, *a place where one can go mad, according to the artist. The painting hangs in the Yale University Art Gallery.*

The Yale University Art Gallery is the home of priceless works and the closest thing to paradise for art enthusiasts in Connecticut.

and *Number 14,* completed in 1939 and 1948 respectively, are included in the Ordway Gallery, filled with works bequeathed to Yale by a collector in 1980. Other modern works, like Alexander Calder's mobiles, are in the same collection.

Works of older illustrious European painters Rubens, Hals, and Bosch can be seen on the third floor. There is a fine collection of colorful medieval Italian religious art — mostly egg tempera on panels — that renders images like the *Madonna Enthroned with Saints* and *Scenes from the Passion.* You will also find on this floor works of American artists like John Trumbull (a major collection), Edward Hopper, Winslow Homer, and John James Audubon.

However, what is considered the most important collection in the entire museum is in the Garvan Galleries of American Art. Located on the second floor, these galleries feature silver, pewter, and other art forms. Many styles of furniture, from William and Mary to Chippendale to Victorian, are also represented here.

After viewing art of varied backgrounds and origins at the gallery, you can cross the street and examine collections focusing upon strictly British art from the Elizabethan era to the mid 1800s. The **Yale Center for British Art** is a modern building, opened in 1978, where you can have your fill of creations like Thomas Gainsborough portraits, John Constable landscapes, and George Stubbs paintings of animals. And more.

Most of the permanent exhibits are on the top floor of this four-story structure, although there are additional ones on the second floor. (Other areas are occupied by temporary exhibitions and classroom space.) The fourth-floor rooms are arranged chronologically, with specific sections devoted to William Hogarth, Constable, J.M.W. Turner, and Stubbs. One of the first paintings you'll see as you step off the elevator is the full-length oil on canvas of the Earl of Newport; the artist, Sir Anthony Van Dyck (1599-1641), is highly regarded today for introducing what has been described as "a refined sense of elegance" into the Elizabethan era.

Individuals' favorites here often depend solely on personal taste. Constable's *Hadleigh Castle, The Mouth of the Thames — Morning, After a Stormy Night,* an oil on canvas painted in 1829, is one noted work. Castle ruins dominate the left half of the painting while the now becalmed water governs the right half. Note the specks of boats on the water and the seagulls that blend right into the clouds. A personal favorite is John Martin's *The Bard.* Known as Mad Martin, this early-nineteenth-century painter is remembered by art enthusiasts for his eccentricity since he spent many years trying in vain to improve London's sanitation system (an effort that pales next to the exploits of his two brothers, one

Artist John Martin spent years vainly trying to improve London's sanitation system (an effort that pales next to the exploits of his brother, who invented a hat to protect an individual from earthquakes).

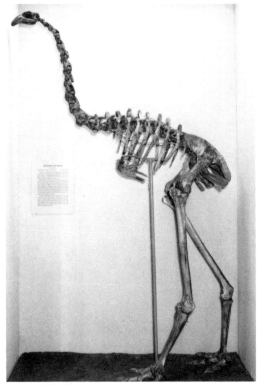

The only place you'll see one of these today is in a museum, like Yale's Peabody Museum of Natural History. It's a dinornis maximus.

Dominating the floor is the massive skeleton of what was once a sixty-seven-foot-long and sixteen-foot-high brontosaurus excelsus.

of whom invented a hat that would protect an individual from earthquakes and another of whom set fire to the grand York Minster in the north of England). *The Bard,* featuring a chasm with gushing water and an evil sorcerer figure on the cliffs on one side and an army of men stretching up a winding road to a castle top on the other, is based on a Welsh legend that says that upon his conquest of Wales, King Edward I ordered all bards put to death.

Other types of violence are the themes of many George Stubbs paintings. *Lion Attacking a Horse,* and *Lion Attacking a Stag,* two vivid oils on canvas painted between 1760 and 1765 for the first Marquis of Rockingham, capture both the brutality and agony of the fights between the animals. Stubbs, son of a Liverpool currier, began studying anatomy at age eight; that, along with his interest in nature, helped direct him toward a specialization in animals and country scenes. In addition to Stubbs's lurid scenes, you'll also find here some of his calmer animal portraits such as *Water Spaniel* and *Zebra,* both painted in the 1760s. Stubbs's works are on the second and fourth floors.

The two-dimensional depictions of animals may serve to whet your appetite for the three-dimensional stuffed versions as well as the assembled skeletons in the **Peabody Museum of Natural History.** This museum, regarded as one of the finest of its ilk in the country, contains a substantial number of animal displays ranging from dinosaurs to musk oxen to a snowy owl. Its cultural displays focus on early residents — humans, other animals, and plants — of North and South America, especially those of present-day Connecticut.

To see some of the first sizable beings that ever roamed the earth, however, you'll want to walk to the biggest display area on the first floor. The massive skeleton of what was once a sixty-seven-foot-long and sixteen-foot-high brontosaurus excelsus dominates the floor; this reptile, whose name translates to mean "thunder lizard," is estimated to have weighed thirty-five tons, and it's calculated that it would have eaten a thousand pounds a day.

In contrast to the reptilian behemoth in the center of the floor, take a look at the limnoscelis skeleton in a glass case in the hall. This collection of bones in the form of a triangular head, backbone, and claws is said to be one of the most important specimens in the museum; it represents a primitive stage in the evolution of the reptile and is, in effect, the ancestor of the gargantuan brontosaurus. This skeleton was found imbedded in red dirt (which you still can notice) in New Mexico, and is regarded as the most complete of its kind.

The European keyboards like the harpischords, spinets, fortepianos, and virginals, most of which are brightly colored and decorated, are perhaps the most eye pleasing.

While there are other skeletons and re-assembled extinct creatures (ranging in time from the 25-million-year-old mastodon to the 300-year-old dodo), you'll also want to study the 110-by-16-foot mural "The Age of Reptiles." The period portrayed here is the Jurassic period of 190 to 136 million years ago. Dinosaurs like the brontosaurus, stegosaurus, and rhamphorhynchus are among many depicted in their natural habitats roaming through a pond, flying across the sky, or nibbling leaves from a tree.

You can travel from past to present by making your way to the third floor and looking at the three-dimensional simulations of North American animals in their native environments. There is a bison standing amid short-grass plains in the foothills of the Rockies, brown bears in Alaskan tundra, and a water moccasin and wood stork making their ways through the Everglades. Farther down the hall is a considerable section devoted to birds of Connecticut; the white snowy owl looks like it came right off the front of the cigar box.

Also representing the college's home state are some creations of early Connecticut Indians. They were excellent craftpeople and while much of their work was created from perishable materials, other products, such as a birch-bark canoe and baskets made from wooden splints, are on view. Displays regarding other Indians, ranging from those who lived on the North American plains to those from Mexico to those from the mountains of Peru, are also available for your examination. The Aztec Calendar Stone, relating the history of the universe by the use of suns, each representing a different age, is fascinating.

There are other antiques to be seen on campus that, compared to the marvels in the Peabody, are almost brand new. Yet if you ever wondered during the course of a modern musical performance where string keyboard instruments evolved from, or if you just wish to see some beautiful old instruments, you'll be interested in taking a look inside the **Yale University Collection of Musical Instruments.**

The majority of the pieces here are of western European origin while about 10 per cent are instruments of other ethnographical origins. The European keyboards like the harpsichords, spinets, fortepianos, and virginals, most of which are brightly colored and decorated, are perhaps the most eye pleasing. For instance, it's not untypical to find paintings of pastoral landscapes or allegorical scenes decorating the instruments; some of the paintings are as beautiful as the items themselves. On the other hand, in the side room devoted to ethnographic instruments, you'll see unusual representations from all over the world. It's easy to think you're familiar with the Southeast Asian gong, but this bronze noisemaker is smaller than you may expect. The stringed Arabian ud, the flat circular stringed moon guitar from China (complete with two pairs of silk strings), and the zither-like Japanese koto are probably instruments that you've never seen before.

Antonio Stradivari, the master violin maker, created one of the violins in the collection. Because of its three-quarter standard size, it was not played regularly; still, this example of excellence in workmanship should be seen. Stradivari made it at the age of ninety-two in 1736, the year of his death. Sebastian Schelle, another famous maker of instruments, created a lute in Nuremberg in 1726 that you can also see. Featured in the design is a carved wooden dolphin holding one string.

From a nineteenth-century Italian bass horn in the

You won't hear pre-adolescents banging out "Heart and Soul" on any of these keyboards. These elegant antiques are displayed at the Yale University Collection of Musical Instruments.

COURTESY YALE UNIVERSITY COLLECTION
OF MUSICAL INSTRUMENTS
THOMAS A. BROWN

shape of a snake (the music came out of its mouth) to a German stockflote (an oboe-like instrument) with a pocket watch at its top to an eighteenth-century French guitar, there are many more items to be seen here. Don't expect to find each instrument displayed every time you visit, however; the collection is so large that only about 20 to 25 per cent of the holdings can be displayed at one time. The rest are rotated periodically.

And that's not the end of Yale's cultural attractions. Beinecke Rare Book and Manuscript Library includes a Gutenberg Bible and some of John James Audubon's original bird prints. In the Sterling Memorial Library, there are collections of Babylonian tablets and historical volumes. In addition, you can take a guided tour of some of the notable buildings and grounds of Yale University. All told there is plenty here to please anyone looking for a fine day of museum hopping.

Here you'll see the stringed Arabian ud, the flat circular moon guitar from China, and the zither-like Japanese koto.

ACCESS

YALE UNIVERSITY ART GALLERY AND YALE CENTER FOR BRITISH ART. Directions: From Interstate 91 exit 47, take the Oak Street Connector, which merges into North Frontage Road; then turn right onto York Street. Park at any garage between Crown and Chapel streets. The museums are on opposite corners of Chapel and York streets. **Season:** All year. **Days:** Tuesday through Sunday. **Admission** free to both. **Allow** at least 3 hours in the Art Gallery and at least 90 minutes in the Center for British Art. **Telephones:** Art Gallery: (203) 436-0574. Center for British Art: (203) 432-4594.

PEABODY MUSEUM OF NATURAL HISTORY AND YALE UNIVERSITY COLLECTION OF MUSICAL INSTRUMENTS. Directions: From Interstate 91 Trumbull Street exit, head west on Trumbull Street. Turn right onto Whitney Avenue, then left onto Sachem Street. The Peabody Museum is on the corner of Sachem and Whitney; the Collection of Musical Instruments is at 15 Hillhouse Avenue, 2 blocks south of the Peabody. Parking is available on side streets. **Season:** All year. **Days:** Peabody Museum: Daily. Collection of Musical Instruments: Afternoons only, Tuesday, Wednesday, Thursday, and Sunday, except closed Sunday in June and July. **Admission** charged to the Peabody, free to Collection of Musical Instruments. **Allow** at least 90 minutes in Peabody Museum, 30 minutes to 1 hour in the Collection of Musical Instruments. **Telephones:** Peabody Museum: (203) 436-0850. Collection of Musical Instruments: (203) 436-4935.

Index

About the Author

Wherever he goes in the course of his research, there's always someone who stares at Mike Schuman as he boards a tour boat or leaves a gondola and asks incredulously, "You do this for a *living?*"

It's not a bad way to earn a paycheck — though, like a restaurant critic or a film reviewer, Mike has to deal with his share of problems on the way to finding the very best. He'd rather forget about the winter carnival that didn't get any snow, the "scenic walk" he had to take in the pouring rain, and the ferry that sank after he rode on it but just before his story was published.

Still, in the course of researching numerous articles as assistant editor of *Yankee Magazine's Travel Guide to New England,* and visiting even more spots for *Favorite Daytrips in New England,* Mike has gotten to know the best of New England, too. And he enjoys traveling enough that his "free" time has been spent visiting thirty-seven other states and twelve other countries on three continents. His travel stories have also appeared in the *Hartford* (Connecticut) *Courant* and the *Asbury Park* (New Jersey) *Press.*

Mike is also an avid sports fan, and before devoting himself to his current "on the road" reports, he was a staff correspondent for *The Baseball Bulletin.* A native of New England, he lives in Keene, New Hampshire, with his wife, Patti.